Experiences of Recent High School Graduates

Experiences of Recent High School Graduates

The Transition to Work or Postsecondary Education

George J. Nolfi
Winship C. Fuller
Arthur J. Corazzini
William H. Epstein
Richard B. Freeman
Charles F. Manski
Valerie I. Nelson
David A. Wise

University Consultants, Inc.
Cambridge, Massachusetts

Lexington Books
D.C. Heath and Company
Lexington, Massachusetts
Toronto

Library of Congress Cataloging in Publication Data

University Consultants.
    Expreiences of recent high school graduates.

    Bibliography: p.
    1. High school graduates—Employment—United States. 2. Occupa-
tional training—United States. 3. Education—Economic aspects—United
States. 4. Vocational education—United States. I. Nolfi, George J.
II. Title.
HD6273.U58 1978   331.1'1'0973   78-2075
ISBN 0-669-02264-0

Published simultaneously in Canada

Printed in the United States of America

International Standard Book Number: 0-669-02264-0

Library of Congress Catalog Card Number: 78-2075

Contents

MAR 5   1980

List of Figures and Tables

Figure

Table

Preface

As the table of contents indicates, this report has five main sections. The initial section is an introduction containing an overview of the entire book. Part I consists of a general analysis of actual post-high school experiences of the class of 1972. Labor market-oriented analysis is presented in part II, followed by part III, which focuses on the development of a model to simulate the demand for higher education. Part IV analyzes secondary and postsecondary vocational education; it examines the strategy of institutional aid and its implications for the effectiveness of public policy implementation are examined.

This book combines the final reports from two contracts performed for the National Center for Education Statistics, Department of Health, Education and Welfare by University Consultants, Inc. These two contracts were "Policy Issues Anaylsis in Postsecondary Education and Work: Transition from High School to Work," Contract Number 300–76–0014, and "Policy Issues Analysis in Postsecondary Education and Work: Demand for Postsecondary Education," Contract Number 300–76–0013. The full combined report, prepared by University Consultants, Inc., has been edited for hardcover publication, removing material of interest only to researchers interested in replicating the exact work.[1] Further, since the two study topics are related, specific complementarity between the studies was planned, and they were performed in parallel as a single research effort. Certain related results between the two projects could most usefully be described through publication in a single book with additional overview chapters, thereby making the combined output of both studies useful to both policymakers and researchers.

Moreover, through the project director, Dr. Nolfi, and the assistant project director, Dr. Fuller, as well as through senior staff member, Dr. Nelson, linkage between the research in the two efforts was encouraged. The ways in which this occurred strengthened the results obtained in both contracts above and beyond that which would have been possible had they been performed in isolation. For example, a greater sensitivity to some of the work and labor market variables was incorporated into the demand analysis; this was the result of its relation to the transition from school to work project and joint direction of the restudies. Hence, the demand analysis model contains a relatively broad specification of labor market alternatives (although its focus remains primarily on the collegiate choice set). Furthermore, the vocational education analysis, originally conceived as focusing on vocational education as an example of federal institutional aid as it relates to the labor market, has been expanded to examine the sensitivity of the relationship between vocational education choices and collegiate choices for young people.

Finally, the labor market analyses have been designed with appropriate consideration to both the issues of educational choice and the tradeoff between investment in education or the pursuit of work. Hence, both individual contracts have produced more useful results than had they been performed in isolation. Because neither the transition to work nor postsecondary education can be considered in isolation, the reports of the two studies have been combined and integrated into this single volume.

Overall, the particular research approach we have adopted reflects a set of beliefs regarding the nature of empirical research and how it can best contribute to policy analysis. Our research strategy had three main objectives. First, as the report describes, we have uncovered several key empirical findings about the transition of youths into school or work. Second, we have advanced the areas of analytic methodology in several crucial respects and laid the groundwork for future analysis not only by our research team, but by others across the country in the research community as well. Third, we have advanced on a tentative basis several controversial challenges to current federal policies.

Our research team has been composed of a number of scholars with expertise in various areas of education and manpower analysis. We have sought to build on their strengths in this study, organizing a set of specific research analyses that collectively addresses the underlying knowledge needed to understand a series of policy issues. Hence, somewhat discrete parts are complementary and form a useful whole. We have sought to maximize the flexibility of individual research team members within their particular areas of expertise, while maintaining for the study as a whole a commitment to and understanding of the policy issues dominating current debate; each scholar has been encouraged to pursue his or her individual research task in depth within the broad outlines of this study.

This volume reflects an appreciation of the value of the NLS and our specific research strategy. The report is not written to provide an all-inclusive analysis of high school graduates; we do not attempt to raise or answer all conceivable questions nor to examine all conceivable policy strategies. Rather, each chapter deals with a specific empirical question, conceptual framework, or methodology, building on past work and advancing our understanding of postsecondary choices. This study does not attempt to provide definitive and comprehensive coverage of all possible questions; rather, it has focused intensively on a limited series of questions that, after lengthy consideration, were generally agreed to be the critical areas of weakness in both the understanding of and, hence, the ability to formulate wise social policy both in education and in youth and labor market issues.

In the overview chapters, highlights of the results in each subsequent chapter are summarized to give policy-oriented readers an overview of the process through which young Americans make the transition from high school to work or postsecondary education (extensive technical detail concerning methodology and results is related in the individual chapters).

Also, several interrelated chapters discuss (from very different perspectives and with different conclusions) the further education and training choices and decisions of high school graduates; see chapters 3, 6, and 10.

Chapter 3 documents, in both detailed and descriptive ways, what has happened to the class of 1972 as its members pursue a variety of different paths; in particular, it discusses the paths actually taken in relation to the expected paths. Although mathematical functions that explain why people with given characteristics at certain times move along particular paths are not developed here, this chapter does present an overall analysis of what types of individuals intentionally or circumstantially end up on certain paths. Subsequent chapters choose selected subgroups and develop considerable mathematical analysis. Moreover, in this initial segment of the study, the entire NLS sample is examined, whereas other chapters employ specific subsamples.

Thus, although chapter 3 is a general analysis of the characteristics of this sample, it is followed by some specialized analyses of various aspects of each of the three major paths that a high school graduate may pursue. The higher education and vocational education choice models presented in chapters 8 and 11 have a limited focus on certain aspects of that broad choice set. This simplification is made for two reasons; first, lack of availability of aggregate data characterizing certain options (although individuals making such decisions almost certainly have the data relevant to their own choice), and second, the necessity to simplify the mathematical model for computation. These simplifications are reasonable, but the results should be compared with the results of other chapters, especially chapters 3, 6, and 10. Chapter 6 focuses less on a choice set but more on the variables that affect the basic decision of whether to pursue additional education. Chapters 10 and 11 analyze how the behavior of institutional providers of educational services is affected by federal policy strategies and how, in turn, these institutional behaviors profoundly affect student choice patterns.

Regardless of particular substantive interests, the reader is encouraged to first read the introductory material before examining the individual chapters. The reasons for the selection of those particular analyses for intensive investigation and their relationship to each as well as to larger policy questions are made clear in this segment. Hence, the specific inquiries and their results can be seen in proper context.

Note

1. G. Nolfi, W. Fuller, A. Corazzini, W. Epstein, R. Freeman, C. Manski, V. Nelson, and D. Wise, *Experiences of Recent High School Graduates: The Transition to Work or Postsecondary Education* (Cambridge, Mass.: University Consultants, Inc., 1977).

Acknowledgments

The study director wishes to express his appreciation to the members of the study team for their respective contributions in this report. Dr. Nolfi, Dr. Fuller, and Dr. Nelson are responsible for chapter 2. Dr. Nolfi and Dr. Epstein with assistance from Dr. Fuller and Dr. Nelson are responsible for chapter 3. Chapter 4 reflects primarily the work of Dr. Corazzini and Dr. Fuller. Chapters 5 and 6 are primarily the responsibility of Dr. Freeman and Dr. Epstein, respectively. Chapter Seven reflects the work of Dr. David Mundel (who was associated with this study during the proposal and initiation phases, before he joined the federal government. His work was completed prior to joining the federal government. Chapter 8 reflects the work of Dr. Wise, Dr. Manski, and Dr. Fuller. Chapter 9 is the combined inputs of Dr. Wise, Dr. Manski, Dr. Nolfi, Dr. Nelson, and Dr. Fuller. Chapter 10 is primarily the work of Dr. Nelson and chapter 11 is the work of Dr. Nelson and Dr. Fuller (the work here also involved an adaptation and respecification of the model developed in chapter 8).

Overall responsibility for the management of computer use rests with Dr. Fuller (Dr. Marcus Lieberman, a research associate at Harvard University provided computer use management advice in the early stages of the project). Overall responsiblity for the organization and management of the several components of the projects and the production of this final report rests with the project director, Dr. Nolfi. Ms. Nancy Bromhead served as project secretary.

All of us involved in the project want to express our appreciation to the staff of NCES, and particularly to Dr. Kenneth Tabler and Dr. Elmer Collins, for their assistance, support, and critical insights throughout the effort. Because these analyses are among the initial ones performed with the NLS data, many problems were encountered in making the data base routinely usable for the specific types of analyses being undertaken. Dr. Kenneth Tabler has been particularly helpful throughout these difficulties in assisting us in obtaining other files for purposes of merging data and in helping us to obtain assistance from other NCES contractors who were responsible for the acquiring the data and preparing the working tapes provided to us at the beginning of the contract. However, responsibility for the production of the necessary working files, cleaned tapes, and other material needed for our specific analyses rests with our own staff entirely.

1 Introduction

During the next several years, the National Longitudinal Survey of the High School Class of 1972 (NLS) will be used to guide policy development in postsecondary education, vocational education, manpower training, public employment, and other major social policy areas. This extensive and representative sample of youth, combined with periodic follow-ups as their educational and career plans are realized, make the NLS particularly important.

During the 1960s and 70s, decisions in many policy areas, including education and manpower, have often been based on swings of opinion and political ideologies, not on hard evidence nor careful scientific research and design. For example, much of the discussion of problems of youth in transition to work has been clouded in uncertainties and rhetoric. In part this has resulted from the fact that minimal good data have been available, as well as from the fashion in academic scholarship to ignore certain questions of great importance to policy-makers.

This book has two objectives: to develop an understanding of the transition from school to work, and to delineate factors in the demand for postsecondary education. To achieve these objectives, we have addressed three distinct tasks. First, we have examined the data on activities of high school graduates for a rough-cut view of the transition to work or school. Second, we have focused on several key new or previously unanswered questions in the literature of empirical and policy analysis. Third, we have directly confronted the inadequacies of existing methodologies and estimation techniques, inadequacies that contribute to biases and misinterpretations of actual events and processes.

This three-pronged approach reflects our judgment of the gaps in the existing literature and of the long-term needs of policymakers. Some applied policy analysis can be undertaken using the NLS data; but, in addition, we perceive the need for more basic research into analytical methodologies and conceptual frameworks. Though we have not carried all of our results forward into explicit policy recommendations in this book, they constitute the building blocks for policy analysis and for future research. Hence, this study is not an all-inclusive analysis, either empirically or in policy terms, but rather a foundation study.

We have confirmed that a number of previous research findings hold true in the case of the NLS. We find, as others have, that much of the process of school choices and work success is currently unmeasurable; luck, random influences, or factors that are beyond measurement with the NLS variables have a very strong impact. For example, only about 15 percent of the variation in wage levels can be explained with the variables in this sample. But, within this

1

limitation, our results are similar to those of other studies. First, high school characteristics appear to have minimal impact on the success of graduates in the labor market. By comparison, measures of family income or socioeconomic status measurably affect student success, whereas ability as such is less important. Finally a pervasive characteristic of this sample is the higher aspirations and greater relative success of white males compared to those of blacks and women.

Also, we have concentrated on several new questions and have uncovered the following findings. Although ability measured by SAT scores or ETS tests has minimal influence on career expectations or on job success, personality and motivational variables appear to have some influence. Second, the process of transition from school to work is characterized by substantial student uncertainty and indecisiveness—many do not make up their minds until just before graduation—and our analysis confirms and amplifies the details of this phenomenon. Third, many students appear to fall short of their expectations by a substantial degree. In particular, many more graduates end up working than had hoped to. Their goal of college or vocational training appears to be stymied, and they thus find full-time work. Fourth, federal support appears to shape public vocational education programs in ways contrary to student wishes. Fifth, both local wage levels and student aid appear to influence graduates' choices of school or work.

In addition, we have developed and refined several key methodological approaches to analysis of this data set. First, we have concentrated on refining estimates of the effects of factors that for one reason or another, are "unobservable" by current variables. Second, we have expanded the conditional logit choice model methodology to incorporate a significantly wider set of choices for high school youth. Third, we have advanced a method of analyzing the impact of institutional aid on the set of students and institutions in the case of vocational education; this method can be extended to other areas of postsecondary education as well.

Given the long-term importance and potential value of the NLS–1972, we have sought to perform a series of "foundation" analyses. This book presents a selected set of related inquiries, each to be pursued in depth, rather than a single overall analytical perspective.

Throughout this study, series of questions that were previously unanswered in the literature and policy discussions have been examined. Over the years, a modest general understanding has emerged in such areas as what happens to people who go directly into the labor market after finishing high school, why some choose to attend college, how choices are made among colleges, to whom is college accessible, and the general area of vocational school choice. Within these critical policy areas, however, many questions continue to plague policymakers. Also, the interrelatedness of these decisions has been insufficiently examined. For example, none of the previous higher education access-choice analyses have looked realistically at the labor market options and tradeoffs that individuals actually must make. Nor has the choice between postsecondary vocational education and higher education ever been adequately examined. That field is particularly important today because many young people now opt for vocational skills in place of higher education.

Thus, we have taken three different analytic perspectives or points of view: the labor market-oriented perspective, the traditional higher education access and choice perspective, and a perspective based on the relationships between supply and demand in a market that previously had not been adequately analyzed. Though the inquiries in each of its three sections thus start from a particular conceptual view, this study yields an integrated perspective wherein student behavior, labor market pressures and opportunities, and the interaction between supply and demand in the training market are examined in the context of one another. Many examples of the ways in which each particular segment relates to the remainder of this report can be cited; for example, the work section includes a discussion of the college choices; the higher education section discusses work and vocational education variables; and the variables used within the vocational education part also implicitly include work and college choices. Thus, most sections of this report are somewhat interrelated, but there are also many highly specialized portions that clearly aim at a particular problem.

It is also apparent that policy considerations have now reached a level of sophistication and refinement in dealing with such issues as a national youth policy, work education issues, and youth unemployment issues; the limits imposed by traditional intradisciplinary perspectives make the findings of many previous analyses inadequate.

For example, there is tension between the economic or rational man view[1] and a more "behavioral and preference" man view[2] of the decision-making process, with neither view being wholly adequate for policy analysis. Both perspectives have been explored here. Indeed, we have deliberately adopted competing analytical approaches in different chapters. For example, we have analyzed decisions to pursue further schooling from two dimensions, one focusing on personality variables (we find that aspirations and parental expectations are crucial), and one focusing on prediction of choice based on non-psychological performance or descriptive characteristic variables.

This study has been undertaken to provide basic analytical results related to many policy issues currently of concern to government and professional circles. Such a "floor" of factual understanding facilitates elucidation of the differences between policies and their likely impact. For example, even the actual post-high school activities of youth (let alone alternative explanations for the facts) are not familiar or well understood within the policy arena.

In more complex policy debates (for example, such as whether to enact an entitlement bill as proposed by Coleman in his *Youth in Transition Report* and by the Carnegie Commission's "2-Years-In-The-Bank" proposal), considerably more must be known about such factors as the market forces and the potential effect of any particular policy strategy. Thus, it is necessary to develop a way of thinking that permits particular policy strategies to be evaluated and compared with their potential rivals. The analyses in this study provide some of the basic tools necessary for such an approach.

The research in each chapter provides both a range of findings and a conceptual framework that contribute to a better basic understanding of the facts which intelligent analysis and decision about a range of policy issues and themes must rest. As a result, several general policy themes run through all four parts of this report; these themes and issues are surveyed next.

First, in the ongoing discussions about youth problems, many policy-makers are becoming concerned with the issue of a national youth policy: for example, the Coleman *Youth in Transition Report*, the current Carnegie Council on Policy Studies in Higher Education research, and numerous bills in Congress dealing with youth unemployment. It has become obvious in recent years that many misconceptions and conflicting information have been historically taken as fact. Thus, analysis in this study attempts to discern more clearly the actual behavior pattern and forces that influence individuals during the period called youth.

Second, some fundamentally new government policy orientations are increasingly being examined. One such idea is the notion of post–high school universal entitlement, which an individual can use in several different ways for entry into further education or the labor market. For example, it could be used to purchase various types of schooling or even for capital investment to start a business; it could also be used to subsidize an employer during a training period or to subsidize wages during employer training. To consider such policy options and alternatives intelligently, it is necessary to know considerably more about such things as the work-education tradeoff and the nature of the training market in which a student might act as a buyer.

A third current theme is the basic question of investment in education. Has too much been invested in education or should we continue to invest at the current high rate? Who should be educated at public expense for what? An example of this question crops up in the debate on limiting appropriations for postsecondary education; such policy deliberations can be conducted in a much more informed manner as a result of this study.

A fourth theme deals with the emerging concern for better integration of society as a whole. One basic question considers better integration of education and work particularly for youth (although the concern for adults as well emerges through movements toward such benefits or paid educational leave in unions.)

A fifth major theme of current policy concern deals with the provision of better information to youth and adults so that they can make intelligent choices. Such projects as the occupational information system experiments by the Department of Labor and the whole movement toward community work-education councils are directed at this perceived problem. The work of others seems to show that students lack good information on labor market opportunities, on the net prices of various educational systems, and so forth. Portions of this report are aimed at this series of questions concerning the availability of information to students.

A sixth major current policy theme deals with the effects of race and sex; virtually every analysis within this report includes some reference to this pair of highly sensitive variables. The results will enlighten discussions of questions of discrimination in such areas as access to further schooling and labor market opportunities.

A seventh policy theme is the question of the determinants of educational pursuits and career success. Different analysts, reflecting different disciplinary points of view, have argued two very different explanatory cases. One group argues that psychological and personality variables such as motivation, family personality characteristics, and attitudes are the most important determining variables, whereas another group has argued equally convincingly that such neutral variables as ability, previous schooling, and price predominate. Sometimes analysts have looked at the same data from these different perspectives and come to exactly opposite conclusions—for example, whether schooling makes a difference in terms of labor market success. Understanding the determinants of the decision to pursue additional schooling and the determinants of labor market success is therefore crucial if social policies aimed at increasing social equity and equality are to be effectively designed and their impact evaluated.

Existing social policies have been heavily predicated on the concept that additional schooling is in fact heavily correlated with greater socioeconomic success, and hence increasing educational opportunity has been seen as a vehicle for social change in the direction of greater equality and equity. Additionally, such issues as career progression and obsolescence, as well as differential access to career advancement opportunities, further complicate understanding the determinants of additional education and career success.

The eighth policy theme concerns a comparability of outcomes from various education and learning options. Increasingly, the substitutability and comparability between learning that takes place in highly varied settings (that is, between formal learning which occurs in colleges, proprietary schools, and other settings, and less formal learning with comparable outcomes which takes place in competency-based curricula, home learning programs, mediated instruction, or employer-education programs) are recognized and the justifications for historically unique public subsidy strategies to only certain forms of teaching and learning have already begun to change. In the 1972 amendments to the Higher Education Act, postsecondary proprietary schools were included as eligible institutions for federal student aid programs. In the early 1970s as well, many efforts to provide academic credit for nonformal learning in nonacademic settings have made substantial progress. Increasingly, public policy must address the clear fact that U.S. citizens learn in a wide variety of formal and nonformal settings, and federal policies to support learning must be responsive to this varied pattern.

A ninth and related policy issue is the relationship between alternative forms of training, job performance, and manpower needs. The historical premise that formal educational institutions are the best place to gain the necessary learning for career performance is being reexamined. Alternative policies involving wage subsidies and training in the work place, customized training, and other forms of career preparation that could take place in employer, union, and related settings rather than in formal educational institutions are increasingly under scrutiny.

A tenth policy issue is the impact of the broadening of access to U.S. postsecondary education. Many writers have observed that postsecondary education is now educating large masses of students that are significantly different from those students who were served by the traditional system (and indeed from those students who are usually served by the more elitist higher education systems of other nations). For these so-called new students, the traditional teaching-learning modes and patterns of postsecondary education may not be the most appropriate. Hence, a range of questions concerning alternative means of serving students with very different learning styles and objectives are increasingly discussed.

An eleventh policy issue relates to the distribution of federal subsidies among alternate potential recipients. In addition to using such information for evaluating program effectiveness, considerations of redistribution of social wealth and social equity have brought to the fore the concerns about the actual impact of alternative federal education and training policies on who actually receives subsidies. For example, the shift toward the strategy of student rather than institutional aid characteristic of federal postsecondary education policy in the early 1970s was largely predicated on the fact that it was the only means to ensure that federal investment would help the students who were most in need and for whom it would have the greatest effect.

A twelfth policy theme, and one that is steadily increasing in importance, deals with patterns of part-time study, recurrent education, and lifelong learning. Large numbers of students are now dropping in and dropping out of postsecondary education, delaying entry, or choosing alternate patterns of education and work. Increasingly public education and manpower policy must be sensitive to the actual patterns of behavior exhibited by young people in the year following high school, particularly their choices in sequencing educational and occupational activities, their patterns of dropping out, return, and transfer; geographic migration; career finding; skills transferability; and so forth. Some of this behavior exhibits rational decision-making and "learning about the world of work"; it may be quite socially efficient. Similarly, some of it testifies to a lack of adequate information that would permit students to make efficient education and work choices by after high school graduation. Some of it also is simply a function of the changing character of the labor market, caused both by long-term trends and also by short-term economic fluctuations and regional variations. Because most employers contend it takes weeks or months to train a fresh graduate from high school or college to the realities of the world of work and to make the new employee a productive member of an economic unit, it is clear that there is much fertile soil for new policies that will better integrate education and work and intersperse periods of education and work over a person's life. The first step in formulating such policies intelligently is understanding the actual experiences and choices of recent high school graduates.

A thirteenth policy issue concerns the long-term variations and trends in attitudes and life-styles of post–high school youth. It is clear that such variation will continue to occur with each succeeding high school class, but the trends and directions are by no means obvious. Students in the mid-1970s, for example, seem to be quite different from the students of the late 1960s, with respect to their attitudes in the years immediately following their graduation from high school. Similarly, the mid-60s cohort of college students, as it approaches the age of settling into careers, appears to be exhibiting behavior significantly different from that which it exhibited a few years earlier. Monitoring closely what, in fact, is happening to recent high school graduates and analyzing their transition to postsecondary education and to work is therefore critically important to wise policy formulation. For example, the trend toward earlier emancipation of students and the increasing numbers of students voluntarily declaring an independent status is undermining one of the major premises on which the family-need-based student financial aid access strategy is predicated.

A fourteenth policy issue relates to the effect on access and choice of different federal intervention strategies. Most basically, the federal government has the option of subsidizing demand or subsidizing supply. Student aid strategy, as a vehicle to educational access and greater social equity, is a demand subsidy strategy. In contrast, supply subsidy strategies of direct institutional aid and provision of service through publicly controlled schools is the norm in vocational education. To determine the actual impact of these different strategies, detailed data on the experiences of students experiencing the different approaches are needed. Analyzing such actual experiences gives some measure of the relative utility and comparative effectiveness of different federal intervention strategies. Moreover, determining exactly what students are doing aids in understanding the extent to which such strategies as financial aid may be reaching the point of exhaustion because of saturation. For example, if it is in fact true, as some contend, that students wanting to pursue postsecondary education can easily find adequate financial aid resources, then increasing financial aid is no longer a viable strategy for increasing access and participation among disadvantaged groups. Rather, efforts may have to concentrate on altering elementary and high school experiences or on specifically attempting to design policies that will alter individual strategies and decision criteria for young people. Some of the variables that affect these strategies and criteria may be very difficult to affect by public policy; an example may be such factors as family styles, labor market shortages, changes in the skills mix in the economy, or political movements.

In conclusion, the research in this study is basic in nature. It was not designed to answer such specific questions as which youth employment bill is best; how much money should the federal government put into higher education; what is the tradeoff between giving vocational education money to students or capital investments or subsidies to institutions; what should be general work-education policy? Rather, our specific analytical results provide an improved understanding of many major questions noted previously that are important to the content of such policy debates. For example, understanding what people might do with a general entitlement requires understanding considerably more about their individual schooling versus their occupation decisions than has been heretofore available. With respect to youth policy, it is necessary to have a better understanding of what it is that seems to affect people's decisions to commit the time and funds necessary to invest in their own human capital. Why do individuals seem to make such educational decisions? General chapters of this study speak to these issues.

Notes

1. This view is assumed in both choice models (chapters 8 and 11).

2. This view is implicit in the finding that father's and mother's expectations are determinants of further schooling (chapter 6).

2

Overview of Findings

The first section analyzes what, in general, has happened to the high school class of 1972 since graduation. It is followed by a series of selected analyses of particular issues that can be grouped into three main areas. The second section looks at those individuals who enter the labor market directly after high school and the third is directed mainly at those individuals who choose to pursue higher education. The question of vocational education is addressed in the last section.

Post–High School Experiences: Expected and Actual

What actually happens to American graduates in the years immediately following high school as they pursue the various paths of transition from high school into various combinations of work and schooling? Specifically, a high school graduate is faced with an array of choices that can be described in 14 basic categories (the expected immediate post–high school activity states). These, plus the 10 categories of actual post–high school activities (in October 1973 and October 1974), are described in table 2-1.

Next, the plans and actual activities of these high school graduates 17 and 29 months following graduation is examined in light of such socioeconomic determinants as sex, race, aptitude, SES, family income, and high school program. A striking conclusion here is that significantly higher proportions of males are working full time and females are homemakers than had planned to be. College attendance is roughly in keeping with expectations, but only half those who expected to both attend college and work simultaneously are actually so engaged. Similar reductions in expectations occur for those hoping to combine work with vocational education. In general, across SES and aptitude categories, those students who hoped to go to school part time are forced to work full time with no school. This condition warrants serious attention as to the reasons for difficulty.

Many more facts, such as white males' aspirations for college not being fulfilled and the effect of aptitude on attitudes toward full-time work, are presented in chapter 3; however, only the more important or the more obvious conclusions that can be derived from this cross-tabular analysis are actually discussed in the body of the report. Next, the substantial variation between

---

This chapter was prepared by George J. Nolfi, Winship C. Fuller, and Valerie I. Nelson.

Table 2-1
Activity State Analysis Categories

Value	Expected Activity States — Definition	Value	Actual Activity States (1973 and 1974) — Definition
1	Full-time work only	1	Full-time work only
2	Full-time college only	2	Full-time college only
3	Full-time vocational training only	3	Full-time vocational training only
4	Full-time apprenticeship or on-the-job training only	4	Part-time work only
5	Full-time work plus part-time college	5	Full-time work plus-part-time vocational training
6	Full-time work plus part-time vocational training	6	Full-time work plus part-time college
7	Full-time college plus part-time work	7	Full-time college plus part-time work
8	Full-time vocational training plus part-time work	8	Military only
9	Full-time on-the-job training plus part-time college	9	Homemaker only
10	Full-time on-the-job training plus part-time vocational training	10	Other
11	Military only		
12	Full-time homemaker only		
13	Full-time homemaker plus part-time college		
14	Full-time homemaker plus part-time vocational training		

students' expectations and their actual activities is further analyzed by comparing plans with actual 1973 behavior, yielding two basic conclusions. First, it is
readily apparent that, for a variety of reasons, many people change their plans.
The figures suggest that for almost the entire sample, individuals have at best a
60 percent chance of realizing their plans. A second major conclusion is that
those planning more complicated activities (such as a combination of work and
college, or of work and vocational training) are much less likely to achieve their
plans. These figures strongly suggest a need for more such opportunities. Especially disturbing is the lack of facilities for combining vocational training with
work; most of these individuals must instead work full time, presumably in a
less skilled capacity.

Quite detailed tables were used to trace the actual activities of these students, delineated by expectation categories, through their actual activities in
1973 and 1974. Certain important results were obtained. In particular, except
for homemakers, no more than 50 percent of any group managed to adhere to
the expectations expressed in 1972. Furthermore, this figure holds for those
intending to do only one thing—that is, work full-time, attend college full-time,
or enter the military. For those whose plans were more complicated (such as
combining work with college or vocational training), the probability of success
is considerably lower.

In summary, many students fail to fulfill their plans and, in particular,
many who had hoped to go to school or seek training are pushed into the work
force full time. On graduation from high school, students appear to be forced
to give up or lower their expectations, at least in the short term. As a more
general conclusion, it can also be stated that any expectation which is a combination of any activities has a lower probability of fulfillment; the more complex the alternatives are, the less likely they are to be fulfilled.

Labor Market Analysis

Part II of this study focuses on a better understanding of where and how students enter the labor market on graduation from high school with several significant findings. First, none of the traditional analyses of labor market entry
patterns had been performed on a data set of such high quality as the National
Longitudinal Survey of the High School Class of 1972. Second, few existing
analyses have aimed at understanding the effects of educational plans on an
individual's expectations with respect to labor market success. Thus, a major
goal of the research in Part II of this book lay, not in advancing analytic capability, but rather in increasing the refinement of several analyses using traditional techniques to deal with questions relating to labor market entry and
success. Several new questions were also examined, especially those relating
to the timing of decisions and the probability of remaining on planned

pathways. Finally a relatively new methodology is employed to examine the effects of schooling versus ability within the framework of several personality and attitude classifications.

This labor market analysis presents an excellent example of the relationship of the specific inquiries within this study to the policy debate themes discussed in chapter 1. In the sense that youth unemployment is the converse of labor market success for youths, an analysis of the determinants of successful labor market entry highlights certain areas that may be among the most effective levers in the youth unemployment policy area.

A summary of those conclusions emerging from the examination of the students entering the labor market directly (chapters 4 and 5) will be considered next, followed by an overview of the analysis of expected earnings and schooling (chapter 6).

Direct Labor Market Entry

For those students who did not intend to pursue any additional training immediately following high school graduation but planned to enter the labor market directly, the transition from plans to actual experiences, the causal determinants of a range of potential outcomes, and the differential impact of a given set of labor market variables on these outcomes for different subsets of that population are analyzed.

With respect to the timing of educational plans, no significant differences are evident by either sex or income among students as to whether they make early decisions about further education. The observed increased labor market success for people who have decided early to go to work is probably the result of better information about the labor market. This would imply that, for late deciders, increased high school counseling about job market opportunities could possibly have a high payoff.

Equally as important is that, when the subsample is examined by race and sex, more blacks and females who decide to go to work are convinced that they have the ability to go on to postsecondary education than is the case for whites and males. Also, more than half the high-income subgroup felt that they had the ability to go to college, even though they chose otherwise. This result should be compared with the additional finding that white males' expectations about postsecondary education tend to be the most unfulfilled of any subgroup.

An examination of the long-run education aspirations of the "chose to go directly to work" subgroup indicated that over 40 percent thought they might evenutally go on to postsecondary education. Thus, a substantial number seem to want postsecondary education tailored to their needs as working adults in the future. This result seems to reflect the partial adoption of a universal access higher education attitude with a recurrent education approach by a significant number of high school graduates.

Apparently, the decision to seek full-time work on high school graduation is complex; this group seems to differ from the high school population as a whole in ways that are not easily captured in the standard variables of race, sex, income, and ability. As a group it may perceive that the payoff to four years of college is not significantly different from the payoff of two years of college, and it prefers vocational training to either of the other two. Once again what is true of the whole group is atypical for those of high measured ability, with the added twist that the brightest apparently prefer four years of college to two years, but vocational education to four years of college.

The career objectives of those planning to go directly to work upon graduation are indicative of sex role stereotyping; some 90 percent of the females in the sample chose either clerical, sales, service, professional, or homemaker, while 75 percent of the males chose to be craftsmen, laborers, operators, professionals, technicians, or protective workers.

The actual job plans of this subgroup indicate that only 50 percent of those planning to go directly to work have definite job commitments, and of that 50 percent three-fifths are people continuing their part-time high school employment. Hence, in general, the picture for this "plan to directly enter the labor market" subgroup is rather pessimistic. It appears that only 40 percent of those hoping to find work on graduation, but with no plans to continue their present employment, have been successful. The best description for this group appears therefore not to be that they have decided to go to work, but that they have decided not to go to school immediately and are uncertain about what they are going to do. Of this group about half indicated a preference or willingness to move, which indicates that this high labor market mobility, if exercised, could alleviate regional pockets of unemployment.

For the group of students who planned neither postsecondary education nor full-time work, five choices (apprenticeship or on-the-job training, military, homemaker, part-time work, and "other") are examined. The timing of the decision not to go to college for these groups were roughly the same as those mentioned earlier, with the exception that a very high percentage (47.5) of the "other" group were still undecided in the twelfth grade. The lowest education aspirations were held by the homemakers, with the military group having very high aspirations for later education (possibly an important indication that the military's voluntary education programs are a good recruitment device). As noted earlier with the subgroup that chose to go directly to work, this too is evidence of increased potential demand for recurrent education.

Also, somewhat more than half of all individuals within any subgroup (except part-time work) are recorded as choosing to be part of that particular subgroup should their choice be unconstrained. It is also worth noting that a significantly high percentage of each group would have preferred to be categorized as "other." This is especially interesting because it appears these people may be indicating that, after high school graduation, they would prefer to do nothing.

Consider next such patterns of actual post-high school activities as school attendance and job characteristics. It is particularly difficult to capture the richness of teen labor activity and labor market success by straightforward measures of employment and unemployment. The group of teenagers who planned to go to work on graduation had come to that decision hesitantly, and the mix of postsecondary school and full-time work plans of the group are intertwined and influenced by the degree of success achieved in pursuing these alternative paths. Lack of high school success may lead many to record themselves as seeking full-time work; subsequent lack of immediate success in the labor market may spawn plans to return to school in some capacity. Better information about wages and salaries available to high school graduates may induce a shift in education and training plans. Moreover, many of these students decided very late in their high school careers not to immediately continue their education on graduation, and many were still undecided about future postsecondary education at the actual time of high school graduation.

The actual patterns of labor market success 4 months and 16 months after graduation reveal several facts. Of those actually attending school, many had been undecided until very late in their high school careers about the prospect of postsecondary school. It is not that they were uncertain whether they had sufficient ability, but simply that they classified themselves as undecided but were most likely not going to be going to school. Importantly, this group consists of roughly an equal percentage of males and females, but a full third of them are nonwhite. Hence, many nonwhite high school graduates make very late decisions regarding postsecondary education, possibly because they were tracked or counseled away from further education in high school even though they realized its value and want it. Or, it may be that, as they see their peers going on to various forms of postsecondary education, they are swayed in that direction. On the other hand, it may be that they see firsthand what their job opportunities are as high school graduates, while they are simultaneously being made newly aware of student aid and educational opportunities. Moreover, this group comes predominantly from the ranks of low measured academic ability, with technical schools and two-year junior colleges appearing to be their overwhelming educational choice. There are also significant differences between males and females in terms of the types of occupations they are being trained for; this can be taken as clear evidence of sex stereotyping.

When considering job characteristics and job mobility of this subgroup, it is clear that many of these high school graduates changed jobs, with no significant difference in the degree of mobility when subclassified by race or sex. An important question that must be raised about this whole phenomenon of high observed mobility is whether it indicates great difficulty in the transition or whether it is actually, in social terms, an extremely efficient way of having young people learn about the labor market so that they can ultimately make rational career choices. This fundamental question is at the bottom of much of the discussions of teenage unemployment and job turnover; it is thus currently being explored further in the author's ongoing research.

Females were employed by the government at nearly twice the rate of males, which could reflect either the increase of opportunities in government for those with clerical skills or compensation for past discriminatory practices. However, the majority of both sexes continue to be employed in industry. Another important phenomenon is that a significantly higher percentage of nonwhites find part-time rather than full-time employment, possibly pointing toward continued racial discrimination.

Transition tables can be constructed for two points in time by 12 status categories for each time period, revealing important transition characteristics. During the first year following graduation, there is a very slight decrease in those that were unemployed and a slight increase of those who are out of the labor force. Surprisingly low unemployment rates of 8.6 percent and 6.6 percent are observed in the two time periods (even considering the fact that dropouts are not in the NLS sample); however, the rates apply only to those who had actually planned to work. For the subgroup working full time while trying to stay in school part time, the unemployment rate is the same for whites and nonwhites (about 6 percent), but twice as high for males as females (8 percent to 4 percent). Overall, nonwhite unemployment rates were twice those of whites, but still considerably below the 25 percent to 35 percent figure usually cited for this demographic group.

Not surprisingly, nonwhites also exhibited higher rates of nonparticipation in the labor force than did whites. More nonwhites were enrolled in school full-time than either working or looking for work. The early marriage of some females probably accounts for the fact that 8.9 percent of the females in contrast to 4.6 percent of the males were not in the labor force and not engaged in any sort of school activity. The males' unemployment rate drops from 5 percent to 2.7 percent if only those not in school are considered, and from 6 percent to 3 percent if those in school part time are included. This movement of individuals between school, work, and unemployment over time is a particularly important phenomenon.

The questions of unemployment, labor force participation, and wage levels have been explored for the "plan to go directly to work" group of high school graduates. The employment regressions revealed that being white and male greatly increases employment prospects immediately on high school graduation. In addition, concentrating on just working, as opposed to also attending school, is an asset in finding employment in the short run. Finally, being from a middle-income family, as well as having a belief in one's control over the environment, is quite important.

It appears that those subjective attitudes which are mainly present in middle-class families have a primary influence on one's chances of being employed. The importance of these attitudes is especially revealed by the significance of a personality variable. In contrast, objective factors such as marital status, high school program, age, physical handicaps, and language deficiencies have little effect on employment possibilities. Local wage rates, unemployment rates, and father's occupation also seem to have no effect.

Labor force participation was examined both for the whole nontraining-oriented sample as well as for four subsamples derived according to sex and actual school attendance. For the entire group, attitudes seem to have different effects on labor force participation than they had on employment; here they become more a factor of class (as measured by father's occupation) than income. In addition, an individual's personality is less likely to matter. Thus, in general, the most consistent results point toward the importance of having on-the-job training and undivided concentration on the job in the sense that one does not attend school. Also of interest is the lack of any effect of either ability or local wage and unemployment rates. At least in this sample, local wage levels are not considered to be an important factor in deciding to participate in the labor force. On the other hand, it is possible that local wage rates are not relevant to the class of jobs that individuals obtain immediately on leaving high school; this market may be segregated from the main labor market.

When those attending school are excluded from the sample, the most striking difference between those males and females not attending school but successfully working is the importance of ability and personality factors for men and their unimportance for women. Whether this effect results from the different mix of jobs offered males and females or different attitudes toward work is an interesting question for further research.

Turning from an examination of labor force participation rates to the regressions dealing with wage rate differentials, it becomes apparent that such factors as being male, on-the-job training, positive attitude, and wealthy parents raise income. Also, not being handicapped and coming from family where English is the primary language helps. And finally, the strongest influence on income is an individual's sex. The remaining variables had no or very little effect. All these variables account for only 15 percent of the variance of income; 85 percent of these differences were caused by other factors such as luck or possibly very specialized abilities.

Thus, regression analysis of labor market status yielded results generally very close to Bowen and Finnegan's analysis of the 1960 census data. Strikingly, males and whites fared better than blacks and females in locating jobs. Interestingly, being employed in 1972 did not result in lower unemployment rates in 1973 than for those who had no job in 1972 (possibly a result of the economic variables at the time). Also, being in any kind of school since graduation greatly lowers one's chances of being employed because the individual is likely to be less committed to those types of jobs which are available to high school graduates. Participating in on-the-job training programs raises employment changes while, finally, parents in middle income brackets significantly increased chances of being employed.

The focus on high school graduates who go into the labor market is continued in chapter 5. There have been relatively few studies of those with less than college training; this preliminary understanding of factors that differentiate young high school graduates in the labor market reveals important facts.

Granting the preliminary nature of the analysis in chapter 5, the calculations reveal some interesting aspects of the determinants of socioeconomic success among high school graduates. Family income in particular is found to have a substantial positive effect on the labor market achievement of persons with the same schooling. Certain personal characteristics, physical handicaps, ability to speak English, and sex also differentiate persons in the market, while other characteristics, notably race, have quite different or less significant effects than have traditionally been found. Several other factors that are often hypothesized to influence socioeconomic success (measures of ability, personality factors, local market conditions, and some characteristics of the high school attended) also have basically no effect. There are, furthermore, certain differences between the determinants of the market positions of men and women.

With respect to the effect of personal characteristics, both the small or non-existent effect of the ability and personality factors and the positive effect on hourly earnings of being black stand out clearly; this positive coefficient on being black could reflect problems with the sample. It is not, however, as odd as it might first appear; calculations with very young men in the National Longitudinal Survey of the Department of Labor also suggest little differences in rates of pay when corrected for various background factors, but larger differences in total earnings caused by greater unemployment and less time worked by blacks. It is also possible that the positive coefficient indicates that blacks are choosing jobs with less training and more immediate rewards than whites.

The most striking aspect of the school variables is their general unimportance. Consistent with other studies, the calculations suggest that the type of school has little or no impact. The only school factor that matters is failure to graduate, which raises wages, presumably due to the odd group covered (1 percent of the whole sample) and the greater work experience of those who left early (the NLS survey does not include early high school dropouts).

Tentatively, family income matters in the economic success of young persons who do not go to college. There is about a 10 percent differential in income between those from the upper 10 percent of the families and those in the lower half. Such a difference is not negligible; it is equivalent, more or less, to a year of schooling or to membership in a trade union. If it persists over lifetime spans, and if individuals make, say, $15,000 per year, it equates to $20,000 at an interest rate of 7.5 percent, a reasonably large "bequest" from upper income levels to their children above and beyond schooling.

When the sample is further broken down by race and sex, several interesting results appear. Although curriculum had no overall effect, it appears to matter differentially by sex. Whereas among young men, both academic education and, to a much less extent, general education are positive factors, those women with vocational training do better than those following academic or general curricula. This raises the possibility that current vocational programs, presumably for commercial clerical work, may serve women students better than the equivalent craft vocational programs for men.

Differences in the effect of background by sex and race also merit further attention. First, the number of siblings appears to have a greater deterrent effect on women than men, which may reflect a greater allocation of family resources to male than female children or the greater sibling care responsibility of female children. A second difference is that black women do markedly better than young white women in this sample, while young black men have only a slight advantage over their white peers. As noted earlier, most of the positive effect of being black occurs among women. Personality variables appear to have little effect on whites but significantly change the position of blacks. Number of siblings and parent income have a sizable effect on whites without being significant for blacks. The bilingual aspect hurts blacks much more than whites in terms of future income achievement, but that may occur simply because of ethnic group differences. Training pays off more for whites than blacks.

However, as noted at the outset, because of the youth of the population analyzed, the high nonresponse rate, and simple tools of analysis, this chapter has yielded only tentative results, which must be checked and verified with additional follow-up data and more detailed models before they can be fully accepted.

Male Earnings and Schooling

As noted earlier, several sections—for example, chapter 6—are based on relatively sophisticated statistical techniques. Interest in relations among earnings, schooling, and other factors such as ability and family background stems from several sources. One is a desire to estimate the contribution of increased schooling to growth in incomes. Other work on earnings functions has concentrated on investigating discrimination by attributing unexplained differences in earnings across groups to discrimination or other market imperfections. This analysis particularly emphasizes the role of ability in earnings and schooling equations. It departs from, or expands on, previous studies in three ways: (1) it attempts to refine the concept of ability by estimating separately such effects as verbal, abstract, and mathematical ability; (2) personality characteristics are added to the equation, as are variables representing parents' desired education for the child; and (3) the effects of characteristics of the high school on earnings and schooling are investigated in detail.

Several major conclusions are reached in this chapter. As in previous studies, all the independent variables together only explain about 30 percent of the variance in earnings and about 35 percent of the variance in schooling.

The net effect of ability is rather small, amounting to about 3 percent on both earnings and schooling. This result for schooling does not agree with earlier studies.

Refinement of the concept of ability into several distinct factors (achievement or academic ability, verbal ability, and abstract ability) is made possible by tests administered during the NLS. These results are unknown to the participants, their teachers, and employers, whereas the individual's class rank is another measure of ability which is known to the student and others.

An important conclusion is that achievement ability is the most significant ability factor contributing earnings success. Both abstract ability and class rank play only a limited role, with verbal ability assigned an intermediate role. For schooling, however, class rank and achievement ability are of approximately equal weight, with verbal and abstract ability playing about the same roles as in the earnings equation. Even though these tests may not measure all types of ability important for schooling and earnings, several important types appear to be distinguishable.

The effects of some personality variables and other indicators of motivation such as the amount of schooling desired by parents for the student on earnings and schooling is explored. The personality variables that attempt to capture the individual's perceived control over the environment are almost 70 percent as effective as achievement ability on earnings and have an effect almost equal to that of achievement ability on schooling. However, in absolute terms, these personality variables are quite unimportant, and thus previous studies that neglected such variables have not erred greatly.

Variables indicating the amount of schooling each parent would like the student to attain are very important; in addition, when contrasted to the other variables discussed thus far, their inclusion in earnings equations lowers the estimated schooling coefficient by 10 percent. These variables have the single most important influence on earnings when compared to the ability and personality variables. Also, in the schooling equation their relative dominance becomes even more apparent. However, other results suggest this effect may be exaggerated because of the use of expected income and schooling. These results do suggest that "objective" indicators of background, such as a father's and mother's actual education or family income, are less important than such "subjective" factors as the amount of motivation received in the home.

Also, an individual's high school has negligible effects on schoolings and earnings. This result is limited to the effects that can be estimated from differences between schools. Most of the variance in these variables is within schools.

This is one of those areas where there is potential for misinterpretation. Should one conclude from this that schooling doesn't matter? It is probably more reasonable to conclude, as did Jencks and Reisman in 1968, that this is the effect of schools being very slow to change their curricula in response to changes in labor market structure. High schools by and large are not known for being immediately responsive to changing needs of the labor market. This lack of responsiveness may be one reason that there is no detectable effect of schooling on labor market success.

Examining the validity of the use of expected, rather than actual, income and schooling and testing for the causes of failure to fulfill plans for postsecondary education reveal two interesting results. One is that parental desires for children's schooling tend to be greater than the children's own desires. Two possible interpretations of this result are that either children are more aware of the decline in the value of college education or that they simply have different utility functions. A more general conclusion is that no "objective" factors such as family income, parents' education, or number of siblings influence the probabilities of disappointment.

Further research with additional follow-up data should explore in more detail the differences that may result from using actual income as opposed to expectations. Other interesting possibilities deal with examination in greater depth the issues related to the realization of schooling plans.

Higher Education Student Demand Analysis

The critical problem in this area traditionally has been a weakness in the available analytic methodology. None of the previous analyses of the demand for postsecondary education (chapter 7) has been adequately sophisticated from a behavioristic standpoint, both because of the poor data bases available and because the range of options used in these models were artificially constrained. The choice model presented in chapter 8 is derived from a much better data base, and it also dramatically expands the range of options available to students. Therefore, this model much more closely represents reality as confronted by students leaving high school. This is especially true in the sense that this choice model assumes that students make simultaneous tradeoffs among a very broad set of alternatives, whereas most previous studies of the demand for postsecondary education have either taken a very constrained view of the range of options open to students or have assumed a hierarchical choice pattern wherein choices are assumed to be made in aribitrary sequences. It is extremely difficult to encompass combinations of various activities within either of these two previously available methodologies.

The nation is committed to a postsecondary aid strategy in higher education that grants aid to students enabling them to make choices, and the choice model provides a tool for examining the differential impact of various policies, strategies, and types of aid. The type of simulation analysis (chapter 9) that can be done with this tool assumes that aid is granted in some particular fashion; this model can then predict the overall distribution of students among various types of institutions and other entities.

The Higher Education Student Choice Model

Several alternatives are assumed to be available to the students in the sample: all colleges to which the student applies and is accepted; the public two-year college closest to the student's home; all public vocational programs to which the student applies and is accepted; all private vocational programs wherein the closest is within 60 miles of the student's home; full-time work; a combined part-time work and part-time school alternative; for males military service; and for females homemaking. The variables assumed to affect individual choices include the quality of the alternative, student academic ability, tuition and fees, room and board costs, transportation, financial aid, income of associated alternatives, family income, sex, and race.

The qualitative features of these parameter estimates reveal that, for a student of given academic ability, the attractiveness of education alternatives first increases with the average quality of other students enrolled in them, peaks at a point where average ability is above the ability of the student in question, and then falls with further increases in average quality. The basic conclusion here is that, as expected, people do not want to be with others whose aptitude is very different from their own. Also, all else equal, the attractiveness of working after high school completion rises as a student's expected yearly income from work increases.

With respect to college attendance, both higher living costs and greater travel distances decrease the probability of attendance. The race variable appears to have a relatively small impact on the probability of college attendance, in the sense that blacks are almost as likely to choose college when all other things are equal. Also, peer group or community characteristics affect the probability of attending any particular type of postsecondary institution in that the higher percentage of a high school's graduates attending a particular kind of school, the more likely it is that a particular student from that high school will choose that type of school.

Furthermore, as expected, increases in tuition decrease a schooling alternative's attractiveness, while increases in scholarship, loan, and other financial aid have positive effects. However, though certain different types of aid are distinguishable in the NLS sample (such as scholarship aid, work aid, loan aid, and direct aid), the myriad of federal programs are not distinguishable. Hence, though data problems make it very difficult to distinguish among these different kinds of programs, the methodology that has been developed here permits such distinctions in forecasting. Also, the same amount of aid information does not exist for all alternatives; unless an institution is actually attended by the student, there is no information available on any alternative other than first-, second-, or third-choice colleges. This makes vocational school aid information particularly unavailable. Thus, although the general characteristic of the aid increasing the probability of attendance is in fact verified, the exact forms of aid need to be specified more carefully to be completely analyzed with this model.

We also find the expected result that as tuition increases, the probability of attendance decreases, but this effect also varies dramatically as a function of program length. Moreover, it appears that a dollar more of scholarship aid is more effective than a dollar less of tuition, but the exact and precise estimate of the magnitude of the difference have not yet been performed.

Analysis for high- and low-income groups separately revealed that all the money variables (cost and aid especially) had less effect on the high-income people than on the low-income people. It seems that, for annual family incomes above roughly $10,000, tuition does not appear to have a substantial effect. This is particularly important in light of the argument that those who can afford to do so should pay higher tuition with the additional revenue being used for scholarship aid to low-income individuals. The access of families with above-median income would not be significantly reduced by increasing tuitions, and yet substantial funds could therefore be raised for scholarships to low-income households. However, this conclusion must be qualified in that the break point chosen for family income was simply the sample average. Hence, although the general conclusion is valid, it is not clear whether the breakpoint is actually at the sample mean. Further work is necessary to determine the precise effects of tuition on various income classes.

Also, the coefficient for expected annual wage is larger for low-income people than for high-income people. In other words, if one comes from a low-income family, a high local wage rate makes the work alternative more attractive than it does for high-income people. Thus, an extremely important result here is that this approach permits us to expose certain subtleties in the student's decision-making process that are of great importance now that the discussion of postsecondary financing policy has reached precisely those subtleties. Previously, for example, work of the National Commission on the Financing of Postsecondary Education assumed that a $100 tuition reduction was the same as $100 of scholarship aid; much earlier work on this subject has been based on similar assumptions.

Finally, chapter 9 forecasts the effects of several hypothetical education policies on the postsecondary decisions of students in our sample. Simulations of the effect of shifts in labor market opportunities suggest that for a "representative" individual, a 10 percent increase in the expected annual wage earnings would lead to an approximately 1 percent increase in the number of persons choosing to work full time. Also, simulations of hypothetical policy alternatives suggest that aid given directly to students, and not conditional on the amount of tuition paid, has a substantially greater effect on educational choices than does aid in the form of tuition subsidies. Again, earlier studies of postsecondary student finance base missed this subtle difference. These illustrative examples are based on policies that give aid to individuals according to their family income. It should be made clear, however, that these simulations primarily illustrate the ways in which a more precisely specified model could be used to analyze alternative policies.

Vocational Education Analysis: Supply versus Demand

The examination of vocational education (chapters 10 and 11) is not directly comparable to the analysis in other sections of this report. Rather than examine such standard methodological and empirical questions as who goes, why, and the role of such factors as parental background, school, or sex, these chapters focus on the behavior of the providers of vocational education in response to a governmental strategy of subsidizing certain suppliers. The starting perspective was to look at the interaction of supply and demand, but especially at the effect of the federal policy of supply subsidy in vocational education. The actual shape of the supply curve, demand curve, or the effect of the subsidy on overall demand are not delineated; however, issues of price and quantity are addressed. Thus, part IV presents a market perspective critically important to any considerations of attendance to the current government strategy of trying to foster a certain kind of vocational training by aiding only a class of publicly controlled institutions.

The Theory of a Two-Price Market

A general theory of the two-price market is outlined in chapter 10, which provides (1) a framework for thinking about a federal institutional aid policy and social service aid in which two-price markets are created through subsidized public institutions and unsubsidized private institutions, and (2) a description of federal legislation in vocational education as a "test case" of the effect on student access and choice of stimulating construction and expansion of enrollment exclusively through subsidies to the supply side of the secondary and postsecondary vocational education market. It also describes some of the problems that policy-makers and researchers have perceived with the public vocational education system and relates them to some of the problems and unique characteristics of the two-price market.

Chapter 10 therefore examines institutional behavior in the face of a strategy of institutional subsidization and fills a gap in the discussion and understanding of supply-demand relationships in postsecondary education. There is a dearth of previous work on the response of the supply side, yet supply side behavior is clearly important. The importance of this analysis lies in the examination of supply subsidization (that is, institutional aid), and it looks at the response of the supply side providers to that strategy; it is then possible to test supply side behavior in relation to the demand side analysis that focuses primarily on the response of students to the net effects of either supply or demand subsidization. For example, in the student response (demand) analysis, examining the effect of low tuition is basically examining the effect of a supply side subsidy strategy. This analysis is therefore important to policy discussions about issues such as institutional aid, the possibility of subsidizing students rather than institutions, and revising vocational and educational policy in general.

Institutional aid approaches that are limited to a single class of institutions in a market (that is, those publicly operated) lead to a "two-price market." The two-price market perspective—specifically, the implications of having both subsidized public institutions and unsubsidized private institutions—is examined. The overriding question is that, in the whole analysis of postsecondary policies, there has been a complete absence of traditional sorts of market perspectives, consideration of market effects, and consideration of supplier response patterns. Certain market forces seem not to have been taken into account in designing the present vocational education aid policies, and certain important results of this lack of appropriate focus are revealed. However, this should not be regarded as stating that the whole philosophy had some potentially very serious weaknesses because it failed to consider some behavior in the training market resulting from certain economic forces. Rather, it has had unintended and unforeseen perverse consequences; too much was expected of the policy. But now, with new realism, it may still be a reasonable policy in that the total costs and benefits of this policy have not been completely examined here. A primary conclusion is that the price-value tradeoff elucidated in chapter 10 is important in students' eyes and is a powerful influence heretofore neglected in analysis.

In summary, the government strategy of institutional aid to public, but not private, vocational schools has been examined. While the complete case study of vocational education may be found elsewhere, nevertheless, it should be apparent that federal legislation with an intent to expand and improve vocational education and a strategy of institutional aid selectively awarded to only public institutions would run into difficulties. Students are consumers quite sensitive to price and nonprice characteristics of schools, and any price advantage of public schools would be noticed; this would, in turn, lead to excess demand for public programs. Normal competitive market pressures on public schools would be muted.

It is clear that problems have developed in vocational education as well as in other social service sectors—for example, problems of misapplied rationing, excessive spending, and nonresponsiveness of teachers and administrators to students' needs. The questions of whether alternative strategies would have produced a better result, or whether, on balance, the benefits of federal aid exceed the costs, have not been addressed here and require careful additional investigation; these questions are being examined by the authors in subsequent work.

The Vocational Education Choice Model

Chapter 11 describes a more rigorous empirical test of one predicted outcome in a two-price market: the development of a price-value tradeoff between public and private vocational schools. The evidence suggests, in fact, that such a phenomenon does occur in response to student preferences and institutional behavior. The tool used here is a choice model, similar to that presented in part III of this report, but with a set of alternatives aimed at detecting student choices within the vocational education sector. It should also be noted that this analysis is a major improvement over survey research approaches because it does not just ask people who have already done something why they think they did it; instead, it examines their behavior and establishes a predictive rationale. Again, however, an evaluation of the relative costs and benefits of institutional aid to public schools is not attempted.

**Part I
Full Sample Analysis**

3 Actual Post–High School Experiences

Choice of Pathway

The U.S. high school senior is faced with a bewildering array of choices as high school ends. At one level there are the choices between further education and work and the various possible part- and full-time mixtures; there are also other options such as the military or homemaking. Each major categorical option at this level may have a dozen specific suboptions, each reflecting a particular institution or type of training or a particular kind of job and career entry.

Not only is the student confronted with choosing among these immediate activities, which, given a large number of schools within easy commuting distance, can easily number in the hundreds for an urban high school graduate, but he or she is also faced with the problem of trying to anticipate the sequential and exclusionary implications of each decision. To begin on certain pathways may begin to exclude other options, although the increased interest in career change in recent years is somewhat ameliorating this. Some pathways have certain logical progressions of activities, while still others erect certain barriers, such as the increased difficulty of entering postsecondary education if one has "stopped out" in the years immediately following high school. Even today, many colleges tend to favor the entry of undergraduates immediately from high school rather than those who have worked for a few years or have engaged in training in a vocational school.

It is significant that the array of choices actually faced by high school seniors is, in fact, so complicated that no single analytical perspective can depict the entire process in its full detail and fully explain the decisionmaking process that occurs. The complicated interaction between individual preferences, predispositions, beliefs, and abilities, and institutional behavior patterns, requirements, and locations, further complicated by economic and social factors, must

This chapter is primarily the work of George J. Nolfi and William H. Epstein with the assistance of Winship C. Fuller and Valerie I. Nelson.

All the tables in this chapter are based on the NLS data set, a random stratified sample of the high school senior population in 1972. The NLS Users Manual provides a set of alternatives weighting schemes that take into account the school sampling pattern and make adjustments for certain nonresponse patterns. These weighting schemes vary for different questions. The effect of the weights would be minor percentage changes in the detailed results of the tables, more of which were deemed of insufficient magnitude so as to significantly alter the results.

be addressed by each graduate with the added complication of varied and inadequate information about each choice.

Rather little is known about the exact way in which people under these circumstances make their decisions. Thus, in various parts of this report, several different perspectives have been taken in an effort to analyze the NLS data in depth and elucidate certain particular aspects of these decisions.

For simplicity, the range of options can be aggregated into the 14 categorical types listed in table 3-1. Clearly for any given individual, each of these particular categories may include one, three, or a dozen or more specific options. The NLS data set permits analysis of students' post-high school expectations in terms of these 14 categories; the actual activity status one and two years following

Table 3-1
Categorization of Activity States

Activity state	Expect[a]	Actual 73[b]	Actual 74[c]
Full-time work only	1	1	1
Full-time college only	2	2	2
Full-time vocational training only	3	3	3
Full-time apprenticeship or on-the-job training only	4		
Full-time work plus part-time college	5	6	6
Full-time work plus part-time vocational training	6	7	7
Full-time college plus part-time work	7		
Full-time vocational training plus part-time work	8		
Full-time on-the-job training plus part-time college	9		
Full-time on-the-job training plus part-time vocational training	10		
Military only	11	8	8
Full-time homemaker only	12	9	9
Full-time homemaker plus part-time college	13		
Full-time homemaker plus part-time vocational training	14		
Part-time work only		4	4
Other		10	10

Note: The analysis presented in the remainder of this chapter is derived from a close examination of crosstabulations of each of these three variables by race, sex, aptitude, socioeconomic status, family income, and high school program. The actual tables used here are available from either the authors or in the full report from which this book is derived.

[a]Expected immediate post-high school activity, March-May 1972.

[b]Actual activities in October 1973.

[c]Actual activities in October 1974.

high school graduation is then examined with the 10 activity state categories also noted in table 3-1. Here again, each of the ten general categories probably includes a multitude of specific activities for each individual. Analysis at the level of those specific activities (which is of course the level at which individual students must make their decisions) is simply impossible with any available data or theoretical constructs. Thus, our analysis is conducted at the level of these general categories.

In this chapter, the actual activities of the class of 1972 are analyzed in terms of the categories in Table 3-1 and some explanations of the observed behavior patterns are presented. In subsequent chapters, specific aspects of several of these categories and pathways are analyzed in more detail. However, the price of this more detailed analysis is a loss of generality through the assumptions that must be made.

What has happened to the class of 1972 as its members pursue a variety of different paths is described in this chapter. In particular, the paths actually taken in relation to the expected paths are analyzed. Though mathematical functions that would explain why people with given characteristics at certain points in time would move along certain particular paths are not developed here, this chapter does present an overall analysis of the types of individuals who intentionally or circumstantially end up on certain paths. Subsequent chapters choose selected subgroups and develop considerable mathematical analysis. Moreover, in this initial segment of the study, the entire NLS sample is examined, whereas specific subsamples are employed in other chapters.

Thus, part I of this book presents a general analysis of the characteristics of this sample; it is followed by some specialized analyses of various aspects of each of the three major paths that a high school graduate may pursue.

Plans and Actual Activities: Socioeconomic Determinants

This section elucidates the contrast between expectations and reality. In particular, anticipated activity in May 1972 is compared with actual activity in October 1973 and October 1974. First, however, the expectations themselves will be described, with special emphasis on differences by sex, race, aptitude, socioeconomic status (SES), family income, and high school program.

About 26 percent of the females intended to work full time, and about 20 percent intended to go to college full time, in contrast to about 23 percent and 18 percent respectively for the males. Vocational training, on-the-job training, and the combination of full-time work and part-time college were the intention of relatively small and approximately equal percentages of men and women. Slightly more men, about 25 percent, intended to go to college full time and work part time, versus 22 percent of the females. About equal numbers of males and females planned to enter vocational training and work. The major differences between men and women existed in the percentage going to the military (7.1 for the males and .9 for females) and percentage planning to be homemakers (.1 percent for males and 6 percent for females). In general, no surprise exists here.

When the class of 1972 is divided into three racial groups—whites (78 percent), blacks (12 percent), and other minorities (10 percent)—somewhat more blacks and other minorities intend to work full time (27 percent and 30 percent) than whites (23 percent). In contrast, more whites intend to go to college full time (21 percent) versus blacks and other minorities (13 percent each). More whites also intend to go to college full time and work part time (24 percent versus 21 percent). This suggests that the availability of work while at college does little to influence the choice between working or attending college, at least as far as racial differences are concerned. More blacks intend to combine vocational training with work (16 percent) than whites and others (4 percent and 11 percent). Otherwise, no great differences are apparent.

Numerous differences exist in the effect of aptitude. About 39 percent of the low-aptitude group intended to work full time, as opposed to 24 percent for the medium-aptitude group and 8 percent for the high. These figures are approximately reversed for full-time college attendance. The same pattern as college full time appears for those intending to attend college full time and work part time. Other categories, such as apprenticeship programs and vocational training, display the same tendencies. About 5 percent of the low-aptitude individuals intended to enter the military, 4 percent of the medium-aptitude, and 3 percent of the high-aptitude; the same trend exists for homemakers. More of the low-aptitude individuals (7 percent) were undecided (said they intended to do something else) versus 5 percent for medium aptitude, and 2 percent for high aptitude.

Interestingly enough, almost exactly the same percentages (within two or three points) exist for low, medium, and high SES categories as appeared in the corresponding aptitude classification. These similarities suggest that low aptitude and low SES are equal handicaps in the pursuit of further education. Furthermore, attempts at equalizing educational opportunities may not have been very successful.

These apparent effects of aptitude and SES are somewhat reduced when students are differentiated only by parents' income. Percentages for those with middle incomes (that is, whose parents earn between $7,500 and $12,000) are almost the same as those of medium SES or aptitude. However, smaller percentages (about 31 percent) of children of low-income parents want to work full time, and higher percentages go to college full time (11 percent). The reverse holds true for high-income parents.

Variations in expectations according to high school program are also distributed much as one would expect. Those in academic programs were much more likely to plan to attend college full time without working (36 percent) than those in general programs (11 percent) or those in vocational programs (4.2 percent). Roughly the same figures pertain for the full-time college and part-time work alternative. Students in vocational programs showed some tendency to obtain additional vocational training. Some 5 percent of those in general programs intended to enter the military, versus 4 percent for those in vocational programs, and 3 percent for those in academic programs; 4.5 percent of those in general and vocational programs planned to become homemakers, versus 1 percent for those in academic programs.

The actual 1973 activity states reveal that 42 percent of the males and 27.3 percent of the females were employed full-time. Thus, approximately the same percentage of females are working full time as expected to so work; however, this percentage for males has almost doubled. Approximately equal numbers of men and women are in college full time while not working (23 percent and 20 percent respectively), and 12 percent of both males and females attend college full time and work part time. The college figures are roughly in keeping with expectations, but only half those who expected to both attend college and work are actually so engaged. Many of these people seem to have chosen to work full time instead. Possibly the earnings from part-time employment simply could not pay college tuition and living expenses.

Differences between reality and expectation in such areas as vocational training, full-time work with part-time college, and part-time work are quite small. With respect to combining vocational education and work, somewhat fewer actually achieved their expectations, regardless of sex. Slightly more men (10 percent) entered the military than had expected, possibly because of rapid pay increases granted during this period. The biggest single shift, mainly among those intending to go to college or to obtain vocational training while working, is to homemakers; about 30 percent of the women became homemakers, whereas only 6 percent intended to be. Thus, for both men and women, those intending to work while furthering their education (either college) or vocational) are more likely than others to be frustrated. Many of the males take full-time jobs, whereas the females tend to become homemakers.

As was the case with sex categories, the racial distinctions show more individuals working full-time than had expected to. However, the numbers actually working are almost equal across racial groups (about one-third), as compared with a markedly lower number of whites expecting to work. Members of minority groups are thus perhaps more realistic about their chances of being otherwise occupied. The number of whites attending college full time while not working (22 percent) is about equal to those expecting to attend, but the percentages of blacks and other minorities actually in college (18 percent and 17 percent respectively) increases over their expectations. The number of those combining college with part-time work decreases sharply, as noted previously, and about equally for all groups; the same effect holds true for the vocational training and work alternative. However, for this latter category, blacks and to a lesser extent other minorities had previously expressed a greater interest than whites; now all groups are about equally represented. Quite possibly some of these minority groups decided to attend college instead. About equal numbers (4 percent) had expressed a desire to enter the military; in reality, blacks are more heavily represented, with about 8 percent. No differences across racial groups are apparent in the percentage actually becoming homemakers. Perhaps the most interesting result is the increased number of blacks and other minorities attending college relative to their expectations. This phenomenon may be at least partly caused by a constant or even increased return to college for blacks during this period versus sharply decreased returns for whites.[1]

The same patterns seen with respect to expectations are apparent in actual behavior for various aptitude groups. More are working full time than had expected to. Though far more low-aptitude people are working relative to desires, twice the expected number of high-aptitude individuals are actually working, versus only a 20 percent increase among low-aptitude individuals. Full-time college attendance while not working shifts in about the same manner. Attendance at college full time while working part time drops more than proportionately for low-aptitude individuals, those presumably least capable of assuming the burdens of both college and work. With respect to the vocational training and work combination, all groups decline relative to expectations, but more or less equally. A slight rise is apparent in the percentage of those entering the military, for all aptitude groups. The number actually becoming homemakers increases greatly over expectations, especially for high aptitude individuals, where 8.6 percent become homemakers relative to the 1.2 percent who so desired. For other aptitude groups the percentages increase by a factor of four. These changes across groups are less striking than those with respect to race or sex classification. The most noticeable change is the proportionately larger number of high-aptitude individuals who revise their plans, especially with regard to work and homemaking. Although these individuals may posses high intelligence, as measured by standardized tests, this ability is not necessarily translated into more accurate predictions for the future. Of course, the declining value of college may have been detected more rapidly by high-aptitude students than by those with lower aptitudes.

As was the case with our expectations data, the actual behavior of students across SES groups is very similar to that across aptitude groups. Thus, our conclusion that low aptitude and low SES have the same relative effect on planning decisions also pertains to actual behavior one year later. The contrasts between high and low SES groups are mitigated when family income grouping is used again confirming our conclusions about planning. Thus, low parental income is not the only handicap faced by low SES children; other factors, such as parents' education, also play an important role.

The number of high school graduates working full time is greater than expected with respect to all the high school programs, with 42 percent from general programs working, 19 percent from academic programs, and 50 percent from vocational programs. Proportionately, the biggest increase relative to high school plans is for the graduates of academic programs. Regardless of curriculum, all groups slightly exceed their expectations with respect to full-time college. All groups are disappointed in attempts to combine work and vocational training; this is especially true for those in vocational or general programs where only between one-fourth and one-fifth of those intending to combine work and vocational training actually succeed in doing so, whereas about half those in academic programs fulfill this desire. This apparent lack of opportunity for combining vocational training with work is quite serious; many of those who need such training cannot afford to pursue it full time and thus need to earn something while learning. Many of these are thus forced to take less desirable jobs on a full-time basis. Also, for all program categories, only half those intending to combine full-time college with part-time work actually do so. Many more than expected become homemakers, especially those in academic programs where 8 percent (versus the 1 percent so planning) actually become so occupied. For the other program categories, this percentage increases only by a factor of four to five. The previously noted deficiency in opportunities for combining vocational training with work is especially apparent here. Remedies for this situation merit careful attention.

These same trends continue into 1974; about 5 percent more men are working full time, and 4 percent more women. College full-time attendance is down about 3 percent for both sexes. Other categories are largely unchanged from 1973 levels. A slight decrease occurs in full-time vocational training and in the combined work and vocational training alternative. The percentage of women who are homemakers increases from 29 percent to 31 percent. Thus, no new trends emerge from the 1974 figures. For all races full-time employment varies by about 6 to 8 percent. Full-time attendance at college decreases for all races, but less for blacks and other minorities than for whites. Thus, the gap between percentages of minorities and whites attending college full time decreases still further. Few other categories change significantly. The percentage of blacks who are homemakers is now exactly the same as the other groups (16 percent); in 1973, 18 percent of the blacks, but only 16 percent of the whites and other minorities, were homemakers. In general then, for race as well as sex, the paths established in 1973 continue, except for the increase in full-time work, the decrease in full-time college, and the small decreases in vocational training.

Like previous categories, all aptitude groups experience an increase of five percentage points in the number working full time. However, because few high-aptitude individuals were working, this amounts to a more than proportional increase for them. All categories decrease in the number enrolled in college full time. However, low-aptitude individuals only decrease one percentage point

(8 percent to 7 percent); medium aptitude individuals, three percentage points (14 percent to 16 percent); and high aptitude individuals six percentage points (40 percent to 34 percent). Proportionately, these decreases are about the same, and thus no group is particularly affected by recent declines in college attendance. Slightly fewer low-aptitude individuals are becoming homemakers (21-19 percent) and slightly more high- and medium-aptitude individuals are doing so (16-17 percent and 9-10 percent respectively). Overall, no major changes occur among the aptitude categories.

In a manner similar to that displayed in 1973, the same trends hold for SES and family income in 1974. Also, the results for high school programs display similar changes, namely a uniform absolute increase in full-time work (a greater than proportional one for graduates of academic programs) and an equal proportionate drop in the numbers attending college. Slight decreases exist for all categories with respect to vocational training and the combined work-vocational training alternative. Other categories are roughly constant.

Degree of Plan Fulfillment

The differences in expectations and actual behavior have been described for various subcategories of race, sex, aptitude, SES, family income, and high school preparation. This section contains a more detailed analysis of students' expectations by tracing each subsamples, delineated by expectations as of May 1972 through their status as of October 1974. In much of this analysis, many of the categories contained too few people to be considered sufficiently important to warrant discussion.

Some 60 percent of those intending to work full time in the spring of 1972 did so in October 1973; of the remaining 40 percent more than half (23 percent) became homemakers instead, with the rest scattered among various activities. Of those planning to enter college full time, 58 percent did so; another 18 percent combined college and part-time work; 11 percent went to work full-time; and 5 percent became homemakers. Only 12 percent who wanted to pursue vocational training full-time succeeded in doing so; another 9 percent did manage to find work combined with vocational training. Of the remaining 79 percent, 43 percent (by far the largest group) went to work full time and 23 percent became homemakers. Only 7 percent of those intending to combine full-time work and part-time college actually did so. Another 45 percent simply worked, while 7 percent went to college full-time, and 22 percent became homemakers. Those planning to combine work and vocational training fared somewhat better. This goal was achieved by 10 percent, while 5 percent became involved with vocational training full time and 55 percent went to work full time. Another 5 percent entered the military and 19 percent became homemakers. Attending college full time and working part time was the combination of work and training most likely to be fulfilled; some 32 percent followed this plan, with an additional 31 percent attending college full time only. Only 7 percent went to work full time and 8 percent became homemakers. Some 56 percent of those planning to enter the military did so, with another 28 percent electing to work full-time, and 6 percent becoming homemakers. Those expecting to be home-makers were the most successful of all groups in achieving their goals, with an 81 percent success rate. Of the remaining 19 percent, 13 percent went to work full time. Only 7 percent of those intending to work part time did so. Almost half (45 percent) went to work full time, and 6 percent went to college full time. With the exception of those planning to be homemakers, a larger percent-age of those planning part-time work became homemakers (29 percent) than any other group. Of those who were unclassifiable with respect to plans, only 3 percent remained unclassifiable in 1973. Many of them (49 percent) went to work full time and another 18 percent became homemakers. Full-time college occupied 10 percent, while 6 percent worked part time, and 6 percent joined the service.

Several conclusions can be drawn from these figures. First, for a variety of reasons, many people change their plans. The highest success rate attained by any group, around 80 percent, is for homemakers; the next two most suc-cessful groups (full-time college and full-time work) succeeded only 60 percent of the time. Because only 3 percent of the 1972 sample intended to be home-makers, these figures suggest that, for almost the entire sample, individuals have, at best, a 60 percent chance of realizing their plans. These figures do not tell whether the problem is simply poor choice of plans, or rather a lack of funds or opportunities for pursuing one's career objectives.

A second major conclusion is that those planning more complicated activi-ties (a combination of work and college, or of work and vocational training) are much less likely to achieve their plans. The relevant figures are 32 percent for the college full time and work part time combination, 10 percent for the work with vocational training alternative, and 7 percent for full-time work with part-time college. These figures strongly suggest a need for more such opportun-ities. Especially disturbing is the lack of facilities for combining vocational train-ing with work; most students must instead work full time, presumably in a less skilled capacity, and may never have the opportunity to upgrade their job skills.

For those expecting to work in 1972, the percentages for the various types of actual behavior in October 1974 are practically identical to those for 1973. With respect to full-time college plans, however, more changes are apparent. Of those expecting to be in college full-time, only 48 percent are now there (versus 58 percent previously) and some 15 percent are now at work (10 per-cent previously); thus about half those leaving college went to work full time with the other half almost equally distributed among those combining college with full-time work and those who are homemakers. Similarly, in 1974 fewer are in vocational training, with the difference mainly entering full-time work

(55 percent as compared to 43 percent previously). A similar trend is observed for those combining full-time work with part-time college, as well as for the combination of work and vocational training. Those expecting to pursue college full time and work part time fare about the same. Some 26 percent are now working full time (as compared to 17 percent previously). About 5 percent of this 9 percent increase comes from the full-time college category with the remainder coming from the full-time work and part-time college category. Other categories are largely unchanged.

Figures for the military are also relatively static. The percentage of those who were planning to become homemakers and actually did so decreases slightly, from 81 percent to 77 percent. All these started working full-time; the other categories are constant. No major changes are apparent in those planning to work part-time only. Still more detailed results comparing 1973 and 1974 activities are available by analyzing separately for each expectation category the various activities through both years.[2]

Of those expecting to work full-time, some 50 percent did so for both 1973 and 1974. The next largest category of this group expecting to work full-time consists of those who were housewives both years (17 percent). About 5 percent were homemakers in 1973 and worked full time in 1974, and about 6 percent did the opposite. Some 4 percent entered the military for both years, and the remaining 20 percent are scattered among the remaining categories, none of which encompass more than 2 percent.

Of those planning only to attend college full-time some 41 percent actually did so for both years. Another 4 percent went to college in 1973 and worked full time the following year, and some 1 percent did the reverse. An additional 9 percent combined full-time college with part-time work. Some 11 percent more went to college the first year, and then continued with college but also worked part time the following year, whereas 5 percent reversed the order. Possibly being in college makes the search for suitable part-time work easier. Only 4 percent actually became homemakers for both years. No other category accounts for more than 2 percent.

Only 2 percent of those intending to pursue only vocational training actually did so for both years; around 5 percent did so the first year and then worked the following year. The largest percentage worked both years (30 percent). The next largest category consists of those who were homemakers both years (18 percent), while 7 percent worked in 1973 and became homemakers in 1974, and 5 percent did the opposite. Finally, 6 percent combined work with vocational training in 1973 and worked full time in 1974.

About 2 percent of those planning to combine full-time work with vocational training managed to acomplish their goal for both years. Another 7 percent were able to combine these functions in 1973 and then worked full-time in 1974; some 1 percent did the reverse. A relatively large proportion (40 percent) ended up working full time both years. The military accounted for

4 percent through 1974. Most of the remaining became homemakers for at least one of the years; some 14 percent were homemakers both years; while 3 percent worked the first year and became homemakers the next year, with 5 percent doing the reverse.

Only 17 percent of those intending to combine full-time college with part-time work actually did so. Another 7 percent did so the first year, and simply attended college in 1974; the same number did the reverse. An additional 17 percent attended college full time both years, while 12 percent worked full time both years. Some 8 percent attended college one year and worked the other, with about half as many picking the reverse order. Here homemakers account for a smaller proportion than in other previous categories; only 6 percent were homemakers both years.

Over half (51 percent) of those intending to enter the military did so for both years. Only 3 percent did so the first year and then worked full time in 1974; some 2 percent delayed their entry into the military while working for a year. Most of the remaining worked full time both years; an additional 3 percent became homemakers for both years. Of those planning to become homemakers, 72 percent did so for both years. An additional 8 percent became homemakers the first year and worked full time the next year, with 5 percent doing the opposite. Working full time both years occupied an additional 7 percent.

The group of students planning to become full-time homemakers were quite successful with some 72 percent actually engaged in this activity both years. Of the remaining 28 percent, almost 8 percent were full-time homemakers the first year and then went to work full time; the reverse of this pattern was followed by about 5 percent of these students. An additional 7 percent worked full time both years, with no other pattern accounting for more than 2 percent of this subsample. When the actual activities of the six other groups whose plans could be categorized prior to high school graduation are examined, by far the largest categories in each of these groups were those individuals who actually chose to work full time.

Some final conclusions can be drawn from these more detailed figures. Except for homemakers, where about three-fourths stuck to their plans over two years, no more than 50 percent of any group managed to adhere to the expectations expressed in 1972. Furthermore, this figure holds for those intending to do only one thing—that is work full time, attend college full time, or enter the military. For those whose plans were more complicated (by combining work with college or vocational training), the probability of success is considerably lower. This seeming lack of opportunities for receiving further education while working at the same time deserves serious consideration. Another consistent phenomenon is that many of those who have other plans actually become homemakers; this is a less common occurrence for those planning to attend college.

Summary Conclusions

First, the various paths that may be taken by students as they make the transition from high school into various combinations of work and schooling are described. Fourteen individual status categories of expected immediate post-high school activity and their actual activity during October 1973 and October 1974 are presented.

Second, plans and actual activities of these high school graduates 17 and 29 months following graduation in light of such socioeconomic determinants as sex, race, aptitude, SES, family income, and high school program revealed the striking conclusion that significantly higher proportions of males are working full time and females are homemakers than expected to be. College attendance is roughly in keeping with expectations, but only half of those who expected to both attend college and work simultaneously are actually so engaged. Similar reduction in expectations occur for those hoping to combine work with vocational education. In general, across SES and aptitude categories, many students who hoped to go to school part time are forced to work full time with no school. This condition warrants serious public policy attention.

Another further striking conclusion is that white males' aspirations for college are the least likely to be fulfilled; also, the effect of aptitude on attitudes toward full-time work are presented. Only the more important or the more obvious conclusions that can be derived from such cross-tabular analysis are actually discussed in the body of the report.

Third, the observed substantial variation between students' expectations and their actual activity leads to two conclusions. It is readily apparent that, for a variety of reasons, many people change their plans. The highest success rate attained by any group, around 80 percent, is for homemakers; the next two most successful groups (full-time college and full-time work) succeeded only 60 percent of the time. Because only 3 percent of the 1972 sample intended to be homemakers, these figures suggest that, for almost the entire sample, individuals have at best a 60 percent chance of realizing their plans. Unfortunately, this analysis does not reveal whether the problem is simply poor choice of plans or a lack of funds or opportunities for pursuing career objectives.

It is equally apparent that those planning more complicated activities (a combination of work and college, or of work and vocational training) are much less likely to achieve their plans. The relevant figures are 32 percent for the full-time college and part-time work combination, 10 percent for the work with vocational training alternative, and 7 percent for full-time work with part-time college. These figures strongly suggest a need for more such opportunities. Especially disturbing is the lack of facilities for combining vocational training with work; most of these graduates must instead work full time, presumably in a less skilled capacity, and may never have the opportunity to upgrade their job skills.

In particular, except for homemakers, where about three-fourths stuck to their plans over a span of two years, no more than 50 percent of any group managed to adhere to their 1972 expectations through 1974. Furthermore, this figure holds for those intending to do only one thing—that is, work full time, attend college full time, or enter the military. For those whose plans were more complicated (combining work with college or vocational training), the probability of success is considerably lower. This seeming lack of opportunities for receiving further education while working at the same time deserves serious consideration. Another consistent phenomenon is that many of those who have other plans actually become homemakers; this is less common for those planning to attend college.

In summary, many students fail to fulfill their plans and, in particular, many who had hoped to go to school or seek training are pushed into the work force full time. After graduation from high school, students appear to be forced to give up or lower their expectations, at least in the short term. More generally, any expectation that is a combination of any activities has a lower probability of fulfillment; the more complex the alternatives are, the less likely they are to be fulfilled.

Notes.

1. R. Freeman, *The Overeducated American*, (New York: Academic Press, 1976).

2. Although the tables containing these results are not included here, they are contained in University Consultants' report to HEW, *Experiences of Recent High School Graduates: The Transition to Work or Postsecondary Education*, by G. Nolfi and others (Cambridge, Mass.: University Consultants, Inc., 1977), on which this book is based.

**Part II
Labor Market Analysis**

4

Analysis of Nontraining-Oriented Graduates

This chapter focuses on that segment of the high school class of 1972 which did not intend to pursue any additional training immediately following high school graduation but intended to enter directly into the labor market. This subsample can be defined as those who responded in categories 01, 03, 04, 09, 10, and sometimes 02[1] to question 31 one in the student questionnaire (SQ).

In contrast, questions 1, 48, and 54 in the first follow-up questionnaire (FQ) allow us to identify what these individuals actually were doing in October 1972 and October 1973. Our intent is to analyze that transition from the plans to the actual experiences of this group as completely as possible.

Measures of Labor Market Success: Cross-Tabular Analysis

The transition from high school to work has been particularly unsuccessful for thousands of American teenagers. The extraordinarily high unemployment rates for those from 17 to 19 years of age are statistical measures of the social and economic frustration faced by many who choose not to go on to college. A variety of current theories purports to offer causal explanations for this lack of labor market success, ranging from simply "lack of skills" arguments to unrealistic expectations about salaries and positions. Recently, Feldstein has argued that the structure of unemployment compensation, reducing as it does the marginal cost of unemployment, may lead to longer voluntary periods of unemployment.[2]

Attitudes at Graduation

This section makes no attempt to offer a new theory of behavior. It is descriptive in that it relies on the sample data, not to formally test any existing or new theory of unemployment, but to begin to describe in some detail the characteristics of those teenagers who leave high school with some intention to enter directly into full-time employment. Our purpose in compiling this descriptive analysis is to glean some insight into how expectations are formed, particularly such questions as, What role if any does counseling play? How

This chapter reflects primarily the work of Arthur J. Corazzini and Winship C. Fuller.

early in the student's high school career does he decide to forego additional education? Does the timing of this decision not to pursue further schooling influence the probability of labor market success? Do blacks and whites differ in the timing of their decisions? Do expectations differ by race? By income level? Does any evidence suggest that increased resources devoted to labor market counseling prior to labor market entry could reduce the extent of teenage employment?

Timing of Educational Plans. We begin with a look at the timing of the decision *not* to pursue higher education. Specifically, working only with that subset of the sample who, in March through May of their last year of high school, were recorded as intending to work full time, we seek information about when in the high school career the decision not to pursue higher education was made. We also investigate whether the timing of that decision varies by race, sex, or income level.

The results are interesting. For the subsample as a whole we find that 19.2 percent are recorded as having decided prior to the tenth grade not to go on to college, but a full 38 percent were still undecided about eventual college careers. It can be argued that the 19 percent come to the labor market far better informed about job opportunities, may have engaged in more job-specific high school training, and may experience significantly greater success in the labor market. Therefore, it is interesting that the percentages of those making early decisions not to go on to college vary with income, race, and sex.

A somewhat greater percentage of low-income students were still unde-cided on college than were higher-income students (40 percent versus 35). There were somewhat more noticeable differences between the percentage of blacks (45.6) and the percentage of whites (35.4) who were still undecided about college in their senior year of high school. Twenty-one percent of the whites but only 14 percent of the blacks in this subsample had decided before the tenth grade not to go on to college. The differences may result from a variety of factors. In general, the expectations of blacks with regard to hoped-for years of education exceed those of whites. However, without further analysis we can not tell whether, for this sample, this is an expectation phe-nomenon or the result of differences in the amount of career option infor-mation available to the two groups. Comparing males and females reveals that 20.5 percent of the males and 18.6 percent of the females made early decisions not to go on to college. The percentages still undecided in the twelfth grade are 40.5 and 35.3 percent respectively. These tabulations are shown in table 4-1.

We emphasize that if early decisions to pursue full-time work are asso-ciated with greater labor market success, they would be consistent with standard approaches to job search behavior that argue that a longer search allows the individual to adjust expectations in the light of information

Table 4-1
Timing of College Decision
(percentages)

	Early decision not to go to college	Twelfth grade decision not to go to college
Subsample total	19.2	38.1
Whites	21.0	35.4
Blacks	14.3	45.6
Males	20.5	40.6
Females	18.6	35.3
Family income less than $7,500	17.7	40.9
Family income greater than $12,000	19.9	35.0

received and to equate the cost of additional search with probable benefits of that search. Clearly, individuals who know at the beginning of their high school careers that they intend to work full time on graduation have far more time to conduct a market search than those who make a late decision. Setting equity questions aside, increased labor market success for "early deciders" might argue for increased high school counseling. Given the critical nature of the ceteris paribus conditions, further speculation on these points ought to wait for the analysis of additional follow-up data.

Although this subset of the sample population intended to go to work on graduation, 52 percent thought they had the ability to go on to college, with the percentage so convinced rising with measured ability and income. Indeed the high-ability group is an interesting subset of all those directly entering the labor market. The survey reveals that 82.2% of these students were convinced of their ability to go on to school, yet they have decided at least a year prior to high school graduation not to do so. The characteristics of this subsample will be examined in more detail later.

Long-Run Educational Aspirations. Given that a significant percentage of the full-time work group is still undecided about further education as they approach high school graduation, it is of some value to look at the educational aspirations of this group in more detail. The timing of any educational plan is, of course, unknown at the outset of the survey; it will be revealed only by picking up individual decisions as they are made and recorded in response to status questions in follow-up surveys.

Approximately 42.4 percent of this subset thought they might eventually go on to post secondary education. Only 2.2 percent aspired to eventual graduate work and the predominant choice of those in the sample was some amount of vocational education with 24.4 percent so interested. However, in the year following high school, only 6 percent would have gone on to vocational technical, even if there were no obstacles in their path. We infer that the obstacles are perceived financial barriers or motivational and aptitude constraints. An additional 8.8 percent would have gone on to either junior college or four-year schools. Table 4–2 breaks up those "plans" and "plans no obstacles" decisions by income, race, sex, and ability levels. The responses seem to indicate higher educational aspirations on the part of blacks and a uniform lack of interest in education beyond four years of college. Junior college seems to be more popular with those with family incomes in excess of $12,000 and with those of higher measured ability.

Apparently, the decision to seek work full time on high school graduation is a complex one. This group differs from the high school population as a whole in ways that are not easily captured in the standard variables of race, sex, income, and ability. As a group it may perceive that the payoff to four years of college is not significantly different from the payoff of two years of college, and it prefers vocational training to either. Once again what is true of the whole group is atypical for those of high measured ability, with the added twist that the brightest apparently prefer four years of college to two years, but vocational education to four years of college. A good answer explaining this preference would add considerably to our understanding of the transition from high school to work. If, of course, the problem is simply one of information, the straight forward recommendations of increased counseling could be stressed. If, as is more likely to be the case, the problem involves motivational and attitudinal factors that are, in turn, influenced by such things as income, race, and sex, the proper course for public policy is less easily described.

Part b of table 4–2, describing the reported unconstrained decision of this group, once again indicates that voc-tech school is preferred to junior college. Indeed, voc-tech is about as popular as four years of college, although the percentages of respondents who indicate a serious immediate interest in pursuing postsecondary education drops considerably relative to the percentage that hope eventually to go on to school. Again the high-ability group is not typical of the sample as a whole and registers a strong interest in four-year colleges relative to voc-tech or junior college.

Career Choices. One final indication of educational aspirations is provided by data on career objectives. Those in the sample were asked to indicate their long-run job goals. Presumably, there should be some link between the intended occupational pursuit and educational aspirations. If career objectives are well thought out, a decision to pursue a career as a professional should be connected with a plan to pursue postsecondary education, even if short-run constraints prevent immediate entry into school. We might then observe that some individuals who are planning on full-time work on high school graduation may also plan to return to school to pursue a career objective. The job search activities of such individuals would again be expected to differ from those with no future educational plans.

Table 4–2
Educational Plans and Desires

	(a) Long-Run Educational Attainment[a] (Highest level eventually planned)					(b) Immediate Educational Desires, No Obstacles[b] (First year after high school)				
	H.S. Deg. or Less	Voc. Tech. Trade Bus.	Jr. Col.	4-Yr. Col. or Univ.	Grad or Prof. Schl.	No Educ.	Voc. Tech. Trade Bus.	Acad. Prog. Jr. Col.	Voc. Prog. Jr. Col.	4-Yr. Col. or Univ.
Overall	57.6	24.4	8.2	7.6	2.2	85.2	6.0	1.3	1.9	5.6
Family Income										
LT $7,500	59.5	25.3	6.0	6.7	2.4	83.8	7.5	1.3	2.0	5.4
$7,500–12,000	59.2	21.8	8.2	8.2	2.7	85.2	5.3	1.5	2.2	5.8
GT $12,000	50.6	27.9	11.7	8.8	1.1	86.1	4.3	1.3	1.7	6.6
Race										
Whites	59.0	23.5	8.6	7.2	1.7	86.1	5.4	1.1	1.9	5.5
Blacks	39.5	30.1	8.7	17.5	4.2	80.9	8.1	2.6	1.0	7.4
Sex										
Males	49.7	26.8	9.7	11.4	2.4	86.0	4.6	1.5	2.0	5.9
Females	62.6	21.6	7.9	5.6	2.2	84.4	6.9	1.3	1.7	5.7
Aptitude										
Low ability	57.8	26.1	7.4	6.2	2.3	87.1	6.5	1.3	1.4	3.7
Medium ability	59.5	23.2	8.2	7.5	1.6	84.1	6.0	1.1	2.1	6.7
High ability	43.5	20.6	12.3	19.3	4.3	80.4	2.4	2.7	2.4	12.1

[a]Base year question 29B.
[b]Base year question 81.

Overall, about one-third of this sample were intending to pursue clerical careers. Again the only real variation in that figure comes from looking at those of high measured ability. Within that group, only 24 percent intended to pursue clerical careers, and 22.5 percent hoped to attain professional job status as compared to 13.7 percent for the sample as a whole. Naturally, this high percentage of clerical careers results from the popularity of this career choice for female high school graduates. A full 54 percent of all females in this sample intended to pursue clerical jobs; in all likelihood, these individuals hoped to enter the market for secretaries and typists.

In many ways comparing the job choices of males and females provides a reasonable feel for the characteristics of this job-seeking population. Fourteen possible career choices were presented to those surveyed, but the responses for the females indicates that 5 of the 14 account for 90 percent of all individuals. These were clerical, sales, service, professional, and homemaker categories. In addition to the 54 percent recorded as seeking clerical careers, 9.3 percent chose service occupations, 14.9 percent professional jobs, 6.2 percent sales, and 6.5 percent homemakers. This last percentage can be interpreted as either revealing unconstrained or somewhat myopic preferences.

Among the males, career choice was more diffuse, although we could account for 75 percent of all those surveyed with six job categories. Twenty-eight percent of the males chose to be craftsmen, 10.6 percent laborers, 9.3 percent operators, 13.3 percent professionals, 6.8 percent technicians, and 6.5 protective workers.

Table 4-3 uses these and occupational categories to look at the choices as differentiated by blacks and whites, high income and low income, and low and high ability.

Job Plans. Answers to three critical questions in the survey give us some idea of the readiness of these teens to enter the labor market. A large number of these teens, although committed to full-time work on graduation, are still undecided about postsecondary education when they reach the twelfth grade. Further, the data suggest that this indecision is reinforced by vague aspirations to continue some sort of education, although most would not begin that training on graduation even if they did not perceive themselves constrained by finances or other circumstances. It is, then, important to look at the responses to the survey questions which asked when the individuals expected to start work, whether they had a definite job lined up, and whether they would be willing to move.

The timing question reveals that 27.6 percent of the respondents expected to start work before June 1 of their graduating year; that data can be taken as coterminous with graduation. The greatest percentage (55 percent of the respondants) planned on starting work sometime within three months of graduation. About 12 percent apparently planned on a free summer with a fall

Table 4-3
Predominant Career Choices[a]
(percentages)

	(1) Females Seeking Full-Time Work						(b) Males Seeking Full-Time Work						
	Cler.	Sales	Serv.	Prof.	Hmkr.	Other	Cftsmn	Lab.	Oper.	Prof.	Tech.	Prot.	Other
Overall	53.9	6.2	9.4	15.0	6.5	9.0	28.5	10.7	9.4	13.3	6.8	6.5	24.8
Race													
White	54.3	6.8	9.6	13.5	7.0	8.8	29.3	10.9	9.7	13.3	6.4	6.8	23.6
Black	50.6	1.8	7.1	24.4	3.0	13.1	20.4	9.7	7.5	16.1	8.6	2.2	35.5
Family Income													
High	57.9	4.7	8.2	13.5	7.9	7.8	26.9	11.1	6.3	18.0	4.8	7.2	25.7
Medium	53.0	6.2	9.9	14.1	7.2	9.6	26.7	11.1	7.0	15.4	7.3	6.5	26.0
Low	52.3	6.8	9.5	17.5	5.2	8.7	28.3	11.1	14.7	8.6	7.8	5.8	13.7
Ability													
High	47.0	4.5	7.9	22.0	10.0	9.5	24.5	5.8	6.5	33.1	3.6	7.9	18.6
Medium	56.6	6.1	8.1	14.1	5.6	9.5	27.2	11.4	9.0	13.6	7.1	6.1	25.6
Low	51.1	7.2	11.6	15.2	6.7	8.2	30.0	10.5	10.5	7.8	7.8	6.6	26.8

[a]Base year question 25A.

starting date and, for various reasons, 5.2 percent did not expect to start work for six months. Clearly the uncertainty of these expected starting dates increases with the length of time between graduation and planned work. Unless plans are extremely well detailed, a decision to begin work within a month of graduation is more accurately a decision to seek work with the hope of finding suitable employment within a month.

The percentage of people who had actually lined up a job, as indicated by their plan to begin work before June 1, varied with income, sex, race, and ability. As a group, males recorded the highest early job success rate, with 33 percent of them stating they would begin work before June 1. In contrast, only 22 percent of the females could count on employment that soon and, among high-ability people, only 20 percent were recorded as starting work that early. The high male percentage may result from their easier access to apprentice programs. However, females may be more confident about job market success and less anxious to commit themselves to any one employer before a search can reveal differences in working conditions. Part a of table 4–4 shows these percentages for the differing groups. The figures are discouraging in that they indicate some 17 percent of this full-time work group has no real intention of beginning work within three months of graduation.

Table 4–4
Work and Employment Relationships

(a) Timing of Decision to Start Work

	To Start Before June 1, 1972	To Start June 1–Sept. 1	To Start Sept. 1–Jan. 1	To Start Jan 1, 1973 or later
Overall	27.7	55.4	11.7	5.2
Males	33.3	53.6	7.6	5.5
Females	22.6	57.1	15.3	5.0
High income	27.2	55.8	12.9	4.1
Middle income	26.6	58.4	11.2	3.9
Low income	30.2	54.0	10.6	5.2
Black	26.0	55.8	9.9	8.3
White	27.9	55.9	11.6	4.5
High ability	20.2	64.9	13.0	1.9
Middle ability	25.5	59.0	11.8	3.8
Low ability	31.8	50.1	10.9	7.2

(b) Percentage Distribution of Employed and Unemployed as of June 1, 1972

	Employed	Unemployed
Overall	49.4%	50.6%
Males	63.4	36.6
Females	38.2	61.8
Whites	53.1	46.9
Blacks	35.5	64.5

As if to confirm the pessimism contained in the first set of percentages, the responses to a question asking whether the graduating senior has a definite job arranged reveal that only 50 percent can answer in the affirmative. Within this 50 percent are the 28.8 percent of the sample for whom the job is a continuation of their high school part-time employment. Recalling that 55 percent of the sample intended to begin work within three months after graduation and 17 percent sometime thereafter, we observed that 20.6 percent are recorded as starting a new job, 18.1 percent haven't looked at all for a job, and 32.5 percent have looked without success.

It appears that only about 40 percent of all those hoping to find work on graduation, but with no plans to continue their present employment, have been successful. Half the group has either not looked for work at all or has not located a job with some amount of job search. However, the sample does not tell us how much effort or what type of search activities were engaged in by the participants.

Finally, about 45 percent of the group either preferred to move or would be willing to move. This reveals a good deal of labor market mobility which, if exercised, could relieve regional pockets of unemployment. Unfortunately, the teen job market has been depressed across most regions of the country, and hence this apparent mobility is likely unimportant in the short run. The percentage distribution of early labor market success by sex and race is given in part b of table 4-4.

Other Nontraining Groups. All these tabulations and discussions are, of course, based on the responses of those in the sample who were recorded as intending to enter the labor market in a fully employed capacity. The student had *five other ways* to indicate that he or she did not intend to continue into post-secondary education immediately on graduation. The respondent could have indicated some intention to (1) enter an on-the-job training (OJT) or apprentice program, (2) enter the military, (3) become a homemaker, (4) engage in part-time work, and (5) engage other activities not described by any of these labels. Clearly one research task to be undertaken during this project should be identifying the causal variables that affect the choices among these various noncollege options. For now we might best describe the groups in terms of our standard measures of income, ability, sex, and race, but with an eye toward identifying possible differences in composition among the various groups.

First, the groups who seek full-time work constitute about 63 percent of all those not going to school. Hence our earlier discussion should serve well as a general guideline to the status and attitude of teens as they enter the labor market. The remaining 37 percent of the noncollege-going group are divided as follows: 6.1 percent apprentice or OJT, 8.5 percent military, 6.6 percent homemakers, 4.9 percent part-time work, and 10.6 percent in other activities. Whereas the full-time work group was divided almost evenly between males and females, 70.4 percent of the OJT group and 88.3 percent of the military group were males. Not surprisingly, all of those in the homemaker group were female. Forty-six percent of those seeking part-time work were male as were 60 percent of those in the "other activities" category. Overall, 50.5 percent of the noncollege-going group were male.

The degree of indecision about further plans appears uniform across these subgroups in that the percentages that make early decisions (before the tenth grade) not to go to college are about the same within each group.

The only figure of note is the extraordinarily high percentage (47.5) from the "other activities" group that were still undecided about college in the twelfth grade. At this stage we can only guess at the actual activities of the group after graduation, but it appears to be a subgroup worth following up in some detail.

Overall, 20.1 percent of the sample had decided before the tenth grade not to go on to college and 37.4 percent were still undecided in the twelfth grade. The student's perception of his or her ability for college was, once again, relatively uniform across the six subsets of this noncollege population. Overall, 54.2 percent of this sample thought they definitely or possibly had college ability, 39.8 percent were not sure or doubted it, and 6.9 percent did not think they had the ability for college.

Comparing the educational plans (aspirations) of the entire noncollege sample reveals some variation across the subgroups. For the sample as a whole, 51.3 percent plan on a high school degree or less, 25 percent on some voc-tech, with only 9.1 percent aspiring to junior college, 10.7 percent to four years of college, and 3.1 percent to graduate work. Our earlier comments about the lack of enthusiasm for four years of schooling beyond high school could be repeated here. Within the sub-groups, the lowest aspirations are held by those females planning on immediate homemaking; 72.4 percent of this group aspired to a high school education or less. Those in this group who do look beyond high school look primarily toward vocational education. The highest aspirations are held by the military group with 6 percent aspiring to graduate school, 28.4 percent to four-year college. Part a of table 4-5 outlines the educational aspirations for these various groups.

An interesting statistic is formed by estimating the percentage of respondents in the sample and within each subgroup who, given no perceived constraint, would have pursued the career goal on graduation that they are in fact pursuing. For example, what percentage of all those who will be homemakers would have chosen that role if their decisions were unconstrained? In the case in point, 56.2 percent of that group indicated they would have made such an unconstrained choice. Obviously the percentage, although interesting, is compiled from the survey instrument and the reliability of the answers is open to question. Just what the perceived constraints were, to what extent they are the result of misinformation, and to what extent the person answering understood the query are all large unknowns.

In general, somewhat more than half the individuals within any one group are recorded as choosing that occupation when unconstrained. It is important to note that only 32.2 percentage of the part-time work groups view that situation as optimal and 19.7 percent would prefer full-time work. Further, 18.4 percent in the OJT group would have preferred full-time work. There is a likely discouraged-worker effect operating here, with a significant percentage of those recorded as doing something other than full-time work forced into those choices by an early lack of success in the job market.

The value of looking at the "other activities" group in more detail was pointed out earlier in the discussion. Interest in this group is confirmed by the fact that, out of 10 percent of the entire noncollege group, 55 percent of people in it say they prefer it that way and 10 to 20 percent of the full-time work, part-time work, and OJT groups would have preferred to be so categorized. If these subgroups mean they would prefer to do nothing, that in itself is worth noting. If those so classified are indeed the group which prefers to stay at home, the phenomenon is even more important in evaluating job market experiences. Part b of Table 4-5 sums up these responses.

Patterns of Actual Activities

Measures of labor market success are social statistics that are subject to a variety of interpretations by various users. The unemployment rate, as it is usually defined and estimated, is a relatively precise concept; it tells us what percentage of all those in the labor force, in a given census week, were not working and were actively seeking work. The percentage can be calculated for a state, a metropolitan, or statistical region, or the United States as a whole. By comparing and contrasting rates among various socioeconomic subsets of the population, one can glean some notion of the relative success with which different groups within the entire population are able to find jobs or find new jobs. The definition used by the Bureau of Labor Statistics counts an individual as employed as long as he or she worked *at all* during the census week—that is, someone who worked 5 hours is considered just as "employed" as someone working 40 hours. Furthermore, the percentage unemployed is calculated using a definition of labor force that includes only those working, looking for work, or temporarily separated from their jobs. All those who are neither employed nor looking for work are considered "out of the labor force." Thus, the full-time housewife is counted as out of the labor force, but so is the individual who has been discouraged by lack of success in finding employment and is no longer actively looking. Obviously, if there are many such individuals, a low unemployment rate can be falsely reassuring to policymakers. Many problems associated with the Bureau of Labor Statistics' definitions have been discussed in the literature and much empirical work has been devoted to estimating the size of the group that would work if the individuals thought jobs were attainable, but who are counted as out of the labor force by the Bureau of Labor Statistics. This phenomenon is labeled "disguised unemployment."

Table 4-5
Educational and Work Plans

(a) Educational Level Desired[a]

	High School or Less	High School plus Voc-Tech	Junior College	Four-Year College	Graduate School
Overall	51.3	25.8	9.1	10.7	3.1
Planning to enter[b]					
Full-time work	56.8	24.0	8.7	8.2	2.3
App and OJT	23.8	61.7	7.9	4.7	1.8
Military	27.8	28.4	8.6	28.4	6.8
Homemaker	72.4	16.4	5.8	3.9	1.6
Part-time work	49.3	17.8	13.3	15.1	4.4
Other	39.8	23.3	13.0	17.2	6.6

(b) Constrained and Unconstrained First-Year Plans (Noneducational options)

		Unconstrained choice[c]						
	Educational Alternative	Full-time Work	OJT	Military	Homemaker	Part-time Work	Other	Same as Plan
Overall	15.0	45.5	6.5	6.8	6.3	4.2	15.7	—
Planned activity[d]								
Full-time work	14.8	62.5	3.7	3.4	2.3	2.3	11.9	62.5
OJT	12.6	18.4	55.7	1.4	0.5	1.0	10.3	55.7
Military	12.3	10.9	2.4	65.4	0.2	1.4	7.4	65.4
Homemaker	14.9	15.3	0.9	0.2	56.2	6.4	6.0	56.2
Part-time work	21.5	19.7	3.0	0.6	3.9	32.2	19.1	32.2
Other	16.7		2.8	2.5	1.5	5.3	55.1	55.1

[a] Base year question 29B.

[b] Base year question 31.

[c] Base year question 81.

[d] Base year question 31.

When considering the labor market success of teenagers, it is particularly difficult to capture the richness of teen labor activity by straightforward measures of employment and unemployment. We have already seen that the group of teenagers who planned to go to work on graduation had come to that decision hesitantly and that the mix of postsecondary school and full-time work plans of the group are intertwined and influenced by the degree of success achieved in pursuing these alternative paths. Lack of high school success may lead many to record themselves as seeking full-time work; subsequent lack of immediate success in the labor market may spawn plans to return to school in some capacity. Better information about wages and salaries available to high school graduates may induce a shift in education and training plans.

The sample of individuals who intended in June 1972 to pursue a full-time work option consists of 4,468 individuals. Many of them decided very late in their high school careers not to attend school on graduation and that many were still undecided about future postsecondary education at the actual time of graduation. We turn now to an analysis of the actual patterns of labor market success, 4 months and 16 months after graduation.

School Attendance. By October 1972, we find that 648 (12 percent) of the 4,468 people in this group were actually in school; they were about equally divided between males and females. The information available allows us to distinguish the type of school for 443 of the 648 going on to school. Apparently, voc-tech and two-year junior colleges are by far the choice of those who decide not to seek immediate employment. Only 40 people (about 9.5 percent) were in four-year schools with 39 percent in voc-tech schools and 29.6 percent in two-year colleges. The remaining 22 percent of those in school were enrolled in a variety of other formal programs.[3]

Many of those actually attending school had been undecided until very late in their high school careers about the prospect of postsecondary school. For example, 68.8 percent of all those attending voc-tech school were either undecided about their postsecondary plans when they graduated, or had made a later decision (twelfth grade) not to go to school. This indecision about future career plans, which was earlier recorded as intent to pursue full-time work, changed to actual enrollment in school. The reasons for the change are not documented in the data; however, we might speculate that initial difficulty in the job market may have induced the shift. We might also infer that the decision to enroll is more the desire to curtail or postpone job search than to receive further training.

Those enrolling in school were drawn predominantly from the ranks of those with low measured ability. Of the 637 for whom data are available, only 60 (9.4) percent) were of high measured ability; more than half (51 percent) were in the low ability category. An extraordinary number were nonwhite, in that about one-third of all those going on to school were so classified. This may be yet another index of the high aspirations of blacks and other minority groups for further education. Those enrolled in school were predominantly in public institutions (85.9 percent); slightly more than half those going on to school were female (52.3 percent).

It is also interesting to detail the training options of those continuing their education. Using the two-digit field of study code employed in the survey, part a of table 4-6 tabulated these responses. (The two-digit code does not capture the diversity of training choices available so that information was available for only 233 of the 639 going on to school. Perhaps this could be improved in future analysis by changing the program code.)

Job Characteristics. Turning now to job and hours worked information, we find that, of the 4,458 in the original subsample intending to go to work full time, 3,174 were recorded as having held some type of job in October 1972, and nearly the same number (3,234) were recorded as holding a job in October 1973. These figures are misleading in that they do not adequately account for the different modes of labor market activity characteristic of the subsample. We have already

Table 4-6
Educational and Job Characteristics

(a)   Field of Study, 1972 (percentages)

	Agri business	Mrktng. & Distrib.	Health Occup.	Home Economics	Bus & Off. Occup.	Tech. Occup.	Trade Indust
Males	2.3	3.4	1.1	3.4	2.3	8.0	79.5
Females	0	15.2	22.1	7.6	42.1	0.7	12.4
Whites	1.3	11.5	10.8	5.7	28.0	3.8	38.9
Nonwhites	0	9.5	21.8	6.8	26.0	1.3	34.2

(b)   Those Holding a Job in October 1972

	Same as 1973		Different from 1973	Total
Overall	1,473	(47%)	1,643	3,116
Whites	1,151	(47%)	1,294	2,445
Nonwhites	322	(47.9%)	349	671
Males	754	(47.5%)	831	1,585
Females	747	(47%)	842	1,589

(c)   Hours Worked, 1972 (percentages)

	Less than 10 hours	10–20	20–30	30–40	More than 40
Overall	2.5	6.1	8.2	60.7	22.6
Males	1.8	5.1	7.0	50.7	34.3
Females	3.1	7.1	9.3	69.2	11.3
White	1.6	5.6	8.6	61.0	23.1
Nonwhite	5.4	7.9	6.9	59.1	20.4

seen that some 648 people who had planned on full-time work were actually in school in October 1972; however, some of these people may also have held part-time or full-time jobs, and some individuals recorded as working may also have been attending school part time or full time. We can, nonetheless, gain some insight into the activity of the group as a whole. We shall then turn to a very detailed analysis of the labor market status of the 4,458 in the subsample.

The 3,234 who were recorded as working in October 1972 divided themselves almost evenly between those who held the same job in October 1973 as they did in October 1972 and those that held different jobs at these two times. We would expect to observe a good deal of job mobility on the part of new entrants in the labor market and this, combined with the fact that those in school are likely to change part-time jobs rather frequently, makes the amount of mobility observed rather unsurprising. The data, as presented in part b of table 4-6 also does not reveal any difference in the degree of job mobility among whites, nonwhites, males, and females.

We can also characterize this group as being employed predominantly by private industry (91 percent), with government the only other major employer (7.7 percent). Females were employed by government at nearly twice the rate of males (10 percent versus 5.5 percent), which reflects the icnreased opportunities in government for those with clerical skills.

Turning to the data on hours worked, we find that in 1972, 60.7 percent of those employed were working 30 to 40 hours per week, 22.6 percent were recorded as working more than 40 hours per week, 8.2 percent at 20 to 30 hours per week, 6.1 percent at 10 to 20 hours, and only 2.5 percent less than ten hours. Some differences in hours by sex and race are also worth mentioning. Relatively more females than males were wokring 10 hours per week or less (3.1 percent versus 1.8 percent), and far fewer were recorded as working more than 40 hours (11.3 percent versus 34.3 percent). (It is hard to accept figures as low as 34.3 percent for males, but it is possible that many reported exactly 40 hours and were thus not included in this category.) Furthermore, it appears that nonwhites are much more likely to have been working for 10 hours or less per week than whites. The summary data is contained in part c of table 4-6.

Detailed Status Analysis. By carefully specifying an extensive set of alternative "status of activity" characteristics of the subsample, we can describe the labor market behavior of this group 4 and 16 months after high school graduation in far greater detail than previously been possible. Specifically, we define four possible labor market situations. An individual can be (1) working full time, (2) working part time, (3) unemployed (in the labor force and out of work but looking), or (4) not in the labor force. For each of these four labor market states, we identify three possible states of educational activity: (1) school full time, (2) school part time, or (3) no school. We can thus generate twelve possible combinations of school and work. For the individuals in the subsample identified as intending to work full time, we can then specify their actual activity 4 to 16 months after graduation.

If we count all those who were working either part time or full time in October 1972, then 80.2 percent of the sample were employed, 8.3 percent were unemployed and looking for work, and 11.5 percent were out of the labor force. One year later, using the identical framework, 81 percent were employed, 6.6 percent were unemployed, and 12.3 percent were out of the labor force. This increase in nonlabor force participation could be caused by either marriages or discouragement.

Following Labor Department practice, we can eliminate those who were in school full time from consideration, counting them as out of the labor force. In October 1972, 10.8 percent of the sample were enrolled in school full time; that total had dropped to 8.1 percent by October 1973. Recalculating the rates of employed and unemployed, though not counting those in school full time or those not looking for work, yields an October 1972 unemployment rate of 8.6 percent and an October 1973 unemployment rate of 6.6 percent. These percentages appear far too low but it should be noted that high school dropouts are not included. If we accept the questionnaire responses as an accurate portrayal of reality, then in 1972 only 276 individuals were recorded as unemployed by the survey, and in 1973 that number had changed to 214. Our subsample of those in the 1972 survey who planned to work full time recorded 3,192 individuals as in the labor force and the 1973 survey counted 3,204.

It is quite possible that these low unemployment rates are accurate for the type of sample we are working with in this analysis. They are, after all, teenagers that had decided to enter the labor market. The overall unemployment rate for 18-year-olds would include all those who had little in the way of post-high school plans (plus high school dropouts).

Table 4-7 records the labor market status in October 1972 and October 1973 for the subsample as a whole and broken down by race and sex for October 1972. Several pieces of information in the table are worth noting. First, for the sample as a whole, 64.8 percent were working full time and not attending any kind of school in October 1972, while 6 percent were attending school and working full time. The percentage working full time and attending school was about 6 percent for both white and nonwhites, almost 8 percent for males and only 4.3 for females. Among nonwhites, only 52.7 percent were working full time and not attending school; thus, in total the nonwhites' full-time work percentage was 58.8 percent, in contrast to 74.8 percent for whites. It was 65 percent for females but 77.2 percent for males. Nonwhite unemployment rates were twice those of whites, although still considerably below the 25-35 percent usually associated with this demographic group. Not surprisingly, nonwhites also exhibited higher rates of nonparticipation in the labor force than did whites,

Table 4-7
Distribution By Labor Market Status, 1972 and 1973
(percentages)

			October 1972			October 1973
Status	*Overall*	*Whites*	*Nonwhites*	*Males*	*Females*	*Overall*
Working full-time with:	70.8	74.8	58.8	77.2	65.0	75.2
School full-time	2.9	2.8	3.0	4.0	1.9	2.4
School part-time	3.1	3.1	3.1	3.9	2.4	3.6
No school	64.8	68.9	52.7	69.3	60.7	69.2
Working part-time with:	9.4	8.8	10.8	7.7	10.9	5.8
School full-time	2.5	2.1	3.4	2.2	2.8	2.0
School part-time	0.6	0.6	0.5	0.6	0.6	0.5
No school	6.3	6.1	6.9	4.9	7.5	3.3
Unemployed with:	8.3	6.2	14.4	6.0	10.4	6.6
School full-time	1.2	0.9	2.1	0.7	1.6	1.1
School part-time	0.4	0.2	1.2	0.3	0.6	0.4
No school	6.7	5.1	11.1	5.0	8.2	5.1
Out of labor force with:	11.5	10.1	15.9	9.0	13.7	12.3
School full-time	4.2	3.6	6.2	3.9	4.5	2.6
School part-time	0.4	0.3	0.8	0.5	0.3	0.3
No school	6.9	6.2	8.9	4.6	8.9	9.4

with the additional interesting caveat that considerably higher percentages of nonwhites apparently were enrolled in school full time, and neither working nor looking for work.

The early marriage of some females probably accounts for the fact that 8.9 percent of females in contrast to 4.6 percent of males were not in the labor force and not engaged in any sort of school activity. There could be other reasons for these differentials, however, including the possible effects of discrimination against women, thereby increasing the incidence of the discouraged worker.

A detailed breakdown of the labor force status of whites, nonwhites, males, and females for October 1973 indicates an increase of about 5 percent in the number of people employed full time; that 5 percent increase is almost uniform across these various population groups. There is a corresponding drop in the extent of part-time work and a decrease in unemployment rates, which is most pronounced for males. Their unemployment rate drops from 5 percent to 2.7 percent if we consider those not in school, and from 5.3 percent to 3 percent if we consider those in school part time.

In contrast, labor force participation drops with the number of nonwhites neither in school full or part time, unemployed, nor looking for work increasing from 8.9 percent to 11.8 percent. There is an identical increase, 8.9 percent to 11.8 percent, in the number of females not in the labor force.

To glean further insight into the movement of individuals between school, work, employment, and unemployment, we have traced the changes in the labor force status of these 3,897 individuals from October 1972 to October 1973.[4] An analysis of the activity states of individuals in each of the two time periods indicates that, of the 113 people working full time and going to school full time in October 1972, 26.5 percent or 30 of them were still in that category one year later. Fifty-nine or 52.2 percent were no longer in school but held full-time jobs. We note with interest the extremely small number of unemployed (4 people, with 2 of them still in school full time). Also, the number of those working full time while in school full time had, by 1973, dropped to 95, 30 of whom were carryovers from 1972. The predominant source of addition to these ranks were individuals who were working full time in 1972 and had apparently decided to continue full-time work while pursuing full-time schooling.

These cross-tabulations can also be used to trace the change in labor force status for key groups within this population. Of the 260 individuals who were unemployed, not in school, and seeking work in October 1972, 155 had found full-time jobs and 17 part-time jobs a year later. Only 6 people in this group were in school while working. Forty-two (16 percent) were still unemployed and 28 (10.8 percent) had dropped out of the labor force.

In October 1972, almost 7 percent of the sample (269 people) were out of the labor force and not recorded as engaged in any school-related activity. Of the 269, 107 (39.8 percent) were working full time one year later and 19 (7.0 percent) were working part time. Also, 26 people recorded themselves as unemployed but looking for work, but 108 (40.1 percent) were still neither employed nor looking for work. By 1973, the ranks of those not in the labor force had grown to 9.4 percent or 368 individuals. These additional people were drawn primarily from the ranks of those who, one year earlier, had been working full-time; there were 175 such people, 112 females and 63 males. As previously mentioned, this disproportionate number of females could be the result of either marriage or discouragement by discrimination.

The material necessary for further detailed analysis of the time paths followed by various groups was also available here. However, it was felt that the limited resources available on this project could be better expended in other areas. Also, some similar discussions have already been presented in chapter 3.

Regression Analysis of Labor Market Status

The preceding cross-tabulations have given some indication of the activities that individuals become engaged in. We then used regression analysis in an effort to investigate the causes of this behavior. Next we discuss the results obtained from the data on unemployment, labor force participation, and wage rates contained in this sample. The analysis here follows quite closely that done by Bowen and Finnigan on 1960 census data. The variables used in this section are defined in table 4–8.

Unemployment

For the purposes of this section, unemployment is defined as looking for a job in October 1973, the time of the first follow-up. Also, those who are unemployed but not looking for work are classified as being out of the labor force and are excluded. In our subsample of 1,936 individuals, 92.7 percent were employed. The sample was distributed such that 48.2 percent were male, 78.6 percent white, 11.4 percent black, and the remaining 10 percent were divided among other minorities, primarily Spanish-American and American Indian. The regression presented in table 4–9 yields the not surprising result that males and whites fare better than blacks and females in locating a job.

Interestingly, unemployment rates in 1973 were not lower for those who had been employed in 1972 than for those who had no job in 1972. In fact, working in a sales or clerical capacity in 1972 had a negative effect on employment chances in 1973 (statistically significant at the 5 percent level), while working as an operative or as a craftsman also yielded a negative coefficient, but the results here were not statistically significant.

Being in any kind of school since graduation greatly lowers chances of being employed; this is not unexpected because the individual is likely to be

Table 4–8
Regression Analysis and Variable Definitions

Variable Name		Definition
EMP	Employment status	= 0 if unemployed
		= 1 if employed
LFP73	Labor force participation 1973	= 1 if individual is in the labor force
		= 0 otherwise
LWPH73	1973 wages	= natural logarithm of hourly wages received in 1973
ACDPG (or ACADPG)	Academic program	= 1 if student in an academic program in high school
		= 0 otherwise
AGEOLD	Age; older	= 1 if born before 1953
		= 0 otherwise
AGE20	Age; 20	= 1 if born in 1953
		= 0 otherwise
BCQ85	Family size	= response to base year question number 85, indicating size of family
CRA72	Craftsman; 1972	= 1 if October 1972, occupation is craftsman or kindred worker
		= 0 otherwise
DIVSW	Postmarital status	= 1 if divorced, separated, or widowed
		= 0 if otherwise
ENGH	English language	= 1 if English is the language spoken in the home
		= 0 if otherwise
FAM45	Family size; level one	= 1 if size of family is four or five people
		= 0 otherwise
FAM67	Family size; level two	= 1 if size of family is six or seven people
		= 0 otherwise
FAM8P	Family size; level three	= 1 if size of family is eight or more people
		= 0 otherwise
FAOC1	Father's occupation; level one	= 1 if father's occupation is professional, technical, kindred worker, nonfarm manager, or administrator
		= 0 otherwise
FAOC2	Father's occupation; level two	= 1 if father's occupation is sales, clerical, or kindred worker
		= 0 otherwise
FAOC3	Father's occupation; level three	= 1 if father's occupation is a craftsman or kindred worker
		= 0 otherwise
FAOC4	Father's occupation; level four	= 1 if father's occupation is farmer, farm manager, farm laborer, or farm foreman
		= 0 otherwise

Table 4-8 (continued)

Variable Name		Definition
FAOC5	Father's occupation; level five	= 1 if father's occupation is service worker
		= 0 otherwise
FF15A	Active personality	= Sum of responses to follow-up questions 15A, 15C, 15D, and 15H; where "agree strongly" = 3, "agree" = 2, "disagree" = 1, and "disagree strongly" = 0
FF15P	Passive personality	= Sum of responses to follow-up questions 15B, 15E, 15F, and 15G (responses are weighted the same as in FF15A)
FRM72	Farmer; 1972	= 1 if October 1972 occupation is farmer, farm manager, farm laborer, or farmer foreman
		= 0 otherwise
GENPG	General program	= 1 if student in a general program in high school
		= 0 otherwise
HCPD	Handicapped	= 1 if student is handicapped
		= 0 otherwise
HDSC	Head of family schooling	= response to base year question 90
HDSC1	Head of family schooling; level one	= 1 if head of family is a high school graduate only
		= 0 otherwise
HDSC2	Head of family schooling; level two	= 1 if head of family has some post high school education but no college degree
		= 0 otherwise
HDSC3	Head of famuy schooling; level three	= 1 if head of family has a four-year college degree only
		= 0 otherwise
HDSC4	Head of family schooling; level four	= 1 if head of family has at least attended some graduate school
		= 0 otherwise
LUNR	Local unemployment rate	= appropriate local unemployment rate (1970) where students are differentiated by sex and by age group (age 16–19 and age 20–24).
LWG	Local wage	= average local wage rate in manufacturing in 1972
SATT	Aptitude	= total SAT scores, if available
		= imputed SAT scores from either ETS or ACT scores
LWG2	Local wage; level two	= 1 if average local wage rate is between $3.30 and $3.90
		= 0 otherwise
LWG3	Local wage; level three:	= 1 if average local wage rate is above $3.90
		= 0 otherwise

Table 4-8 (continued)

Variable Name		Definition
MAR73	Marital status	= 1 if married by October 1973
		= 0 otherwise
NOGRAD	Nongraduate	= 1 if not a high school graduate
		= 0 otherwise
OJT	Training	= 1 if participated in on-the-job training, registered apprenticeship, manpower training, personal enrichment, or correspondence courses (not regular school or college or armed forces training)
		= 0 otherwise
OPL72	Operative-laborer; 1972	= 1 if October 1972 occupation classified as a nontransport operative or a nonfarm laborer
		= 0 otherwise
PLMAR	Marital plans	= 1 if marriage planned within 12 months
		= 0 otherwise
PMG72	Professional-manager; 1972	= 1 if October 1972 occupation classified as professional, technical, kindred worker or nonfarm manager or administrator
		= 0 otherwise
PY	Parents' income	= continuous measure
PY1	Parents' income; level one	= 1 if parent's income is between $3,000 and $6,000 per year
		= 0 otherwise
PY2	Parents' income; level two	= 1 if parents' income is between $6,000 and $9,000 per year
		= 0 otherwise
PY3	Parents' income; level three	= 1 if parents' income is between $9,000 and $12,000 per year
		= 0 otherwise
PY4	Parents' income; level four	= 1 if parents' income is between $12,000 and $15,000 per year
		= 0 otherwise
PY5	Parents' income; level five	= 1 if parents' income is between $15,000 and $18,000 per year
		= 0 otherwise
PY6	Parents' income; level six	= 1 if parents' income is greater than $18,000 per year
		= 0 otherwise
RACEB	Race—black	= 1 if black
		= 0 otherwise
RACEW	Race—white	= 1 if Caucasian
		= 0 otherwise
SCAT	School dropout–attendance index	= score derived from school questionnaire items 16, 17A, and 17B

Table 4–8 (continued)

Variable Name		Definition
SCHOOL	Schooling	= 1 if attended a college or university, service academy, business school, trade school, technical institute, vocational school, or community college
		= 0 otherwise
SCL72	Sales–Clerical; 1972	= 1 if October 1972 occupation classified as sales, clerical, or kindred worker
		= 0 otherwise
SCPB	School positive factor index	= index derived from School Questionnaire Items Number 3T, 20A, 22, 25, and 34
SEX	Student's sex	= 0 if female
		= 1 if male
SRV72	Service; 1972	= 1 if October 1972 occupation classified as a service worker
		= 0 otherwise

less committed to those types of jobs which are available to high school graduates. Participating in on-the-job training raises employment chances and is significant at about the 7 percent level.

Parents in the middle-income brackets (between $9,000 and $12,000) significantly increased chances of being employed. However, parents who either are quite poor (earning less than $3,000 a year) or relatively affluent (greater than $15,000 a year) had almost no effect on employment opportunities. Not much effect on employment possibilities is apparent from fathers' occupations, except that children whose fathers are employed in service occupations exhibited higher unemployment rates; these results are merely suggestive of possible interesting relationships because they were not statistically significant. The importance of fathers' occupations as a determinant of social prestige or class suggests that those values or attitudes which aid an individual in his or her quest for employment are a function of income and not social class. It must be remembered, of course, that this entire analysis is only for those who expressed a desire to work full-time immediately on graduation from high school, and thus applies only to jobs requiring no college education.

The final significant variable is one measuring personality attributes. Those who seem to believe that they have only a limited amount of control over their environment by agreeing with such statements as "Good luck is more important than hard work and success" and "Planning only makes a person unhappy since plans hardly every work out anyway" are less likely to be employed. Once again this finding is consistent with our general contention that attitudes are an important determinate of labor market success.

Of relative unimportance are such variables as type of high school program, marital status, age, innate ability (as measured by SAT scores, if available, or

Table 4-9
Unemployment Regression

	Dependent Variable:	EMP = 0	if unemployed
		= 1	if employed
		(EMP = .927;	σ = .261)

| Sample Size = 1,936 | | R^2 = .080 | |

Variable	Mean	Coefficient	t value
SEX	.48244	.79497D-01	5.688
GENPG	.39411	-.18686D-01	-1.448
ACDPG	.14153	-.28260D-01	-1.515
HCPD	.63533D-01	-.16176D-01	-0.673
ENGH	.90909	-.10459D-01	-0.497
MAR73	.26601	.14813D-01	1.071
PLMAR	.16994	.19152D-01	1.182
DIVSW	.11364D-01	.22880D-01	0.416
RACEW	.78616	.42903D-01	2.074
RACEB	.11364	-.89576D-01	-3.425
PMG72	.11880D-01	.29460D-01	0.548
SCL72	.15289	-.43342D-01	-2.555
CRA72	.49587D-01	-.41677D-01	-1.508
OPL72	.12242	-.35429D-01	-1.887
FRM72	.46488D-02	.15712D-01	0.182
SRV72	.70248D-01	-.58259D-02	-0.251
NOGRAD	.13430D-01	.43623D-01	0.857
OJT	.29029	.23449D-01	1.827
SCHOOL	.26136	-.45398D-01	-3.386
PY1	.13378	.29253D-01	1.493
PY2	.21591	.28869D-01	1.683
PY3	.18595	.36559D-01	2.035
PY4	.11364	.29265D-01	1.378
PY5	.50103D-01	-.57480D-03	-0.020
PY6	.67149D-01	.97063D-02	0.379
AGE20	.22676	-.43784D-02	-0.183
AGEOLD	.54752D-01	.23686D-01	0.712
FAOC1	.16116	.76117D-02	0.405
FAOC2	.11312	-.36346D-01	-1.750
FAOC3	.30888	-.68830D-03	-0.045
FAOC4	.68698D-01	-.90069D-02	-0.360
FAOC5	.72831D-01	.26218D-01	1.090
CONSTANT	1.0000	.79154	6.473
LWG	3.4912	.20659D-01	1.030
SATT	691.43	.45418D-04	1.165
FF15A	8.4236	.13651D-02	0.463
FF15P	3.7438	-.62546D-02	-2.040
LUNR	7.7479	-.43897D-03	-0.075

else by the results of the tests administered during this survey), local wage and unemployment rates, and whether the individual is handicapped or deficient in English.

In summary, being male and white greatly increases employment prospects immediately on high school graduation. Concentrating on working, as opposed to attending school part time or full time, is also an asset in finding employment in the short run. Finally, being from a middle-income family, as well as believing in one's control over the environment, is quite important. Because of the lack of influence of fathers' occupations on unemployment, it may be that those subjective attitudes which are mainly present in middle-class families have a primary influence on one's chances of being employed. The importance of these attitudes is especially revealed by the strength of the personality variable. In contrast, such objective factors as marital status, high school program, age, physical handicap, and language deficiencies have little effect on employment possibilities. In addition, local wage and unemployment rates seem to have no effect.

Labor Force Participation

Labor force participation was defined as either holding a job or looking for one. The total sample of 2,224 was obtained by restoring those individuals eliminated in the unemployment regressions as being out of the labor force. To expand the analysis, these regressions were also run on four separate subsamples (males in school, males not in school, females in school, and females not in school) as well as on the entire sample. October 1973 is the point in time at which an individual's status is defined; thus, "in school" is clearly distinguishable from the variable measuring attendance at a school at any time since graduation.

For the entire sample as presented in table 4-10, about 13 percent were out of the labor force. As expected, being male and white produced a strong positive effect on labor force participation. However, in contrast to the unemployment regression, blacks did not fare worse than other minorities.

As before, working in 1972 provided little toward increasing labor force participation. In fact, working as an operative sharply decreased one's chances of being in the labor force in 1973. Working in a sales or clerical capacity also had a negative effect on the probability of being in the labor force, though this effect was only statistically significant at the 6 percent level.

Being in school at any time greatly lowered chances of being in the labor force, indicating that those going to school did little to combine schooling with part-time work. Those participating in on-the-job training were more likely to be in the labor force. Again, these results closely parallel those for unemployment.

Table 4-10
Labor Force Participation Regression: Whole Sample

	Dependent Variable:	LFP73 = 0　if out of labor force	
		=1　if in labor force	
		(LFP73 = .871, σ = .336)	
	Sample Size = 2,224	R^2 = .074	
Variable	*Mean*	*Coefficient*	*t value*
SEX	.46448	.84117D-01	5.008
GENPG	.40513	-.51978D-01	-3.354
ACDPG	.14209	-.24369D-01	-1.081
HCPD	.66547D-01	-.44278D-01	-1.566
ENGH	.91007	-.26069D-01	-1.025
MAR73	.28642	-.81053D-01	-4.901
PLMAR	.16547	-.53004D-02	-0.269
DIVSW	.11241D-01	-.96348D-02	-0.145
RACEW	.77338	.64187D-01	2.608
RACEB	.12320	-.21527D-01	-0.703
PMG72	.11241D-01	-.54999D-02	-0.083
SCL72	.15827	-.37494D-01	-1.856
CRA72	.49011D-01	-.55342D-01	-1.656
OPL72	.12860	-.84659D-01	-3.830
FRM72	.44964D-02	-.17970D-01	-0.170
SRV72	.72842D-01	-.40642D-01	-1.481
NOGRAD	.13489D-01	.90562D-02	0.149
OJT	.27563	.68190D-01	4.363
SCHOOL	.27743	-.76233D-01	-4.782
PY1	.13040	.36282D-01	1.531
PY2	.21673	-.82435D-02	-0.402
PY3	.18795	-.15294D-01	-0.711
PY4	.11331	-.79448D-02	-0.312
PY5	.50809D-01	-.14646D-01	-0.430
PY6	.62500D-01	.61814D-01	1.946
AGE20	.23471	-.20499D-01	-0.710
AGEOLD	.55306D-01	.11294D-01	0.283
FAOC1	.16502	-.41619D-02	-0.187
FAOC2	.10791	.66524D-01	2.620
FAOC3	.30171	.46015D-01	2.496
FAOC4	.69245D-01	.13734D-01	0.459
FAOC5	.70594D-01	.62340D-01	2.135
CONSTANT	1.0000	.75900	5.210
LWG	3.4901	.14652D-01	0.614
SATT	690.73	-.55072D-04	-1.180
FF15A	8.4236	.54443D-03	0.154
FF15P	3.7257	.56546D-02	1.539
LUNR	7.7286	.81673D-02	1.145

The not-too-implausible conclusion emerging from both the unemployment and labor force participation regressions is that, unless an individual participates in on-the-job training (about one-fourth of this sample did so) and concentrates exclusively on his or her job (does not attend school), the likelihood of being unemployed or of simply leaving the labor force greatly increases. Furthermore, an individual should be working in the right job; in particular, working either in a clerical or sales position or as an operative decreases both labor force participation and employment.

The effect of parents' income on labor force participation is less important than it was in the employment variable; only those whose parents were in the highest income bracket had an increased probability of participation. Though fathers' occupations generally have an important effect here, individuals with fathers working in clerical or sales positions, as craftsmen, or as service personnel have a significantly higher chance of being in the labor force. Two possible explanations are that (1) individuals from such families are more likely to believe in the value or necessity of working; and (2) in addition, such parents are less likely to subsidize their children in the pursuit of idleness. In contrast to the unemployment results, the attitudes affecting the decision to participate in the labor force are more a function of class than income. Here the high school program becomes an important variable, with being in the general program having a strong negative effect. However, since this category is not very well defined, not too much emphasis should be placed on this result. Also important here is the effect of being married, which decreases the probability of labor force participation. The personality variables have now become insignificant, joining those variables identifying handicapped individuals, non-English-speaking households, age, innate ability, and local wage and unemployment rates.

In summary, attitudes have different effects on labor force participation than on employment. Here they become more a factor of class (as measured by fathers' occupations) than income. In addition, an individual's personality is less likely to matter. Thus, in general, the most consistent results point toward the importance of having on-the-job training and undivided concentration on the job in the sense that one does not attend school. Also of interest is the lack of any effect of ability and local wage and unemployment rates. At least in this sample, local wage levels apparently are not considered an important factor in deciding to seek employment or to participate in the labor force. On the other hand, it is possible that local wage rates are not relevant to the class of jobs that individuals obtain immediately on leaving high school; this market may be segregated from the main labor market. The unimportance of the local unemployment rates may result from possible discrepancies in these figures. Both for this sample and for the Parnes data, youth unemployment rates are lower than those in the BLS statistics usually used. One possible explanation could be that in this study, each individual is asked directly, whereas in the BLS figures only one member of the household is interviewed.

In the subsample regressions (except for no-school females), it became necessary to delete the dummies representing parents' income ($PY1$–$PY6$) in an effort to obtain an adequate sample size.[5] The number of in-school males was 158, with a quite high percentage (22) of this sample being out of the labor force. Possibly because of the small number of observations, very few variables here are statistically significant. In fact, the F-statistic for the significance of all the coefficients (except the constant) is significant at only the .09 level.

Although being white continues to increase the probability of being in the labor force, the only other significant variable in this regression is marital status, with the effect now becoming positive. This result can be explained if we bear in mind that the overall regression contains both males and females; the negative sign associated with marital status in that calculation is probably produced by the behavior of females who marry and drop out of the labor force. In the regression for males only, marital status should thus be expected to induce more labor force attachment.

In this sample, 924 males were out of school; of these, about 7 percent were not in the labor force, less than the corresponding figure for the whole sample. Here the F-statistic is quite significant at the .0001 level. One noticeable difference from the total sample is that blacks now fare significantly worse than other minorities. Another important difference is that on-the-job training and attending school (here, of course, it applies only to attendance at some other time) have very little effect on labor force participation; this latter result is not surprising because the sample now excludes those attending school in 1973.

Two final differences should be noted. The coefficient for ability is negative and significant at the .057 level. In short, high aptitude actually decreases labor market participation. Another quite surprising result is the positive coefficient for our personality variable identifying an individual lacking a sense of strong control over his or her environment. It is likely that those people with a strong sense of control over their environments do not find the mix of jobs available on graduating from high school very appealing and thus drop out of the labor force. In other words, for out-of-school males, the available jobs appeal to those with lower ability and ambition.

There were only 129 females in school, with 31 percent of this subsample not in the labor force. However, in contrast with the males, the coefficients are statistically significant as a group at the .000001 level. Variables for race have little effect here. Working as an operator in 1972 had a sharply negative effect on labor force participation in 1973. As with the previously mentioned subsamples, on-the-job training has little effect. Ability plays no role here, but again the personality variable standing for limited control over the environment is very strong. Interestingly, marital status or plans seem to have little effect on labor force participation, but the sample here is too small to make definitive statements about these results.

There were 1,057 females out of school, with about 14 percent not in the labor force. Because of the larger sample size, dummies could also be included in this regression to account for parents' income; however, they proved to be insignificant, further reinforcing their initial exclusion. In general, the results here are quite similar to those obtained for the total subsample; this is not surprising because these individuals constitute the major bulk of those analyzed in table 4-10.

Being married has an extremely strong negative effect on labor force participation, as was expected from the total sample results. Working either as an operative or in a sales or clerical capacity also greatly diminishes labor force participation. For the first time, being handicapped has a significantly negative effect, but racial variables seem to play no role. On the-job training is again important, but having previously attended school has no effect. Finally, the result of one's father working in the clerical or sales occupations or in service occupations increases labor force participation. Both ability and personality variables are insignificant.

In conclusion, the most striking difference between males and females (out of school) is the unimportance of ability and personality factors for women and their importance for men. Whether this effect is caused by the different mix of jobs offered males and females or by different attitudes toward work is an interesting question for further research.

Wage Levels

An analysis of wages involves regressing the natural logarithm of wages per hour on a number of dependent variables. There is some theoretical controversy over the validity of such a functional form; in any event, the coefficients in such a regression can be interpreted as representing percentage changes in income.

Because a greater number of variables were used in this subsample, a smaller number of observations were available because those individuals lacking the necessary data were deleted. Thus, the total sample for this regression consists of 1,116 individuals. Two versions of this regression were tested; in the first, certain variables were used in a continuous manner, whereas, in the other, a series of dummies were used to test for any significant nonlinearities.

The R^2 for both regressions are around .15, which means that only 15 percent of the variance in earnings is explained by the independent variables; this is within the range usually obtained for such formulations of wage equations. F-statistics for the significance of all the coefficients are extremely high in both regressions.

In the version containing the continuous variables, as presented in table 4-11, being male is very significant, leading to about a 25 percent increase in income. Interestingly enough, being white decreases income, though this dummy is significant only at the 7 percent level. Being handicapped reduces income by 13.5 percent, while the age variables seem to have little effect, possibly because of the small amount of variation.

Table 4-11
Wage Regression: Continuous Variables

Dependent Variable:	LWPH73	=	natural logarithm of hourly wage received in 1973
	(LWPH73	=	$.979; U = .431$)
Sample Size = 1,116		$R^2 = .147$	

Variable	Mean	Coefficient	t value
BCQ85	2.1013	−.43859D-02	−0.631
HDSC	10.496	−.40709D-02	−1.232
FF15A	8.4346	.12285D-01	1.975
FF15P	3.7267	.91913D-03	0.141
SATT	702.76	−.32808D-04	−0.400
SCAT	2.3272	−.70155D-02	−0.557
SCPB	−.35476	.12708D-01	0.174
PY	8453.4	.90219D-05	3.862
SEX	.52061	.24661	9.608
LWG2	.21416	.40344D-01	1.292
LWG3	.21685	.23504D-01	0.739
GENPG	.39964	.29259D-02	0.107
ACADPG	.14516	.37071D-01	0.947
HCPD	.59140D-01	−.13506	−2.593
ENGH	.91487	.13466	3.019
RACEW	.82437	−.65989D-01	−1.835
NOGRAD	.12545D-01	.30775	2.800
OJT	.28943	.81496D-01	3.024
SCHOOL	.24104	.70472D-02	0.244
AGEOLD	.50179D-01	−.47256D-01	−0.808
AGE20	.24552	.13068D-01	0.446
FAOC1	.15412	−.67832D-01	−1.683
FAOC2	.10484	−.33294D-01	−0.734
FAOC3	.34677	.20252D-01	0.636
FAOC4	.66308D-01	−.28872D-01	−0.545
FAOC5	.64516D-01	.22294D-01	0.417
CONSTANT	1.0000	.65972	5.999

As far as schooling is concerned, quite significant and surprising is the positive effect of not graduating from high school. However, only about 1 percent
of the sample falls in this category, and thus this result cannot be taken too
seriously. Participating in on-the-job training programs increases income by
8.1 percent and is very significant. Åttending school since graduation has no
effect on wages; the same holds true for the high school program variable.

Also included were various family background variables, such as number
of children dependent on parents, father's education, father's occupation, and
parents' income. Only parents' income had a statistically significant effect;
however, this effect is quite small, with each $1,000 increase in parents' income
only raising wages by about 1 percent.

Among the ranks of the insignificant were several variables attempting to
measure school quality such as percentage of attendance, percentage of children

of professionals, and number of library books. The same was true of the dummies measuring local wage rates.

Finally, the same ability variables as used in previous regressions had no effect on wages. However, our indicator of personality which measured, in some sense, one's positive attitudes proved to have a significant though small effect on wages, raising them about 1.2 percent.

Substituting dummy variables for the continuous measures of number of dependents in the family, fathers' education, and parents' income had little effect on the results. For fathers' education, being in the middle of the distribution has a significantly negative effect of 1.1 percent; this holds for fathers with some college and for those who attended business school or adult education programs. Little effect is noted for fathers with more or less education. Dummies for the other variables confirm previous results. As expected, the higher the level of parents' income, the greater is the increase in wages received.

In conclusion, then, being male, having on-the-job training, positive attitudes, and wealthy parents raises income. Also, not being handicapped and coming from a family where English is the primary language helps. And finally, the strongest influence on income is an individual's sex. The remaining variables had no or very little effect on income. It must be remembered that all of these variables account for only 15 percent of the variance of income; 85 percent of these differences were caused by such other factors as luck or possibly such very specialized abilities as hitting a baseball.

Conclusions

This chapter is the first of three chapters focused on a better understanding of where and how students enter the labor market. Several conclusions emerged from an initial examination of existing information on labor market entry on graduation from high school. First, none of the traditional analyses of labor market entry patterns had been performed on a data set of such high quality as the National Longitudinal Survey of the High School Class of 1972. Second, little analysis has been aimed at understanding the effects of educational plans on an individual's expectations with respect to labor market success. The major goal of this research was to increase the refinement of several analyses using traditional techniques to deal with questions relating to labor market entry and success.

Thus, this chapter has examined those students who did not intend to pursue additional training immediately following high school graduation but planned to enter the labor market directly. For this group, the transition from their plans to their actual experiences, with additional focus on both the causal determinants of a range of potential outcomes and the differential impact of a given set of labor market variables on these outcomes for different subsets of that population, is explained. The dual nature of the approach taken is demonstrated in that the cross-tabular analysis of both student attitudes on graduation and the patterns of their subsequent activities is followed by regression analysis of unemployment, labor market participation, and wage rates.

Also, the first section of this chapter makes no attempt to offer a new theory of behavior. It is descriptive in that it relies on the sample data, not to test any existing or new theory of behavior formally, but to begin to describe in some detail the characteristics of the teenage population that leaves high school with the intention of entering directly into full-time employment. The purpose of this descriptive analysis is to glean some insight into the process by which expectations are formed and then realized or frustrated in the years immediately following high school graduation. A summary of the major conclusions developed here follows.

In general, the picture for this "plan to directly enter the labor market" subgroup is rather pessimistic. It appears that only 40 percent of those hoping to find work on graduation, but with no plans to continue their present employment, have been successful. The best description for this group appears therefore not to be that they have decided to go to work, but that they have decided not to go to school immediately and are uncertain as to what they are going to do. Of this group about half indicated a preference or willingness to move, which indicates that this high labor market mobility, if exercised, could alleviate regional pockets of unemployment.

After examining student attitudes on graduation, an analysis of patterns of actual post–high school activities, such as school attendance and job characteristics, was presented. When considering the labor market success of teenagers, it is particularly difficult to capture the richness of teen labor activity by straightforward measures of employment and unemployment. The group of teenagers who planned to go to work on graduation had come to that decision hesitantly and that the mix of postsecondary school and full-time work plans of the group are intertwined and influenced by the degree of success achieved in pursuing these alternative paths. Lack of high school success may lead many to record themselves as seeking full-time work; subsequent lack of immediate success in the labor market may spawn plans to return to school in some capacity. Better information about wages and salaries available to high school graduates may induce a shift in education and training plans. Moreover, many of these students decided very late in their high school careers not to attend school on graduation and many were still undecided about future postsecondary education at the actual time of high school graduation. Thus, it is appropriate to examine the actual patterns of labor market success 4 months and 16 months after graduation.

This movement of individuals between school, work, and unemployment over time is a particularly important phenomenon. Thus, for the sample that was planning to work full time on high school graduation, detailed tables of data are presented that permit analysis of the various paths followed by any sub-group of those individuals who have decided not to attend postsecondary education immediately. Not all subgroups are analyzed in detail in the text, but certain tables do allow examination of many of the possible permutations.

Regression analysis of labor market status yielded results generally very close to Bowen and Finnegan's analysis of the 1960 census data. Strikingly, males and whites fared better than blacks and females in locating a job. Interestingly, being employed in 1972 did not result in lower unemployment rates in 1973 than for those who had no job in 1972 (possibly a result of the economic variables at the time). Also, being in any kind of school since graduation greatly lowers chances of being employed, since the individual is likely to be less committed to those types of jobs that are available to high school graduates. Participating in an on-the-job training program raises employment chances, while, finally, having parents in middle-income brackets significantly increased chances of being employed.

Notes

1. Insofar as 02 represents graduates who are actually working or training on the job, as indicated by SQ questions 21 and 22.

2. Martin Feldstein, "The Economics of the New Unemployment," *The Public Interest* 33 (Fall 1973).

3. "Other formal programs" refers to response 4 to first follow-up questions 26b and 32b. The NLS data bank did not indicate what they might be.

4. The analysis here is derived from tables where reading across the rows yields information on the 1973 activities of individuals who, in 1972, were recorded as being in one of the 12 labor force categories listed in the left-hand column. Reading down the columns yields information on the 1972 activities of individuals who, in 1973, were recorded as being in one of the twelve labor force categories listed across the top of the table.

A further breakdown of these tables by race and sex yielded no particularly startling results. All tables are contained in the full report, *Experiences of Recent High School Graduates: The Transition to Work or Postsecondary Education* by Nolfi and others (Cambridge, Mass.: University Consultants, Inc., 1977).

5. While the actual coefficient estimates for these subsample regressions are not presented here, they are contained in the full report, ibid.

5 High School Graduates In The Labor Market

The labor market position of persons who graduate from high school but do not go to college varies widely. Some graduates end up as managers with high incomes, others as well-paid union factory operatives or craftsmen; others, however, fall to the bottom of the occupational and income structure. Despite the fact that most young persons today do not go to college,[1] there have been relatively few studies of the determinants of the market success of those with less than college training. Human capital analyses have concentrated on the economic effects of schooling, with differences in the economic position of those with the same level of schooling ignored or treated as the result of experience. Recent work on the falling economic value of college has focused on the market for new college graduates, with little attention given to the particular alternatives facing those who elect not to go.

Sociological studies of the determinants of social mobility generally analyze the impact of family background on achievement in the whole population, with background often operating largely through schooling. The possibly differential effect of background on various education groups has seldom been studied. Traditional labor market studies of blue-collar job markets have focused on the institutional features of the market, regulating the personal and background determinants of economic success within the blue-collar world.

This chapter presents some preliminary results of analyzing the factors that differentiate young high school graduates in the labor market in 1973, using the National Longitudinal Survey of the Class of 1972. The results are preliminary in three ways. First, because the young persons analyzed have just begun their work careers, their current position is a potentially frail indicator of lifetime success; follow-up analyses of the class in future years are needed for firmer results. Second, the analysis is preliminary because of the peculiarities of the sample covered. Because of the way in which the data were gathered, many observations are missing, raising the possibility of serious response bias. Thus, any findings should be checked with other survey data to draw significant conclusions; however, initial examination of the whole sample points toward the biases being small. Third, the statistical modeling used is also relatively simple; because of the data problems, it was not deemed fruitful to apply more advanced techniques than ordinary multiple regression analysis. The use of sophisticated unobservables methodology on a potentially highly unrepresentative sample was rejected.

This chapter is primarily the responsibility of Richard B. Freeman

Granting the preliminary nature of the analysis, the calculations reveal some interesting aspects of the determinants of socioeconomic success among high school graduates. Family income, in particular, is found to have a substantive effect on the market achievement of persons with the same schooling. Certain personal characteristics, physical handicaps, ability to speak English, and sex also differentiate persons in the market; other characteristics, notably race, have quite different or less significant effects than have traditionally been found. Several other factors that are often hypothesized to influence socioeconomic success (measures of ability, personality factors, local market conditions, and some characteristics of the high school attended) also have basically no effect. There are, furthermore, certain differences between the determinants of the market position of women and men.

Differences in Achievement of High School Graduates

At the outset, it is important to recognize the significant dispersion in the economic position of persons with the same level of schooling *even* at the beginning of their careers. Table 5-1 presents some national data on the dispersion of incomes and occupational position of high school men and women, taken separately, in recent years. Lines 1 and 2 show that, for either sex, there was a marked dispersion in incomes, even for those working full-time year-round. The variance in the incomes of year-round full-time white male high school graduates aged 19 in 1973 was on the order of 75 percent of the mean. Though some of this variation results from different lifetime career strategies, with some taking lower pay now to invest in training and obtain higher pay in the future, the variation is still impressive. The occupational attainment data in line 3 shows that, even in the weakened job market in the mid-1970s, some *new* high school graduates obtained "good" white-collar jobs, a sizable number got into the skilled crafts, and others did relatively poorly.

The extent of variation in market positions in the NLS sample under study here is examined in table 5-2. The measure of position to be analyzed is the hourly pay of workers. This measure has several disadvantages as an indicator of market position for such a young group of workers. As previously noted, some of those with low wages may have chosen jobs in which they implicitly "pay" for training, so that current wages are a fallacious measure of their true position. Similarly, those with low wages could be in temporary jobs which they intend to leave shortly, again providing an underestimate of their "true" earnings potential. These disadvantages notwithstanding, wages are still very good measures of market position and merit analysis. In contrast to indicators of socioeconomic status, they relate to individuals rather than average characteristics of groups and thus vary more. Studies that look at the effect of background variables on wages and occupational status tend to yield similar findings, making it unlikely that changes in the measure would alter results. Some control on the possible bias on wages caused by on-the-job training is possible with data from the tape. Future

Table 5-1
Variation in the Market Position of Young High School Graduates

		Male	Female
1.	Earnings, 19-year-old white high school graduates, 1973		
	Mean	5188	3375
	Standard Deviation	2915	2122
2.	Earnings, 19-year-old white high school graduates, year-round, full-time workers in 1973		
	Mean	6101	4710
	Standard Deviation	3234	1693
3.	Occupational distribution of high school graduates in the high school class of 1974, in October 1975 (in percentages)		
	Professional	2.7	4.0
	Managerial	3.7	2.9
	Other white collar	12.1	52.6
	Craftsmen	18.4	2.5
	Operatives	28.5	10.9
	Service workers	10.2	25.3
	All other	24.4	1.8

Source: Lines 1, 2 tabulated from March 1974 *Current Population Reports*, Survey. Line 3, U.S. Department of Labor, Bureau of Labor Statistics, *Special Labor Force Report 1911*, table f, p. A–14.

Table 5-2
Variation in Hourly Pay for the NLS Class of 1972 Sample

		Log Hourly Pay	
	Sample Size	Mean	Standard Deviation
Total	1,623	.97	.43
Men	812	1.09	.44
Women	811	.85	.39
Black	284	1.03	.50
Nonblack	1,339	.93	.42

Source: Calculated from NLS Class of 1972 Tape.

work should, however, test occupational status (along the lines of the work presented in chapter 6) as well as wages.

Column 1 of table 5-2 gives the number of persons in the NLS sample, by sex and race, for whom sufficient data existed for analysis. Column 2 gives the mean of the log of hourly earnings in October 1972, obtained by dividing earnings by time worked as reported in the first follow-up survey. It shows a male-female differential of about 22 percent (= exp .24) and, surprisingly a black-white differential of 7 percent (= exp .07) *in favor of blacks*. The higher wage of blacks is due, however, primarily to an advantage among women (see table 5-5) and may be suspect because of the high nonresponse rate among blacks. Even so, the absence of any sharp differential against blacks is striking. Finally, column 3 of table 5-2 records the standard deviation in the log of wages. The variation is larger for men than for women and for blacks than for nonblacks. Its general magnitude is similar to that found in other data sets.

Factors Affecting Wages of New High School Graduates

This section reports the results of some basic multiple regression calculations designed to evaluate the *measured* variables that influence the wages of persons with the same level of schooling, young high school graduates. It should be viewed as an extension of the analysis presented in the third section of chapter 4.

1. *Family background characteristics*: the education of the head of household of the young person (PAREDUC); the occupational position of the father (PAROCCUP); the income of the parental household measured in thousands of dollars (FAMINC); the number of siblings (SIBS); whether or not English is spoken in the home (ENGL).
2. *Personal characteristics*: (SEX) as reflected in a dummy variable, with male = 1; (RACE) as reflected in a dummy variable, with black = 1; (ACTIVE) obtained by summing responses to statements 1, 3, 4, and 8 to question 15 in the follow-up; (PASSIVE), obtained by summing responses to statements 2, 5, 6, and 7 of the same question; and a measure of ability (ABILITY), either SAT, ACT, or ETS tests (the latter administered during the base-year questionnaire), depending on availability (all tests were scaled to have the same variance); (AGE); and whether the person has any physical handicap (HANDCPD).
3. *Schooling characteristics*: dummy variables for whether the high school program was general (GENRL) or academic (ACAD) as opposed to vocational; whether the person had some post-high school education (POST); and a dummy variable (NOGRAD) for those who did not manage to graduate (about 1 percent of the sample).
4. *Market job characteristics*: the unemployment rate in the local market (UNE); and whether the individual regards his or her job as offering on-the-job training (OJT).

The results of regressing the log of hourly earnings on these variables for the entire population are summarized in table 5-3, which differentiates the four types of variables into three classes, depending on their estimated effect. The family background variable with the greatest impact is family income, which obtained a substantial positive coefficient; in contrast, the parental

**Table 5-3
Effects of Various Factors on Wages
(OLS estimates, entire population)**

Impact of Variables	Family Background		Personal Characteristics		School Characteristics	Market/Job Characteristics	
1. Substantial effect	FAMINC:	0.061 (3.1)	SEX:	0.25 (11.0)	NOGRAD: 0.19 (2.1)	OJT:	0.08 (3.5)
	ENGL:	0.10 (2.7)	RACE:	0.08 (2.7)			
			HNDCPD:	.10 (2.3)			
2. Marginal impact	SIBS: − 0.0074 (1.3)						
3. Little or no impact	PAREDUC PAROCCUP		ACTIVE PASSIVE ABILITY AGE		POST ACAD	UNE	

Note: Summary Statistics R^2 = 0.2; F = 9.1; t statistics in parentheses

occupation dummies and parental education variables were found to have little effect. Whether or not English is spoken in the home is also important. The number of siblings has a modest impact. The strong effect of family income suggests that social origin has an impact on market position for persons with the same years of schooling, but also suggests that parental occupation and education variables do not provide a good measure of the relevant background characteristics.

For personal characteristics, what stands out are (1) the small or non-existent effect of the ability and personality factors, and (2) the positive coefficient on being black. It is presumably possible to obtain larger ability or personality effects through the use of instrumental variable techniques that correct for measurement error in these factors (see chapter 6), but their negligible role is unlikely to be greatly altered.[2] The positive coefficient on being black could, as noted earlier, reflect problems with the sample. It is not, however, as odd as it might first appear; calculations with very young men in the National Longitudinal Survey of the Department of Labor also suggest little differences in rates of pay, when corrected for various background factors, but larger differences in total earnings due to greater unemployment and less time worked by blacks. It is also possible that the positive coefficient indicates that blacks are choosing jobs with less training and more immediate rewards than whites.

The most striking aspect of the school variables is their general unimportance.

Consistent with other studies, the calculations suggest that the type of school has little or no impact. The only school factor that matters is failure to graduate, which raises wages, presumably because of the odd group covered (1 percent of the whole sample) and the greater work experience of those who left early.

Finally, the on-the-job training variable shows that persons in jobs with such training (as they perceive it) have higher wages than others, contrary to the prediction of human capital theory. There are, of course, possible ways of reconciling this result with the theory, for instance, by arguing that the comparisons do not control adequately for the alternatives available to individuals, but the prime facie case is against the theory. This is consistent with C. Brown's work on the NLS (Parnes) tape, which also found the human capital model not readily applicable to young men just beginning their careers.

Overall, family background seems to matter in the position of young high school workers, as do certain personal characteristics, while local unemployment has no effect and perceived on-the-job training appears to work in the "wrong" direction. The school variables have no apparent impact.

The effect of family income on the hourly earnings of young workers in the market is examined further in table 5–4, which records the results of decomposing the family income variable into a set of dummy variables. Measuring income in this way provides an estimate of the curvature of the family background effect and is a stronger test of its impact: we expect coefficients to rise fairly steadily as the income classes rise. The results are high reasonable, with little difference found among those from families in the first three classes, followed by rising differences thereafter. Roughly speaking, there is a 10 percent differential between those from the upper 10 percent of the families and those in the lower half (compare the coefficients for the two top groups in table 5–4 with those from the bottom three groups, in terms of income). Such

Table 5–4
Curvature of the Impact of Family Income on Wages
(Sample size = 1,623)

	Coefficient	Percentage of Sample
$ 3,000 per year	—	.11
$ 3,000–6,000	−.02	.13
$ 6,000–9,000	−.006	.23
$ 9,000–12,000	.03	.20
$12,000–15,000	.05	.12
$15,000–18,000	.10	.05
+$18,000	.12	.06

Source: Calculated from NLS tapes.

a difference is not negligible: it is equivalent, more or less, to a year of schooling or to membership in a trade union. If it persists over the lifetime, and if
individuals make, say, $15,000 per year, it cumulates to $20,000 at an interest rate of 7.5 percent, a reasonably large "bequest" from upper-income levels
to their children above and beyond schooling.

Differences Among Subgroups

To what extent, if any, do the family background, personal, school, and mar-
ket/job characteristics examined here have different effects on different groups
of persons?

This section presents estimates of the impact of the variables of concern
on log hourly earnings for subsamples of the basic population, Part a of
table 5-5 compares coefficients by sex, while part b compares coefficients

Table 5-5
The Impact of Variables on Wages

(a) Comparison by Sex

	Coefficients			
Variable	*Male*		*Female*	
SIBS	−.001	(.07)	−.015	(1.9)
Family Income	.068	(2.3)	.053	(2.1)
ENGLISH	−.08	(1.5)	−.18	(2.4)
RACE	.04	(.08)	.14	(3.3)
HNDCP	−.08	(1.5)	−.18	(2.4)
ACAD	.07	(1.5)	−.03	(.6)
GEN	.02	(.6)	−.05	(1.6)
OJT	.06	(2.0)	.08	(2.7)
Size of Sample	812		811	

(b) Comparison by Race

Variables	*Black*		*Nonblack*	
ACTIVE	.025	(1.8)	−.00	(.27)
PASSIVE	−.026	(1.9)	.01	(.01)
HDCPD	−.03	(.25)	−.12	(2.051)
SEX	.25	(3.8)	.25	(10.6)
ENGL	−.25	(3.3)	.03	(0.7)
Family Income	−.00	(.01)	.07	(3.6)
SIBS	.00	(.60)	−.001	(1.8)
OJT	.02	(.40)	.09	(3.9)
Sample Size	284		1,339	

Source: Calculated from NLS tapes, *t* statistics in parentheses. (Calculations
include all other variables used in the regressions in table 5-3.)

by race. Because the subsamples have, of necessity, many fewer persons than the total sample and may be subject to differential response bias, the computations should be viewed solely as suggestive. Given the sample sizes and confidence intervals, few if any are statistically significant, though they might be in larger populations.

There are several interestingly different coefficients between men and women in table 5-5. first, the number of siblings appears to have a greater deterrent effect on women than men, which may reflect the greater allocation of family resources to male than female children. It would be fruitful to decompose the SIBS variable more finely. A second difference is found in the RACE coefficient, which shows young black women doing markedly better than young white women in this sample, while young black men have only a slight advantage over their white peers. As noted earlier, most of the positive effect of being black occurs among the women. Third, and perhaps most significant as a guide to future work, is the different coefficients obtained on the type of curriculum. Whereas among young men, both academic education and, to a much less extent, general education are positive factors, those women with vocational training do better than those following academic or general curricula. This raises the possibility that current vocational programs, presumably for commercial clerical work, may serve women students better than the equivalent craft vocational programs for men. If this differential effect is confirmed with larger, better samples and with more precise measures of programs, it deserves attention in policy analysis and formation.

The comparisons of variables by race in table 5-5 also reveal some interesting differences in the effect of various factors in the hourly earnings of black and nonblack persons in the sample. One striking difference is in the impact of the two "personality" variables on wages; whereas these factors have no effect on whites, they do have an impact on the position of blacks, with persons rated highly in the ACTIVE variable doing somewhat better and those rated highly in the negative PASSIVE variable doing somewhat worse than others in the sample. One possible interpretation is that blacks face a wider range of opportunities than whites, with discrimination in some sectors and various affirmative action and related aid programs in others; this may make the personal drive variables more important.

Another noticeable difference is the impact of family background characteristics. Number of siblings and family income have no effect on blacks compared to a sizable effect on whites. By contrast, when English is not spoken in black homes, there is a large loss in income compared to essentially no impact in white homes. Possibly the differential ENGL coefficients reflect differences in the ethnic groups, with some lacking English in black homes compared to a more diverse group of persons in nonblack homes. The most discouraging differential in coefficients is that found on on-the-job training, which shows a markedly greater effect of training for whites than blacks; this bodes ill for the future of rough parity in incomes by race.

Conclusions

As noted at the outset, because of the youth of the population analyzed, the high nonresponse rate, and simple tools of analysis, this chapter has yielded only tentative results that must be checked and verified with additional data and models before they can be accepted. The principal findings, tentative as they are, can be summarized briefly:

1. Family income matters in the economic success of young persons who do not go to college.
2. Curriculum has no overall effect but may matter differentially by sex.
3. Racial differences in hourly earnings are essentially nonexistent in the sample analyzed, though this could be an artifact of the response rate.
4. Differences in the effect of background by sex and race merit further attention.

Notes

1. *Current Population Survey*, p-20, no. 103, p. 9.

2.   However, correcting for errors of measurement not only increases the size and significance of the coefficients, but also reduces the variation in the explanatory variable, so that the contribution to differentials in the sample does not change markedly.

6

Schooling and Occupation Decisions

Interest in relations among earnings, schooling, and other factors such as ability and family background stems from several sources. One is a desire to estimate the contribution of increased schooling to growth in incomes. Other work on earnings functions has concentrated on investigating discrimination, by attributing unexplained differences in earnings across groups to discrimination or other market imperfections. (See Griliches, 1975a, for a survey and bibliography.) This chapter places special emphasis on the role of ability in earnings and schooling equations for men only, for reasons given below. It departs from or expands on previous studies in three ways: (1) it attempts to refine the concept of ability by estimating separately such effects as verbal, abstract, and mathematical ability; (2) personality characteristics are added to the equation; and (3) the effects of characteristics of the high school on earnings and schooling are investigated in detail. The results are presented in two parts. The basic regressions are presented, along with the results of more advanced estimation techniques, in the first section. The second section deals with the effects of high schools. Technical discussions of both the identification of the models presented and of the nonlinear maximization program have been deleted here.

The National Longitudinal Study of the High School Class of 1972 has several advantages and disadvantages as compared with other surveys. The chief advantages of this data set are the good information available on the ability and attitudes of the individuals, and also on the individual's high school. Six different tests, all purporting to measure different categories of ability—for example, verbal, mathematical, abstract, and reasoning skills—are available. However, that each test was very brief; all six were administered in a span of a little more than an hour. In addition, the individual's class rank is also listed. The results of the test scores, as opposed to class rank, are unknown to the student, his or her school, college, and employer. Thus, if education has primarily a "screening" effect (as discussed, for example, by Spence, 1974), then these measures of ability should have little effect relative to class rank. In addition, class rank is certainly not a function of pure ability alone. Drive and motivation probably play a role. In fact, it is conceivable

This chapter is a condensed version of an unpublished Ph.D. thesis submitted to the Department of Economics at Harvard University with the same title in January 1977 by William H. Epstein.

that class rank measures that combination of those unobservable factors most relevant for economic success.

Another advantage of such multiple tests is that of distinguishing among the relative importance of different types of ability. Gary Chamberlain (1975a and 1975b) has suggested the distinction between that kind of ability relevant to schooling success and that relevant to earning success. These different tests permit both the identification of various types of ability and, as a result, some testing for the relative importance of different types of ability.

Other researchers have had far inferior measures of ability. Griliches and Mason (1972) only had the Armed Forces Qualifying Test scores. The Parnes data (discussed in Parnes and others, 1970-73) contain two possible measures of ability: (1) the so-called IQ test, and (2) a "knowledge of the world of work" test. The IQ test relies on different sources for different individuals. For some the IQ score may be the result of one of the many different IQ tests; for others the score may be a scaled version of their class rank. The problems with such measures, as opposed to a battery of tests administered under controlled circumstances at the same point of an individual's life, are evident. The tests in this study will be discussed in greater detail when the specific variables used here are presented.

A second advantage of this data set concerns its wide range of data on attitudes. Questions are available, for example, on the advice and desires regarding further education received from parents, teachers, and peers. In addition, numerous questions dealing with opinions on the relative importance of job attributes such as money, serving society, and having leisure time are asked. Further questions deal with such personality attributes as individual self-confidence and attitudes on the role of luck. Sherwin Rosen, in his survey of human capital theory (1976), remarks that the lack of such variables in earnings equations is a serious deficiency in these models.

An important disadvantage of these data is that, by concentrating exclusively on high school graduates, the lowest achievers in terms of education and social class are omitted. Thus, the sample is not representative of the entire population. Because many government programs are directed especially at this lowest class of achievers, the utility of this survey is diminished for the purpose of policy recommendations concerning the mitigation of poverty and other problems. It might be argued that this problem is alleviated because of the selection of a more than proportional number of schools from communities located in low- income areas and with high percentages of minorities. Though, via these means, an adequate percentage of minorities might be achieved, nevertheless, given the comparatively small percentage of high school graduates among minorities (see Current Population Survey, P-20, no. 295, p. 13), those individuals so selected will still not be representative of the minorities.

Another serious problem with these data is that students themselves filled out the questionnaires. Thus, several types of error are possible. Students did not have to fill out the entire base-year or follow-up questionnaire. Rather, based on their experience and aspirations, different students filled out different portions. Obviously, some could fill out the wrong portion. In addition, especially in the follow-ups, some questions required students to write in a program or number, rather than, as in most of the questions, simply circle a number corresponding to the desired response. Finally, students were conspicuously reminded of their option not to answer any question that they or their parents would consider objectionable. Many of these problems are mitigated in such surveys as the Parnes data, where an interviewer asks the respond-dent the question, and can thus ensure that correct portions of the questionnaire are answered and omit any patently unreasonable result.

Attempts were made to ensure that certain basic questions were answered; otherwise, questionnaires were returned or the respondent was otherwise contacted. In addition, because students gave such information as parents' income, desired schooling for student, and actual schooling, a small number of parents were contacted to verify the data in the base-year survey; this survey of parents was performed several months after the students had completed the questionnaires. In addition, before the parent was surveyed, the student's permission was requested. As might be expected, parents and students did differ on some matters. These discrepancies will be discussed in connection with the actual variables used in this chapter.

As in all such surveys, individuals "disappear," though this difficulty is now lessened because of the end of the draft. One problem is that not all students completed the base-year questionnaire and tests; about 6,000 students could not be contacted during their senior year, but were surveyed in the first follow-up and asked a few of the most important base-year questions. About 93 percent of those contacted completed the first follow-up.

Perhaps the most serious problem with this data set for the purposes of investigating earnings and schooling is the relative youth of the sample. At the time of the first follow-up, individuals have completed only one year of either college or work. Thus, using current earnings would pose severe problems for two reasons. One is that for a large fraction, about 60 percent, earnings would not be available because they are in college, and working at best part-time, and in jobs likely to be unrelated to their future career. For those already working, it is likely that they are still engaged in extensive on-the-job training, and thus their earnings are unrepresentative of their anticipated returns from schooling.

For this reason, following Griliches (1975a), it was decided to use *expected* schooling and earnings. The advantages and disadvantages of this procedure have been discussed by Griliches. The major advantage is that one can ignore the problems caused by on-the-job training, and use a larger and more representative group such as one that includes those now in college.

In addition, such a concept more closely approximates the concepts dealt with in models of optimal levels of schooling as discussed by Becker (1967), Rosen (1975), and Wallace and Ihnen (1975). In fact, such concepts can be thought of as approximating Mincer's "overtaking point" (1974), at which earnings from prior on-the-job training cancel out current investments in on-the-job training. At this point, in short, it is possible to obtain estimates of the effects of schooling uncontaminated by on-the-job training.

An obvious disadvantage is that one is dealing with expectations, rather than reality. A more serious problem concerns not so much the use of expected earnings as such but the method used both here and in the Griliches study of imputing expected earnings to individuals. In this data set no questions deal with expected earnings directly. Rather an individual is asked what he or she expects to be doing at age 30. Unfortunately, only 14 categories are available concerning the choice of job. Each category was given an expected income based on the median income for men for that profession as reported by the 1970 census. The logarithm of this variable is denoted W30. (A complete list of all variables used in this study is contained in table 6-1.) Herein lies another major problem; one loses all variation within occupations. In addition, the link between the imputed expected earnings and the actual expected

Table 6-1
Variables Used

W30	Logarithm of expected income at age 30
AS	Realistically anticipated amount of schooling
ES	Desired amount of schooling
TEST	Average of the six tests
VOCABT	Test of vocabulary
PICTT	Test of short-term memory
READT	Test of reading comprehension
LETGP	Test of matching letters
MATHT	Test of basic mathematical skills
MOSAT	Test of recognizing patterns of mosaics
CLRANK	Student's high school class rank
FF15P	Index of personality suggesting an individual perceives only a limited control over his environment
FF15A	Index of personality suggesting an individual is confident of himself
SIBDEP	Number of siblings still dependent on parents
FAMINC	Parent's before-tax income from all sources
BB94A	Measure of families' affluence
BB94S	Measure of "culture"
FED	Father's education
MED	Mother's education
PACA	Student's high school program academic or college-preparatory
BLACK	Student is black
STCOM	Student's high school in rural or small community
SREG	Student's high school located in the South

earnings is somewhat tenuous. More basically, then, this method of imputing expected earnings would suggest regressing it on *mean* schooling, *mean* ability, and so forth. If such an approach were valid, then, as Griliches and Chamberlain (1976) point out, the use of *actual* schooling, ability, and so on would lead to biases. However, as shown by Griliches and Chamberlain (personal communication), such a regression using the means implicitly assumes the residual term has no group structure, a dubious assumption. For this sample, regressions using such means yield meaningless results. Thus, the extent of the distortions and biases induced by this procedure of calculating expected income remains uncertain.

One defense is that Griliches (1975) also used actual earnings, and found the results to be quite similar to those based on expected earnings. In that study, using the Parnes data, he had a reasonably broad sample of those already out of school and employed in professional areas as well as some who had already been working for several years and thus were more settled in their careers. Such a comparison would be quite meaningless for this data set, for all individuals are of roughly the same age, and further, as already noted, actual incomes are only available for individuals in subprofessional areas.

For expected schooling two variables are available. Follow-up question 12 asks: "How far in school would you like to get?" Choices are high school only, vocational school (less than two years, greater or equal to two years) and college (some college, B.A., M.A., and Ph.D.). Question 14 of the follow-up asks: "As things stand now, how far in school do you think you actually will get?" Thus, these two questions attempt to distinguish between how much schooling an individual would like to get and how much he actually thinks he will get. The first measure will be denoted as ES, the second as *AS*. *AS* would appear to be more relevant in terms of a model of optimal schooling or human capital investments. In most cases, therefore, only estimates for AS will be presented.

The six aptitude tests available are (1) vocabulary (5 minutes) (VOCABT); (2) picture-number (10 minutes) (PICTT), which required students to look at pictures of such items as desks and pens and numbers next to them; after a few minutes, students had to turn the page and then were given the pictures and had to supply the numbers (in short, this test can be viewed as a memory test); (3) reading comprehension (15 minutes) READT); (4) letter groups (15 minutes) (LETGP), in which students were given five combinations of letters and asked to choose the combination that differed from the others; (5) mathematics (15 minutes) (MATHT), more a test of basic computational skills than of abstract mathematical ability; and (6) mosaics (9 minutes) (MOSAT), a test of recognizing patterns of mosaics. Also used at times in the following regressions is an average of the six tests (TEST). The raw scores are transformed versions so that each mean is 50 and the standard deviation is 10.

These tests seem to measure three different concepts of ability. VOCABT, READT, and MATHT appear to measure basic scholastic achievement. The first two tests indicate competence in verbal skills, with MATHT measuring competence in fundamental computational mathematics. LETGP and MOSAT measure abstract nonverbal ability. Of course, the precise measurement and definition of this type of ability is tenuous, and thus any test attempting such measures must have some uncertainties associated with it. Finally, PICTT is an indicator of short-term memory. As already noted, the brevity of these tests is disturbing but obviously cannot be remedied.

Two indicators of personality are derived from the answers to the following statements posed in follow-up question 15. Answers were coded to be 0 for disagree strongly, 1 for disagree, 2 for agree, and 3 for agree strongly (average responses are in parentheses):

1. I take a positive attitude toward myself. (2.43)
2. Good luck is more important than hard work for success. (1.93)
3. I feel I am a person of worth, on an equal plane with others. (2.44)
4. I am able to do things as well as most other people. (2.39)
5. Every time I try to get ahead, something or somebody stops me. (1.24)
6. Planning only makes a person unhappy since plans hardly ever work out anyway. (1.08)
7. People who accept their condition in life are happier than those who try to change things. (1.50)
8. On the whole, I am satisfied with myself. (2.12)

In some sense (see Coleman, 1966), affirmative responses to questions 1, 3, 4, and 8 can be identified as indicative of positive attitudes (in terms of self-perception), and affirmative responses to the rest as indicative of negative attitudes (in terms of locus of control). Two variables defined as the sum of the four positive attitudes (FF15A) and the sum of the four negative attitudes (FF15P) are used as indicators of the student's attitudes.

Finally, the following background variables were used:

1. SIBDEP—number of siblings still dependent on parents.
2. FAMINC—parent's before-tax income from all sources. Students tended to underestimate high-income parents and to overestimate low-income parents. Student nonresponse was also a problem, especially with families with high income.
3. BB94A—measure of "affluence": index as to whether family possesses color TV, dishwasher, tape recorder, record player, two cars. Coded so as to award one point for possessing each of the listed items; the maximum score is 5, the minimum 0.
4. BB94S—measure of "culture": index as to whether home possesses place to study, newspaper, dictionary, encyclopedia, magazines, typewriter.

With respect to a place to study, parents tended to report such a place existed much more frequently than did students. Coded in the same manner as BB94A.

5. FED—father's education.
6. MED—mother's education.
7. PACA—student's high school program: academic or college-preparatory. Unfortunately, there is no uniform definition of what does or does not constitute such a program. Nevertheless, schools and students were both asked, without further definition of the terms, whether the student was in a general, academic or college-preparatory, or vocational-technical program. PACA is set equal to 1 when both student and school agree on his being in an academic program, 0 otherwise. About 80 percent of those students which the school considered to be in an academic program agreed with the school.
8. BLACK—set equal to 1 if student is black.
9. STCOM—student's high school in rural or small community.
10. SREG—student's high school located in the South.

In any large set of data, the actually usable sample size will be considerably smaller than the total sample size because of missing information. As mentioned previously, this problem is especially likely to occur with this data set because the students themselves filled out the questionnaires.

Women have been deliberately omitted from these samples for several reasons. Preliminary results for females displayed less explanatory power and at times unreasonable results, perhaps because 1970 earnings for men were used to impute expected income. (Using average female earnings was rejected since, for many professional careers, these figures are distorted by part-time work.) Possibly there is need for a more general model explicitly incorporating the marriage and child-bearing decision. For these reasons as well as those of economy and compatibility with previous studies, it was decided to concentrate exclusively on roughly 11,500 males who composed about 50 percent of the sample.

About 3,500 of these men (about a third of the sample) failed to answer questions relating to the dependent variables (W30, AS, and ES) or did not report their race or age. Lost via this route were a disproportionate number of students with low aptitudes. About 20 percent of the lowest third in aptitude did not answer the questions on expected schooling or occupation, as opposed to only 10 percent for the highest third in aptitude. With respect to SES (socioeconomic status) the situation is less severe. Some 14 percent of the lowest third failed to answer the question on expected occupation versus 10 percent for the highest third. For schooling the equivalent figures are 13 percent and 8 percent. About 18 percent of the racial minorities did not respond to the expected occupation question, versus 14 percent for whites. For schooling, these figures are 16 percent and 12 percent. In addition, those stating they expected to be full-time homemakers, to enter the military, or not to work at all were excluded. If those lacking information on the dependent variables as well as on race and age are excluded, the sample is reduced to 8,058 males.

A further reduction to 3,470 males was obtained by excluding those lacking test scores, class rank, family income, father's and mother's education, and father's and mother's desired education for the student. One of the main reasons for this big reduction in sample size is the fact that about 25 percent of the overall sample did not participate in the base-year questionnaire and thus did not take the series of aptitude tests. Because one major advantage of this survey is the availability of the aptitude tests, it was considered worth the reduction in subsample size to be able to utilize them. Ideally, weighted variables should be used with these smaller samples so that those groups, if any, that were susceptible to leaving out certain variables would not be underrepresented. However, no weights are currently available for item nonresponse.

One possible technique that has been used to circumvent the problem of missing observations on certain variables is to substitute the mean for the sample for the missing observations and then to add a dummy variable indicating where this was done (see Dagenais, 1973, and Griliches, 1975b). Such techniques were tried for all variables, including test scores, class rank, and the other variables listed in the preceding paragraphs, with no major changes in results.

The means and standard deviations for both the large and small subsample are given in table 6-2. The values calculated for the small subsample (3,470) are given in the lower row for each variable. As can be seen, excluding those students lacking data on test scores, family income, father's and mother's education, and father's and mother's desired education slightly lowers average scores on the tests by about two points, or one-fifth of a standard deviation. Likewise, mean values for family income and parents' education are slightly lower. Perhaps the major changes are a considerably lower percentage of blacks, from 11.8 percent in the large subsample to 6.3 percent, and a larger number enrolled in academic or college-preparatory courses, from 31.9 percent to 42.6 percent.

Finally, before discussing the empirical results, some discussion of functional form is necessary. The literature on optimal human capital accumulation leads to no specific functional form for the relation between earnings and schooling, but does contain considerable criticism of the conventional semi-log form (see Ben-Porath, 1967; Rosen, 1973; and Wallace and Ihnen, 1975). As derived by Mincer (1974, p. 19), the standard semi-log form can be viewed as coming from a cost function where the only elements are the rising interest costs of foregone income. The basic criticism of this model is that it assumes no optimization—that is, everybody is taken as having the same amount of initial human capital and thus is indifferent to the schooling

Table 6–2
Means and Standard Deviations[a]

	Mean	S.D.		Mean	S.D.
W30	9.090	.264	ES	15.502	2.244
	9.119	.254		15.791	2.239
AS	14.956	2.176	TEST	50.260	7.362
	15.252	2.189		51.896	6.620
VOCABT	50.629	9.918	PICTT	49.239	9.799
	52.185	9.667		50.383	9.562
READT	50.528	9.934	LETGP	49.712	9.936
	52.328	9.344		51.658	8.766
MATHT	51.999	9.921	MOSAT	49.453	9.821
	54.018	9.241		50.803	9.185
CLRANK	48.071	27.650	FF15P	3.544	1.887
	51.635	27.297		3.343	1.817
FF15A	8.710	1.974	SIBDEP	2.066	1.493
	8.809	1.913		2.030	1.684
FAMINC	11.459	5.306	BB94A	3.481	1.206
	12.106	5.071		3.604	1.149
BB94S	4.997	1.151	FED	12.286	2.855
	5.137	1.098		12.588	2.848
MED	12.097	2.233	PACA	.319	–
	12.316	2.159		.426	–
BLACK	.118	–	STCOM	.495	–
	.063	–		.488	–
SREG	.350	–	Large subsample	N = 8,058	
	.306	–	Sample used	N = 3,470	

[a]Lower row is for the sample used in this study.

level chosen. In short, why some choose more schooling, or how ability and other factors enter, is completely obscured by this empirical form. Nevertheless, the semi-log form is quite strongly favored by the empirical evidence and is practically the only one used in empirical research. Using Box and Cox transformations (1964), Heckman and Polachek (1974) show that the semi-log form yields the best result. For the schooling equation, simple linear forms are utilized; there is no a priori best functional form, and thus the linear one was chosen for its simplicity.

Role of Ability and Personality

This section analyzes the ways in which variables designed to measure ability levels and personality characteristics affect future expected income levels (W30) and both anticipated and desired amounts of schooling (*AS* and *ES*). Ordinary least-squares estimation techniques will be used initially. The relevant models will also be estimated using techniques that allow for the "unobservable" nature of variables such as ability or personality; that is, no one test can capture all the complicated factors that make up intelligence.

Ordinary Least-Squares Estimates

Table 6-3 gives the basic ordinary least-squares regression results, using W30 as the dependent variable; although not presented here, the results with *ES* substituted for *AS* are quite similar except that the return to schooling is always about 0.3 percent to 0.5 percent less. This result is in keeping with prior expectations; realistic estimates of the amount of desired schooling should yield higher rates of return than those subject to no constraints except foregone earnings.

Among the background variables, SREG, STCOM, and PACA stand out, especially the last, which has an effect on income close to that of one more year of schooling. Parents' educations, especially that of the mother, are also significant but not very large. Four years of education increases expected income by only 1.5 percent. The relative importance of mothers' educations is in agreement with empirical results obtained by A. Leibowitz (1974) who argued, on the basis of human capital theory, that efficiency and time spent in child care should increase with mothers' educations.

The addition of personality variables (FF15P and FF15A) changes the background coefficients marginally, as is evident from column 2 of table 6-3. These personality variables have the expected signs but are rather small in size; a one standard deviation increase in FF15P reduces income by less than 1 percent, while for FF15A, the same increase raises income by about two-thirds of a percentage point.

The third column of table 6-3 gives the coefficients of the background variables when the ability variables are included in the equation; the coefficients of the ability variables are presented in table 6-4. Not much changes in the background variables except that the coefficient of BLACK increases substantially because blacks score lower on the tests than others, and the coefficient for PACA drops. The schooling coefficient drops only slightly, in keeping with other studies. When all six tests are included along with CLRANK, the three achievement tests and PICTT stand out. CLRANK and the two abstract ability tests are much less important. However, none of the tests, even when combined, are very important. A one standard deviation increase in all of the ability variables[1] raises income about 3.8 percent, roughly the same effect that would be achieved by such an increase in just the three achievement tests. A similar increase in just the abstract ability tests has a small negative effect on earnings. Thus, the achievement tests alone seem to account for the influence of ability on income. As might be expected, native

Table 6-3
Basic Regressions with W30 as the Dependent Variable

	Basic Equation	Including Personality Variables	Including Ability Variables[a]
R^2	.300	.302	.307
SEE	.213	.213	.212
AS	.0530 (.00194)	.0518 (.00197)	.0503 (.00203)
SIBDEP	.00145 (.00219)	.00125 (.00219)	.00165 (.00219)
FAMINC	−.0000006 (.0000009)	−.0000006 (.0000009)	−.0000007 (.0000009)
BB94A	.00113 (.00367)	.00092 (.00366)	.00168 (.00366)
BB94S	.00350 (.00395)	.00321 (.00394)	.00241 (.00394)
FED	.00322 (.00171)	.00338 (.00170)	.00229 (.00171)
MED	.00431 (.00210)	.00404 (.00210)	.00329 (.00211)
PACA	.0493 (.00831)	.0486 (.00833)	.0320 (.00906)
BLACK	.0189 (.0160)	.0199 (.0158)	.0415 (.0163)
STCOM	−.0292 (.00747)	−.0298 (.00746)	−.0293 (.00746)
SREG	.0188 (.00809)	.0192 (.00808)	.0193 (.00810)
FF15P		−.00478 (.00207)	
FF15A		.00330 (.00193)	

Note: Standard deviations of coefficients in parentheses.

[a]See table 6-4 for remaining coefficients.

ability must be combined with some actual knowledge before any effect on earnings is noticed.

When similar equations using *ES* were estimated, few significant differences were apparent, except that FED and the personality variables had stronger effects.[2]

Next discussed are equations measuring the effect of the background variables on the level of schooling; *AS* will be examined as a dependent variable. The basic estimates are given in table 6-5; all coefficients, with the exception of FAMINC and BB94A, are significant. Especially strong are (1) FEL, where a

Table 6-4
Coefficients of Ability Variables
(dependent variable = W30)

	$.302^a$	$.307^b$	$.308^c$	.307	.305	.304	.306	.303	.305	.302	.302
R^2											
SEE	.213	.212	.212	.212	.212	.212	.212	.213	.212	.213	.213
AS	.0518	.0503	.0495	.0496	.0505	.0511	.0505	.0511	.0503	.0517	.0509
	(.00197)	(.00203)	(.00205)	(.00201)	(.00200)	(.00198)	(.00199)	(.00199)	(.00201)	(.00198)	(.00204)
TEST				.00354							
				(.00069)							
VOCABT		.00102	.00103		.00179						
		(.00052)	(.00052)		(.00044)						
PICTT		.00104	.00103			.00134					
		(.00043)	(.00043)			(.00040)					
READT		.00108	.00100				.00197				
		(.00056)	(.00056)				(.00044)				
LETGP		.00016	.00013					.00130			
		(.00057)	(.00057)					(.00046)			
MATHT		.00082	.00082						.00187		
		(.00064)	(.00064)						(.00048)		
MOSAT		-.00022	-.00024							.00041	
		(.00044)	(.00044)							(.00041)	
CLRANK		-.00010	-.00011								.00029
		(.00017)	(.00018)								(.00010)

Note: Standard deviations of coefficients in parentheses.

[a] This regression contains only background and personality variables.

[b] This regression contains only background and ability variables (from table 6-3, column 3).

[c] This regression also includes background and personality variables, as do all succeeding regressions (from table 6-3, column 2).

Table 6-5
Basic Regressions with AS as the Dependent Variable

	Basic Equation	Including Personality Variables	Including Ability Variables[a]
R^2	.275	.300	.344
SEE	1.866	1.835	1.788
SIBDEP	−.0642 (.0191)	−.681 (.0188)	−.0525 (.0183)
FAMINC	.00002 (.000008)	.00002 (.000008)	.00002 (.000008)
BB94A	−.0327 (.0321)	−.0381 (.0316)	−.00045 (.0307)
BB94S	.0849 (.0345)	.0732 (.0340)	.0533 (.0330)
FED	.150 (.0147)	.150 (.0145)	.120 (.0142)
MED	.0824 (.0184)	.0719 (.0181)	.0619 (.0177)
PACA	1.553 (.0679)	1.480 (.0673)	.833 (.0745)
BLACK	.764 (.138)	.767 (.136)	1.109 (.136)
STCOM	−.308 (.0652)	−.314 (.0641)	−.319 (.0623)
SREG	.156 (.0708)	.163 (.0696)	.125 (.0679)
FF15P		−.140 (.0177)	
FF15A		.102 (.0166)	

Note: Standard deviations of coefficients in parentheses.

[a]See Table 6-6 for remaining coefficients.

one standard deviation increase raises expected schooling by half a year;
(2) BLACK, which increases schooling by two-thirds of a year; (3) STCOM,
which reduces schooling by one-third of a year; and especially (4) PACA,
which raises schooling by 1.5 years.

Both personality variables are extremely significant, but not very strong.
A one standard deviation increase in FF15P drops expected schooling by
about one-third of a year, while the same increase for FF15A raises schooling
somewhat less. There are few changes in the background coefficients when
the variables are added. As demonstrated in table 6-6, the various ability
tests yield approximately the same results as were obtained in the earnings

Table 6-6
Coefficients of Ability Variables
(dependent variable = AS)

R^2	.344[a]	.358[b]	.332	.320	.309	.317	.313	.326	.303	.347
SEE	1.778	1.759	1.792	1.809	1.823	1.812	1.818	1.800	1.831	1.772
TEST			.0744 (.00572)							
VOCABT	.0172 (.00437)	.0170 (.00432)		.0376 (.00373)						
PICTT	.00829 (.00358)	.00771 (.00354)			.0233 (.00340)					
READT	.00580 (.00470)	.00343 (.00466)				.0351 (.00374)				
LETGP	.00644 (.00480)	.00543 (.00476)					.0323 (.00393)			
MATHT	.0129 (.00535)	.0127 (.00529)						.0468 (.00402)		
MOSAT	-.00362 (.00372)	-.00417 (.00368)							.0138 (.00353)	
CLRANK	.0157 (.00145)	.0150 (.00144)								.0199 (.00125)

Note: Standard deviations of coefficients in parentheses.

[a]This regression contains only background and ability variables (from table 6-5, column 3).

[b]This regression also includes background and personality variables, as do all succeeding regressions (from table 6-5, column 2).

equation. The achievement tests are still strongly significant, with the exception of READT, and the effect of abstract ability is somewhat stronger, especially LETGP. PICTT no longer stands out, suggesting perhaps that pure memorization is less important for schooling aspirations than for earnings. When all ability tests and CLRANK are increased by one standard deviation, an increase of slightly less than a year of schooling results, with the effects of CLRANK and the tests being about equal; among the tests, those of achievement are still dominant. However, CLRANK was completely insignificant in the earnings equation; thus, one can conclude that CLRANK measures an ability peculiar to success in schooling. Yet it is also possible that a high level of CLRANK, however achieved, gives a student enough confidence to increase his schooling aspirations. Coefficients for BLACK and PACA are similar to those in the earnings equation. Many other background coefficients also decrease somewhat.

When actually anticipated schooling (AS) is compared to schooling subject to no contraints (ES), several differences result.[3] The total effects of ability are about the same, but when ES is the dependent variable, the importance of the achievement tests increases as that of CLRANK decreases. This is quite plausible; because an individual's classroom performance is an important factor in determining the availability of further schooling, it should have more effect on realistically anticipated schooling than on desired schooling. The greater importance of achievement for ES is more difficult to rationalize. Among the background variables, the most noticeable difference is the greater effect (by a factor of 3) of the cultural index, BB94S, in the AS equation. In absolute terms, however, this index is not very important in either equation.

In conclusion, these ordinary least-squares (OLS) results reinforce previous conclusions concerning the relatively small net effects of ability on earnings. As in the Griliches study (1975b), ability can be said to contribute about 1 percent toward the explanation of variations in income. Likewise, the effect of ability on the estimated schooling coefficient is quite small, reducing the coefficient by at most 4 percent. These results show, in addition, that achievement ability matters more than abstract ability or CLRANK; short-term memory is also quite important. The effects of the personality variables are negligible. For expected schooling, the ability variables continue to be unimportant, but CLRANK assumes a more prominent role. Personality variables, though quite significant, are also not very large.

*Estimates Incorporating the Unobservable Nature of
Ability and Personality*

In the regressions presented thus far, the various tests of ability and the personality variables are likely to contain errors that obscure their true values. Both ability and personality are examples of "unobservables," factors that are impossible to measure or estimate accurately; if this characteristic of these variables is ignored, biased estimates can result. It is, however, possible to develop estimates of the influence of the unobservable factors contained in an ability or personality test by using advanced estimation techniques. The following discussion illustrates the techniques employed.

Tests of personality variables are assumed to include an error along with the true value of the ability or personality factor. Only the true measure is relevant for scholastic and economic success. The error can be interpreted in this context as a test-retest error, which can be eliminated through repeated administration of the test. Thus, because the variable measures the relevant characteristic with error, estimates of the importance of the personality or ability factor are biased downward and the other coefficients biased upward, according to well-known errors-in-variable results. If, however, there is another aptitude or personality variable measuring the same influence and possessing an error term uncorrelated with that in the first variable, then it is possible to obtain consistent estimates of the personality or ability coefficient; this is done simply by using one variable as an instrument for the other.

More formally, the regression equations used alone constitute the following model:

$$F \quad = \quad\quad\quad\quad\quad B\gamma_1 \; + \; v_1$$

$$AS \quad = \quad\quad\quad \delta_S F \; + \; B\gamma_2 \; + \; v_2$$

$$W30 \; = \; \beta AS \; + \; \delta_I F \; + \; B\gamma_3 \; + \; v_3$$

where F stands for the complex of ability and personality variables and B stands for the background variables. In developing our more elaborate model, incorporating the unobservable nature of ability and personality, the residual term is assumed to have a different structure. In addition, δ_S and δ_I are set equal to 0, for reasons explained below. For the simplest case of two ability personality variables, the model has the following structure.

$$T_1 \quad = \quad\quad\quad B\gamma_1 \; + \; \lambda_1 f \; + \; \epsilon_1$$

$$T_2 \quad = \quad\quad\quad B\gamma_2 \; + \; \lambda_2 f \; + \; \epsilon_2$$

$$AS \quad = \quad\quad\quad B\gamma_3 \; + \; \lambda_3 f \; + \; \epsilon_3$$

$$W30 \; = \; \beta AS \; + \; B\gamma_4 \; + \; \lambda_4 f \; + \; \epsilon_4$$

where T_1 and T_2 represent any pair of ability or personality variables, f the unobservable factor in the ability or personality variables that is relevant for the earnings and schooling equation, and ϵ_i the errors. By construction, f is assumed to be independent of the background variables; that is, one simply interprets f to be that part of the unobservable ability or personality factor which is uncorrelated with the background variables. Thus, the coefficients of the background variables, γ_i, measure the total effect of the background coefficients, both their direct effects and the indirect effects due to the correlation between the background variables and f. More formally, using the "dot" notation for regression coefficients (as given in Johnston, 1972, pp. 56–57):

$$b_{f \cdot B} \;=\; (B'B)^{-1} B'f$$

Rewrite

$$B\gamma_k + f\lambda_k = B\!\left(\gamma_k + b_{f \cdot B}\lambda_k\right) + \left(f - Bb_{f \cdot B}\right)\lambda_k$$
$$= B\widetilde{\gamma}_k + \widetilde{f}\lambda_k$$

Thus, the γ's of our model, when transformed to $\widetilde{\gamma}$, can be interpreted as the direct and indirect effects of the background variables. Likewise, it is evident that λ is estimated correctly and the $\widetilde{f}$ is the pure ability factor, after the effect of the background variables are netted out. It can also be seen that, by construction, $\widetilde{f}$ and B are orthogonal.

In addition to the restrictions placed on the residuals, two further alterations are evident relative to the model estimated by ordinary least squares. The test scores themselves no longer enter the schooling and earnings equations; only the intrinsic factor that they represent does. A possible argument for including the tests themselves in the income equation could be that scores on the tests themselves, as opposed to innate ability, are the important factors; that is, the tests may serve as a screening device. But because nobody knows their test scores, this hypothesis is not tenable for the equations analyzing individuals' expectations. On the other hand, it is indeed quite plausible when CLRANK is considered; that possibility will be examined later in this chapter.

Identification criteria for these models must, of course, be satisfied before estimation is possible. The general rule is that at least two indicators are needed to identify one factor. Thus, only one personality factor can be identified, and similarly, with five test scores, only two factors can be identified. The sixth test, PICTT, does not appear to be related to any other kind of ability. When one attempts to group the test scores, LETGP and MOSAT are one obvious combination; the remaining three tests, VOCABT, READT, and MATHT, are somewhat more difficult to group. Theoretically, one can conceive of two possible types of measurable ability here. One is verbal ability, which could be measured by VOCABT and READT. Another less well-defined factor might be labeled "academic" or "achievement" ability—that is, that ability to master fundamental skills in reading and mathematics, or more generally the ability to do well in school. This factor may also involve the willingness to do regular assignments. All three tests might be used here with the additional possibility that READT and MATHT could do the job without VOCABT. There is no a priori way of deciding whether models containing a verbal ability factor are superior to those containing an academic achievement factor. Thus, most models presented below are estimated with a verbal factor and again with an achievement factor. The most general model possible would have an academic ability factor, an abstract ability factor, and then load VOCABT on the abstract and academic ability factors. A testable restriction of this model is to have VOCABT load only on academic ability. The models incorporating only one ability or personality factor will be presented initially, followed by more general models incorporating several factors.

The procedure for estimating these models begins with the estimation of the reduced form including either personality or ability variables, each taken (as in the OLS regressions) to be exogenous when the effect of the other is estimated. The residuals from these regressions are then used as variables in the LISREL (Joreskog et. al., 1973) program, greatly reducing the computer costs of estimating these types of models. This program is designed to produce maximum likelihood estimates for this type of model. Assuming (by construction) that the factors are orthogonal to the background variables is a necessary prerequisite for this procedure.

Contained in part a of table 6-7 are estimates for the coefficients of verbal aptitude (VOCABT and READT), academic achievement (READT and MATHT), and abstract ability (LETGP and MOSAT) when they are included in both the the income and schooling equations. The expected effect is that the use of a "true" measure of ability, such as f, should reduce the schooling coefficient and raise that of ability. This prediction is verified by the results in that the schooling coefficient drops a little in all these estimates. The finding that correcting for errors in the tests alters the results only slightly is very much in keeping with previous studies. The implied R^2 (equal to $1 - (\sigma_v^2 / \sigma_{W30}^2)$) for the earnings equation is .306, almost identical to that attained in our previous estimates. The effect of a one standard deviation increase in the achievement or verbal factor (all factors being constrained to have a variance of one) is about 2 percent, and for abstract ability, the effect is about 1 percent. For the schooling equation the R^2 is unchanged, and the factors measured by the tests continue to have small effects, with the verbal and achievement factors dominating the abstract ability factor. Nevertheless, the influence of this abstract ability factor is considerably larger in both the schooling and earnings equation relative to the OLS equations.

The reliabilities of the tests (implied R^2), as derived from the calculated factor loadings and error variances, are presented in part b, table 6-7. When compared to the others, MOSAT is clearly inferior with respect to reliability. In the sense of being explained by a verbal achievement factor, the vocabulary and reading tests are about equal. Academic achievement is more important in

Table 6-7
Models with One Ability Factor

(a)   Income and Schooling Equations

Income Equation	Verbal Ability	Academic Achievement	Abstract Ability
AS	.0491 (.0020)	.0488 (.0021)	.0507 (.0020)
f	.0220 (.0045)	.0220 (.0046)	.0121 (.0045)
σ_v^2	.0448	.0448	.0451
Schooling Equation			
f	.416 (.0372)	.468 (.0382)	.303 (.0476)
σ_v^2	3.194	3.148	3.276

(b)   Test Reliabilities from Models with One Ability Factor

	VOCABT	Verbal Ability	READT Academic Achievement	MATHT	LETGP	MOSAT
Implied Reliability	.666	.609	.539	.528	.763	.218
% explain by factor	39.5	38.6	31.5	38.2	56.8	14.1
% explained by background	27.2	22.4	22.4	14.6	19.5	7.6

the composition of mathematical achievement than in reading achievement.

When the two personality variables, FF15P and FF15A, are used to construct a single personality factor, one would expect FF15P to have a negative loading and FF15A a positive one if the factor appears in the earnings and schooling equation with positive signs, because higher scores for FF15A indicate more positive attitudes; these predictions are verified in table 6-8. Here the correction for errors-in-variable bias makes a considerable difference. The coefficient of schooling drops more than it did when ability was included, although still by only a small amount. Thus, according to table 6-8, it seems that an influence about equal to that of achievement factors is evident when personality is included in the earnings and schooling equations. This increased effect is not surprising since both measures of personality have low implied reliabilities (roughly .2).

Thus this simplest method for correcting for errors-in-variable bias produces

Table 6-8
Income and Schooling Equations with One Personality Factor

	Income Equation	Schooling Equation
AS	.0475 (.0024)	
f	.0193 (.0076)	.508 (.0611)
σ_v^2	.0447	2.914
	FF15P	FF15A
Implied Reliability	.205	.160
% explained by factor	14.5	15.3
% explained by background	6.0	.6

no great changes in the results for ability, although the effects of abstract ability are somewhat enhanced. The relative importance of academic achievement or verbal ability when compared to abstract ability in both the schooling and earnings equations (especially the latter) continues. However, for the personality variables, a much greater influence surfaces; this brings the importance of personality attributes up to about the same level as ability. It is important to note that such techniques can never increase the contribution of ability or personality variables toward explaining the variance in income or schooling. Because the personality variables contain larger error components than most of the ability variables, the effects of the underlying components of personality are more obscured in ordinary least-squares regressions than are those of ability. These techniques therefore only isolate this underlying component.

Previous estimates of different types of ability in schooling and earnings equations were obtained by Chamberlain (1975b). Using the Malmo sample, consisting of two tests taken at different points of the individual's lifetime, he develops the following model.

$$H = B\pi + f$$

$$T_1 = \lambda_1 H + \gamma_1 g + \epsilon_1$$

$$S = B\delta + \lambda_2 H + \gamma_2 g + \epsilon_2$$

$$T_2 = \beta_1 S + \lambda_3 H + \gamma_3 g + \epsilon_3$$

$$Y = \beta_2 S + \lambda_4 H + \epsilon_4$$

where B refers to background variables, Y to actual earnings, S to actual schooling, T_i to the two tests, ϵ_i to the disturbances; f and g are unobservable factors.
The basic idea is that the unobservable f and the background variables B are
assumed to enter the income equation; in addition, the tests also include another
factor, g, that is relevant to academic achievement and attained schooling, but
not for income. For the model to be identified, the background variables and
f must enter the earnings equation with proportionality restrictions. As before, f
is independent of B by construction, and g is assumed to be independent of B and
f. As recognized by Chamberlain, this last assumption is somewhat dubious.
Ideally, one would like to have g uncorrelated with B and f by construction;
however, attempting to do so breaks the proportionality constraints on the
background variables, and thus the model is no longer identified.

The availability of several test scores makes testing for the existence and
effect of several ability dimensions considerably easier because the different
factors can simply be added to the equations to determine how important each
one is. Thus, not only is it no longer necessary to make restrictive assumptions
about the nature of the unobservable factors entering the schooling and earnings
equation, but we can also get some clue as to what each of these factors actually
are (such as abstract, achievement, or verbal ability). Still, we cannot reject the
hypothesis that the tests contain other factors relevant to schooling but not to
earnings. But if they do, no adequate remedy is available with this data set
short of making the dubious assumption that these additional factors are uncorrelated with the background variables.

In formal terms, the model with several ability factors or one ability and
one personality factor, is the following:

$$T_1 \; = \; B\gamma_1 \qquad\qquad + \; \lambda_{11}f_1 \qquad\qquad + \; \epsilon_1$$

$$T_2 \; = \; B\gamma_2 \qquad\qquad + \; \lambda_{21}f_1 \qquad\qquad + \; \epsilon_2$$

$$T_3 \; = \; B\gamma_3 \qquad\qquad\qquad\quad + \; \lambda_{32}f_2 \; + \; \epsilon_3$$

$$T_4 \; = \; B\gamma_4 \qquad\qquad\qquad\quad + \; \lambda_{42}f_2 \; + \; \epsilon_4$$

$$AS \; = \; B\gamma_5 \qquad\quad + \; \lambda_{51}f_1 \; + \; \lambda_{52}f_2 \; + \; \epsilon_5$$

$$W30 \; = \; B\gamma_6 \; + \; \beta AS \; + \; \lambda_{61}f_1 \; + \; \lambda_{62}f_2 \; + \; \epsilon_6$$

T_1 and T_2 refer to one pair of ability or personality variables, and T_3 and T_4
to another. Each factor's variance is set equal to 1, but the correlation between
them is not constrained. It might be easier to think of a model in which each test
includes both factors (such as verbal tests containing both verbal and abstract
ability factors). In this case, however, the factors would be taken as orthogonal.

However, this factor structure merely represents a different normalization. Simply let f_1 in the last model equal the combination of factors measured by the first two tests, and f_2 equal the combination measured by the last two tests. (For a good discussion of factor analysis, see Lawley and Maxwell, 1971).

Intuitively, each member of the pair of ability variables can be thought of as an instrument for the other. An additional condition is that both pairs of tests do not measure the same combination of factors, which would make it impossible to distinguish among the factors in the income and schooling equations.

The results for estimating the two ability factors, verbal and abstract ability, and academic achievement and abstract ability, are presented in part a of table 6-9. As previously noted, the R^2 for the equations are not affected.

Verbal ability has an effect about five times that of abstract ability, with a one standard deviation increase in verbal ability raising income almost 2 percent. In the schooling equation, verbal ability is stronger than abstract ability, but not to the extent of the earnings equation; both factors are significant. The restriction that all four tests measure the same factor is rejected with a $\chi^2 (3) = 260$.

When substituted for the verbal achievement factor, the academic achievement factor is very strong in the earnings equation, with a one standard deviation increase raising income almost 3 percent. The abstract ability factor becomes negative but its coefficient is also insignificant. The same effect is observed in the schooling equation where the achievement factor accounts for six-tenths of a year of schooling; the abstract ability factor continues to be negative and insignificant. Thus, the achievement tests capture all of the ability factor that is relevant for earnings and schooling, leaving little for the abstract ability tests. The restriction to just one factor is rejected with a $\chi^2 (3) = 72$.

The reliabilities for these results are given in part b of table 6-9. READT now captures considerably more of the verbal ability factor than it previously had, and thus it has an increased reliability. MATHT behaves in a similar fashion for the achievement factor. In conclusion, the relative importance of academic achievement ability, particularly in the earnings equation, is strengthened.

With this data set it is of course possible not only to have a model with two ability factors, but also to add a personality factor. The results of estimating such a model are contained in table 6-10. The results are similar to those obtained previously. When verbal ability is included in the income equation, the personality factor dominates both ability factors, but the achievement factor becomes predominant when it is included. The same pattern holds true for the schooling equation, except that the abstract ability factor is more significant, especially when included with the verbal ability factor. Together, a one standard deviation increase in the achievement ability and personality attributes raises expected schooling by almost a year.

With five tests available, the most general model would permit VOCABT to depend on the academic achievement factor and the abstract ability factor,

Table 6-9
Models with Two Ability Factors

(a) Income and Schooling Equations

	Income Equation	Schooling Equation		Income Equation	Schooling Equation
AS	.0497 (.0020)			.0489 (.0021)	
Verbal factor (f_1)	.0174 (.0050)	.260 (.0440)	Achievement factor (f_1)	.0287 (.0107)	.584 (.0945)
Abstract factor (f_2)	.0034 (.0052)	.167 (.0460)		−.0104 (.0105)	−.165 (.0944)
σ_v^2	.0449	3.228		.0448	3.154
$\sigma_{f_1 f_2}$	.508			.804	

(b) Test Reliabilities from Models with Two Ability Factors

	VOCABT	READT		MATHT
		Verbal Ability	Academic Achievement	
Implied Reliability	.515	.850	.495	.765
% explained by factor	24.3	62.6	27.1	44.4
% explained by background	27.2	22.4	22.4	32.1

	LETGP		MOSAT	
	Verbal Ability	Academic Achievement	Verbal Ability	Academic Achievement
Implied Reliability	.779	.757	.214	.219
% explained by factor	58.4	56.2	13.8	14.3
% explained by background	19.5	19.5	7.6	7.6

Table 6-10

Income and Schooling with Two Ability and One Personality Factors

	Income Equation	Schooling Equation		Income Equation	Schooling Equation
AS	.0482 (.0023)			.0473 (.0023)	
Verbal factor (f_1)	.0156 (.0053)	.188 (.0495)	Achievement factor (f_1)	.0276 (.0114)	.506 (.104)
Abstract factor (f_2)	.0021 (.0054)	.122 (.0495)		−.0119 (.0109)	−.185 (.101)
Personality factor (f_3)	.0168 (.0073)	.501 (.0669)		.0172 (.0074)	.484 (.0666)
σ_v^2	.0447	3.076		.0446	3.007
$\sigma_{f_1 f_2}^2$	.523			.812	
$\sigma_{f_1 f_3}^2$	.278			.297	
$\sigma_{f_2 f_3}^2$	.240			.244	

or on just one of these factors, preferably the academic achievement factor. Formally, this model is as follows:

$$\text{VOCABT} = B\gamma_1 \qquad + \lambda_{11}f_1 + \lambda_{12}f_2 \qquad + \epsilon_1$$
$$\text{READT} = B\gamma_2 \qquad + \lambda_{21}f_1 \qquad + \epsilon_2$$
$$\text{MATHT} = B\gamma_3 \qquad + \lambda_{31}f_1 \qquad + \epsilon_3$$
$$\text{LETGP} = B\gamma_4 \qquad + \lambda_{42}f_2 \qquad + \epsilon_4$$
$$\text{MOSAT} = B\gamma_5 \qquad + \lambda_{52}f_2 \qquad + \epsilon_5$$
$$\text{FF15P} = B\gamma_6 \qquad + \lambda_{63}f_3 + \epsilon_6$$
$$\text{FF15A} = B\gamma_7 \qquad + \lambda_{73}f_3 + \epsilon_7$$
$$\text{AS} = B\gamma_8 \qquad + \lambda_{81}f_1 + \lambda_{82}f_2 + \lambda_{83}f_3 + \epsilon_8$$
$$\text{W30} = B\gamma_9 + \beta AS + \lambda_{91}f_1 + \lambda_{92}f_2 + \lambda_{93}f_3 + \epsilon_9$$

Estimating the model in this form produces almost no changes in any coefficient. The restriction that VOCABT depends only on achievement ability ($\lambda_{12} = 0$) is rejected, with a $\chi^2(1) = 184.93$. Thus, READT and MATHT appear to identify a factor that is contained to a significantly lesser degree in VOCABT.

In conclusion, it can be stated that the five tests define three factors. One clear factor is that of abstract ability as measured by LETGP and MOSAT.

This plays almost no role in determining earnings, but does have a significantly positive effect in the schooling equation when included with verbal ability, and an almost significantly negative effect when accompanied by achievement ability. The three tests, VOCABT, READT, and MATHT, contain two factors that cannot be estimated simultaneously. VOCABT and READT identify a verbal ability factor, and READT and MATHT an academic achievement factor. The latter factor is considerably stronger, accounting for a 2.8 percent increase in income, and half a year of schooling, as opposed to 1.6 percent increase in income and about one-fifth of a year of schooling for verbal ability. One possible explanation is that verbal ability is more specialized than academic achievement ability. Thus, the equality specialized ability represented by LETGP and MOSAT is expected to assume greater importance when accompanied by verbal ability; however, achievement ability is anticipated to capture most of the complex of abilities needed for earnings and schooling success, and thus leaves little room for abstract ability.

The personality factor is about as strong as the achievement factor. However, in absolute terms, all personality and ability factors are still quite small, and thus our previous findings are left relatively undisturbed by the introduction of the several ability factors and a personality factor.

A simple extension of the above model can be used to test for the causes and effects of CLRANK. Unlike the previous measures of ability, the student and others, including parents, schools, and employers, are cognizant of the outcome. In addition, CLRANK is usually the result of several years of work as opposed to the 15 minutes or less available for the completion of each test. Finally, it is possible that it is a weighted sum of the ability and personality variables that would best capture the complex of unobservables most relevant for schooling and/or earnings success. It is added to the model in the form of a third equation, much the same as the test or personality equations. The schooling and earnings equations are then changed so as to include CLRANK. In formal terms:

$$T_1 = B\gamma_1 \qquad\qquad + \lambda_{11}f_1 \qquad\qquad\qquad + \epsilon_1$$

$$T_2 = B\gamma_2 \qquad\qquad + \lambda_{21}f_1 \qquad\qquad\qquad + \epsilon_2$$

$$T_3 = B\gamma_3 \qquad\qquad\qquad\quad + \lambda_{32}f_2 \qquad\quad + \epsilon_3$$

$$T_4 = B\gamma_4 \qquad\qquad\qquad\quad + \lambda_{42}f_2 \qquad\quad + \epsilon_4$$

$$P_1 = B\gamma_5 \qquad\qquad\qquad\qquad\qquad + \lambda_{53}f_3 + \epsilon_5$$

$$P_2 = B\gamma_6 \qquad\qquad\qquad\qquad\qquad + \lambda_{63}f_3 + \epsilon_6$$

$$CLRANK + B\gamma_7 \qquad + \lambda_{71}f_1 + \lambda_{72}f_2 + \lambda_{73}f_3 + \epsilon_7$$

$$AS = B\gamma_8 + \delta_S CLRANK \qquad + \lambda_{81}f_1 + \lambda_{82}f_2 + \lambda_{83}f_3 + \epsilon_8$$

$$W30 = B\gamma_9 + \delta_I CLRANK + \beta AS + \lambda_{91}f_1 + \lambda_{92}f_2 + \lambda_{93}f_3 + \epsilon_9$$

where f_1 refers to verbal or achievement ability, f_2 to abstract ability, and f_3 to personality.

Two sets of results for a model with CLRANK are given in table 6-11, one including verbal ability and the other with achievement ability. When calculated the implied reliability of CLRANK is only .387 in the verbal ability model and .479 in the achievement model. The percentage of the variance explained by the three factors is 10.5 percent in the first model and 48 percent in the second. All of this difference results from the much stronger effect of achievement ability relative to verbal ability. In fact, achievement ability accounts for 43.5 percent of the variance of CLRANK, while 37.4 percent of the variance is explained by background in the first model and zero in the second model. Personality factors, as well as abstract ability, are very unimportant in explaining CLRANK.

Table 6-11
Income and Schooling with Three Factors and CLRANK

	Income Equation		
AS	.0482 (.0023)		.0477 (.0023)
CLRANK	.0001 (.0002)		.0003 (.0002)
Verbal factor (f_1)	.0180 (.0062)	Achievement factor (f_1)	.0329 (.0138)
Abstract factor (f_2)	.0014 (.0066)		$-.0137$ (.0120)
Personality factor (f_3)	.0165 (.0074)		.0175 (.0074)
$\sigma_{f_1 f_2}$	.578		.821
$\sigma_{f_1 f_3}$	.289		.295
$\sigma_{f_2 f_3}$	.259		.248
σ_v^2	.0447		.0446
	Schooling Equation		
CLRANK	.0145 (.0015)		.0122 (.0019)
Verbal factor (f_1)	.124 (.0544)	Achievement factor (f_1)	.291 (.120)
Abstract factor (f_2)	.0280 (.0573)		$-.121$ (.105)
Personality factor (f_3)	.462 (.0655)		.470 (.0651)
σ_v^2	2.969		2.950

As in our previous results, achievement ability is particularly dominant in the earnings equation. CLRANK is completely insignificant in both models. These results appear to reject the notion that it is only ability as perceived by others that counts in earnings. When placed in the earnings equation, it is achievement ability that dominates. For the schooling equation, on the other hand, CLRANK is reasonably important. A one standard deviation increase in CLRANK has almost the same effect as an equivalent increase in the personality variable. CLRANK serves as more of a substitute for the other measures of ability here.

Role of the High School

The effects of the high school on academic achievement have been studied extensively, especially since the publication of the Coleman report in 1966. In contrast, only a limited number of studies have dealt with the effects of high schools on either schooling or occupational success and aspirations. Some studies explore these effects indirectly by examining such attributes as student-teacher ratios, class size, or teacher salaries. The effect of these variables on such things as schooling and earnings in the context of this data set will be discussed later in this chapter. None of these variables, however, captures the entire influence of the high school.

For a proper investigation of the total high school effect, it is necessary to be able to group students by high school. This feature is one of the major advantages of the NLS. It was also possible in the Project Talent data set. An exhaustive investigation of this data by Jencks and Brown (1975) concluded that the effects of the high school are very small. They estimate, by adding school dummies to a regression similar to those already considered in this chapter, that at most 2.2 percent of the variance in expected education one year after high school is due to the high school. This figure drops to about 1 percent for education five years after high school. Measurement of the effect of high school on occupational status is, they concluded, obscured by local labor market conditions.

Another study by Hauser, Sewall, and Alwin (1976) came to similar conclusions. Their data set was from the Milwaukee school district, combined with a sample of students in the entire state of Wisconsin. Adding dummies for each school to a regression including miscellaneous variables showed that high schools account for only 2 percent of the variation in educational attainment for the Milwaukee sample; for the state sample, the effects were even smaller. For both occupational status and ultimate educational attainment, adding school dummies produced practically no changes.

For our NLS sample, table 6-12 gives the within-school standard deviations and the percentage of variance between schools for our variables. As has been demonstrated by Chamberlain and Griliches (1975), consistent estimates of the population standard deviations are obtained when the

Table 6-12
Standard Deviations Within Schools

Number of students = 3,408
Number of schools = 773
p = average number of students per school = 4.4088[a]

Variable	Standard Deviation	Percentage of Variance Between Schools	Variable	Standard Deviation	Percentage of Variance Between Schools
W30	.213	15.81	AS	1.821	10.51
TEST	5.419	13.34	VOCABT	7.813	15.47
PICTT	8.201	4.87	READT	7.895	7.65
LETGP	7.429	7.12	MATHT	7.661	11.11
MOSAT	6.870	27.65	CLRANK	23.793	1.73
FF15P	1.455	2.99	FF15A	1.682	0
SIBDEP	1.455	3.47	FAMINC	3.956	21.30
BB94A	.931	15.13	BB94S	.877	17.53
FED	2.263	18.33	MED	1.755	14.52

[a]The use of subsamples reduced this well below the 18 students per school who were initially sampled

estimated standard deviations are corrected by the factor of $\sqrt{\bar{p}/(\bar{p}-1)}$, where $\bar{p}$ is the mean number of students per school. This correction factor is incorporated into the estimates of between-school variance. About 15 percent of the variance of W30 is between high schools, whereas only 10 percent of the variance of AS is. Between 15 percent and 20 percent of the variance of most SES variables, such as FED, MED, or FAMINC, are attributable to the school. Personality variables have only a very weak school component. The ability tests range from 5 percent for PICTT to 28 percent for MOSAT. As expected, CLRANK has a very small school component. Actual between-school variance is likely to be less than the values reported here because some of this variance in variables like FED, MED, and FAMINC is likely to reflect regional variations in such variables.

The regression results of inserting individual constant terms for each high school into the earnings equations are given in tables 6-13 and 6-14. As shown by the F-statistics, the hypothesis that the individual constant terms can be ignored is rejected. However, given the large sample size, this result is not surprising. The R^2 increases from about .3 to almost .5, but this change is largely due to the addition of over 770 dummy variables to the equation. In the earnings regression with just background variables and schooling, the schooling coefficient is about 0.1 percent lower than in our initial model. No other coefficients change significantly. The addition of personality and ability variables changes little. Thus, for this sample, the omission of school effects has

Table 6-13
Basic Regressions with Individual Intercepts for Each High School
(dependent variable = W30)

	Basic Equation	*Includes Personality*	*Includes Ability*[a]
R^2	.482	.483	.488
SEE	.208	.208	.207
AS	.0515	.0504	.0489
	(.00196)	(.00199)	(.00205)
SIBDEP	.00098	.00091	.00137
	(.00219)	(.00219)	(.00219)
FAMINC	−.000001	−.000001	−.000001
	(.0000009)	(.0000009)	(.0000009)
BB94A	.00053	.00056	.00132
	(.00374)	(.00373)	(.00373)
BB94S	.00040	.00025	−.00013
	(.00393)	(.00393)	(.00393)
FED	.00320	.00338	.00242
	(.00170)	(.00170)	(.00170)
MED	.00577	.00545	.00497
	(.00210)	(.00211)	(.00211)
PACA	.0561	.0545	.0378
	(.00884)	(.00887)	(.00981)
BLACK	.0111	.0139	.0327
	(.0191)	(.0191)	(.0195)
STCOM	−.0191	−.0197	−.0173
	(.0127)	(.0127)	(.0126)
FF15P		−.00569	
		(.00207)	
FF15A		.00141	
		(.00191)	
F-statistic	1.653	1.652	1.654

[a]See table 6-14 for remaining coefficients.

no significant effect on the earnings equation. Much the same is true of the schooling equations presented in tables 6-15 and 6-16. In short, correcting for school effects has little effect on the earnings or schooling equations.

To test further this hypothesis, a few of the nonlinear equations were reestimated using only within-school moments. The results for a model with two ability and one personality factors are presented in table 6-17. Most noticeable are the reduced effects of the verbal and achievement factors in both equations. This is not surprising because these factors are the ones most

Table 6-14
Ability Variables Included with Individual Constant Terms for Each School
(dependent variable = W30)

	.482[a]	.488[b]	.488[c]	.487	.485	.485	.486	.485	.486	.483	.483
R^2	.482[a]	.488[b]	.488[c]	.487	.485	.485	.486	.485	.486	.483	.483
SEE	.208	.207	.207	.207	.207	.207	.207	.207	.208	.208	.208
AS	.0504	.0489	.0483	.0480	.0490	.0496	.0492	.0495	.0487	.0501	.0496
	(.00199)	(.00205)	(.00207)	(.00204)	(.00202)	(.00200)	(.00201)	(.00201)	(.00203)	(.00200)	(.00206)
TEST				.00379							
				(.00072)							
VOCABT		.00116	.00114		.00176						
		(.00053)	(.00053)		(.00046)						
PICTT		.00111	.00109			.00138					
		(.00043)	(.00043)			(.00040)					
READT		.00088	.00078				.00181				
		(.00055)	(.00055)				(.00045)				
LETGP		.00050	.00043					.00148			
		(.00058)	(.00058)					(.00467)			
MATHT		.00112	.00113						.00198		
		(.00066)	(.00066)						(.00050)		
MOSAT		-.00019	-.00019							.00068	
		(.00053)	(.00053)							(.00048)	
CLRANK		-.00030	-.00031								.00022
		(.00019)	(.00019)								(.00016)
F-statistic	1.653	1.654	1.687	1.655	1.648	1.652	1.645	1.655	1.653	1.652	1.648

[a]This regression contains only background and personality variables (table 6-13, column 2).

[b]This regression contains only background and ability variables (table 6-13, column 3).

[c]This regression also includes background and personality variables, as do all succeeding regressions in this table.

Table 6–15
Basic Regressions Including Individual Constant Terms for Each High School
(dependent variable = AS)

	Basic Equation	Includes Personality	Includes Ability[a]
R^2	.466	.484	.515
SEE	1.819	1.789	1.734
SIBDEP	−.0581	−.0618	−.0428
	(.0191)	(.0188)	(.0183)
FAMINC	.00001	.00001	.00001
	(.000008)	(.000008)	(.000008)
BB94A	−.0127	−.0146	.0191
	(.0327)	(.0321)	(.0313)
BB94S	.109	.0980	.0688
	(.0343)	(.0338)	(.0329)
FED	.133	.132	.102
	(.0147)	(.0145)	(.0141)
MED	.0806	.0719	.0638
	(.0183)	(.0181)	(.0176)
PACA	1.612	1.542	.848
	(.0722)	(.0716)	(.0809)
BLACK	.628	.662	1.042
	(.167)	(.164)	(.162)
STCOM	−.175	−.200	−.134
	(.111)	(.109)	(.106)
FF15P		−.121	
		(.0177)	
FF15A		.116	
		(.0163)	
F-statistic	1.675	1.674	1.658

[a]See table 6–16 for remaining coefficients.

likely to be connected with the high school. The implied R^2 also rises, as was the case with the OLS equations.

Therefore for both the OLS and the more complex models the within-school results differ little from our previous estimates. This result is not unexpected because most of the variance is within schools. The ability factor most susceptible to influence by the school (achievement or verbal ability) is reduced somewhat in importance.

The following model can be employed to test further the hypothesis of marginal high school effects.

Table 6-16
Ability Variables Included with Individual Constant Terms for Each School
(dependent variable = AS)

R^2	.515[a]	.588[b]	.508	.499	.490	.495	.494	.505	.487	.519
SEE	1.734	1.598	1.745	1.762	1.778	1.770	1.771	1.752	1.783	1.727
TEST			.0776 (.00592)							
VOCABT	.0194 (.00446)	.0188 (.00441)		.0393 (.00384)						
PICTT	.00692 (.00361)	.00567 (.00357)			.0220 (.00342)					
READT	.00242 (.00463)	−.00430 (.00459)				.00325 (.00378)				
LETGP	.00569 (.00484)	.00455 (.00479)					.0322 (.00395)			
MATHT	.0153 (.00549)	.0158 (.00543)						.0493 (.00410)		
MOSAT	−.00144 (.00477)	−.00226 (.00442)							.0196 (.00412)	
CLRANK	.0153 (.00157)	.0148 (.00155)								.0204 (.00129)
F-statistic	1.658	1.660	1.670	1.682	1.665	1.653	1.674	1.693	1.687	1.674

[a]This regression contains only background and ability variables (see table 6–15, column 3).
[b]This regression also includes background and personality variables, as do all succeeding regressions in this table.

Table 6-17
Income and Schooling with Three Factors and Individual Constant Terms for Each School

	Income Equation	Schooling Equation		Income Equation	Schooling Equation
AS	.0465 (.0023)			.0455 (.0024)	
Verbal factor (f_1)	.0110 (.0047)	.136 (.0438)	Achievement factor (f_1)	.0207 (.0094)	.446 (.0873)
Abstract factor (f_2)	.0048 (.0047)	.113 (.0428)		−.0062 (.0091)	−.173 (.0858)
Personality factor (f_3)	.0140 (.0067)	.443 (.0591)		.0148 (.0067)	.437 (.0577)
σ_v^2	.0331	2.260		.0330	2.197
$\sigma_{f_1 f_2}$	.503			.804	
$\sigma_{f_1 f_3}$	.311			.293	
$\sigma_{f_2 f_3}$	.262			.265	

$$\text{TEST} = \alpha_1 B \qquad\qquad\qquad + \gamma_1 \left(f_i + g_{ij} \right) + u_1$$

$$\text{AS} = \alpha_2 B \qquad + \delta_1 \text{ TEST} + \gamma_2 \left(f_i + g_{ij} \right) + u_2$$

$$\text{W30} = \alpha_3 B + \beta AS + \delta_2 \text{ TEST} + \gamma_3 \left(f_i + g_{ij} \right) + u_3$$

B refers to background variables and TEST to the average of the six ability tests given the students. The term $(f_i + g_{ij})$ represents the effects of the school; it is separated into f_i representing the common effect of the school on all the students and g_{ij} representing the effect of the school on each individual student. In short, the unobservable school effect is given a certain structure: the restrictions imposed by this structure can identify the model, as has been demonstrated for a similar model examined by Chamberlain and Griliches (1975).

Unfortunately, the above model is not identified. In such circumstances, a more general theorem of Chamberlain (1976) may establish bounds for a key parameter of this model. If the bounds are reasonably small, the rest of the model can be estimated using several possible values within the bounds; quite possibly estimates of the other parameters might be insensitive to the precise values chosen for the key parameter. Actual attempts to estimate this model are discussed elsewhere.[4] The estimated range between the bounds was very large, and thus the model could not be estimated. Quite likely this failure results from the absence of variation between schools.

Another set of attempts to measure the effects of schooling have concerned themselves with examining such objective manifestations of school quality as student-teacher ratio, expenditures per pupil, and percentage of teachers with advanced degrees. An example of this work is in Wachtel (1975). In a model very similar to the initial one presented in the first section of this chapter, Wachtel (1975) includes a variable representing "amount school expenditures per student in average daily attendance for school district in which respondent attended high school." This variable is significant in the earnings equation but not in the schooling equation. The magnitude of its effect on earnings is as small as that of the other background variables. Wachtel's R^2 for the earnings equation is .194 and for the schooling equation .102; these equations include the expenditure variables.

Also Jencks and Brown (1975) tested five school characteristics in a similar manner. These variables were school's annual expenditure per pupil, mean starting salary for teachers, percentage of teachers with master's degrees, average years of experience of teachers, and average class size. The first two variables had no effect at all. Experienced teachers and percentage of teachers with master's degrees were significant for occupational success for males only. They were not significant for female occupational success, nor for educational attainment. Finally, average class size had a positive effect, and significantly so, for male occupational success and for a measure of educational attainment. Because of this anomalous result, the authors caution against taking any of the results too seriously.

For our study, the following variables were selected as possible indicators of quality: DROT (the percentage of students that drop out before graduating), SBW (the percentage of white students), FBW (the percentage of white faculty), SPRTC (the percentage of children with fathers employed in professional or technical fields), CLCO (the percentage of students going to two-or four-year colleges), TED (the percentage of teachers with advanced degrees), and STR (the student-teacher ratio). Each of these variables was appended, one at a time, to each of two equations: an earnings equation including all background variables as well as personality and ability variables, and a schooling equation including the same variables. The results are given in table 6-18.

For each variable, the top row shows the increase in R^2 when the variable is added, the middle row gives the coefficient, and the bottom row contains its standard error. As for earnings, the only significant variable is the student-teacher ratio, and, in keeping with the results of Jencks and Brown, the coefficient has the wrong sign. One would expect that decreasing the student-teacher ratio, all else equal, would raise income rather than decrease it. In the schooling equation, attending a school with a low percentage of minorities decreases expected schooling. This coefficient is significant but very small, since increasing the number of whites by ten percentage points would lower expected schooling by less than one-twentieth of a year. Positive and significant effects

Table 6-18
Effects of School Quality on Income and Schooling

Dependent Variable	W30	AS
DROT	0 −.00034 (.00062)	0 −.00026 (.00516)
SBW	.001 −.00033 (.00018)	.002 −.00446 (.00150)
FBW	.001 −.00024 (.00027)	.001 −.00218 (.00221)
SPRTC	.001 .00074 (.00039)	.002 .0103 (.00319)
CLCO	.001 .00034 (.00023)	.006 .0109 (.00188)
TED	.001 .00020 (.00019)	.001 .00329 (.00156)
STR	.001 .00162 (.00073)	0 .00727 (.00608)

are evident for SPRTC, CLCO, and TED; however, a 10-point increase in any of these percentages would raise schooling by at most one-tenth of a year. It is surprising that effects of TED and STR are both negative and insignificant. However, all coefficients are trivial in terms of absolute magnitude.

Thus, such measures of school quality as teacher's qualifications, student-teacher ratios, and such indicators of the general SES status of the students and community as the percentage going to college and the percentage of children in upper SES groups have little effect on anticipated earnings or schooling. However, the statement depends only on results based solely on variations across schools; because of "tracking" and similar phenomena, a good deal of the variation in such variables is within schools. Thus definitive conclusions must await detailed data on the variance of these variables within the school.

Conclusions

Before summarizing the conclusions of this study, some further material deleted because of space limitations will be briefly discussed. Full details are available elsewhere.[5]

Another set of variables in the survey describes the amount of schooling the father and mother, respectively, would like the student to attain. These variables can be viewed as possible proxies for the amount of motivation or encouragement the student receives from his parents, not only toward more education but also toward achieving other career ambitions. Both simple regression and more complicated models were employed. Relative to any variable previously considered, these variables constituted the most important influence on earnings (except for schooling) and the overwhelming influence on schooling.

An attempt was also made to analyze the differences between reality and expectations. Throughout this chapter, expectations have been treated as equivalent to actual earnings and schooling, as previously discussed. An attempt was made, however, to investigate the differences between reality and expectations. Although data on actual earnings are not available, a comparison can be made between planned schooling, as expressed in the base-year questionnaire, and actual schooling, as revealed by the first follow-up. Thus an analysis has been made only of the causes of unfulfilled expectations with regard to schooling, particularly the variable AS. This variable is more suitable than ES, for it measures realistic plans, as opposed to plans if there were no constraints (see previous discussion of variables). Because this is a qualitative dependent variable—that is, the student realized or did not realize his plans—logit techniques only have been employed. The major conclusions are that ability raises an individual's chances for achieving schooling expectations, whereas parents' desired schooling increases the chances for disappointment. Two possible reasons for this latter effect are that children may be more aware of recent declines in the value of college education or that children and parents simply have different utility functions. These findings also suggest that the strong effects of parents' desired education discussed in the preceding paragraph may apply more to expected schooling and income as opposed to the actual values.

Several major conclusions stem from this chapter. As in previous studies, all of the independent variables only explain about 30 percent of the variance in earnings and about 35 percent of the variance in schooling. The net effect of ability is rather small, amounting to about 3 percent in both the earnings and the schooling equations. This result for the schooling equation is not in agreement with earlier studies, which might be explained by such factors as the restricted range of schooling (high school or greater) or the use of expected schooling as opposed to actual schooling.

One feature of this study concerns the refinement of the concept of ability into several distinct factors—academic achievement, verbal ability, and abstract ability. Indicators of these ability factors are available in the tests administered during the survey; these results are unknown to participants, teachers, and employers. In contrast, individual class rank is another measure of ability that is known to the student and others.

An important conclusion is that academic achievement is the most significant ability factor contributing to earnings success. Both abstract ability
and class rank play only a limited role, with verbal ability assigned an intermediate role. For schooling, however, class rank and academic achievement
have approximately equal weight, with verbal and abstract ability playing about
the same roles as in the earnings equation. Even though these tests may not
measure all types of ability that are important for schooling and earnings, it
has been possible to distinguish among several important types.

A second feature of this study concerns the measurement of the effects
of some personality variables on earnings and schooling. The personality variables that attempt to capture individuals' perceived control over their environment are almost 70 percent as important as academic achievement in the earnings equation and have an effect almost equal to that of achievement ability
on schooling. However, in absolute terms the personality variables are quite
unimportant, and thus previous studies that neglected such variables have not
erred greatly.

Another important conclusion is that the high school has negligible effects
on schooling and earnings. These findings are similar to those obtained in
other studies. These results, however, are limited to the effects that can be
estimated from differences between schools. Much of the variance in those
variables influencing schooling and earnings is within schools.

Notes

1. This is actually achieved by summing the products of the standard
deviations and the regression coefficients of each variable mentioned. This
sum of products is the net effect on the dependent variable.

2.   Though these estimates are not presented here, they are contained
in the full report *Experiences of Recent High School Graduates; The Transition to Work or Postsecondary Education*, Nolfi and others (Cambridge, Mass.:
University Consultants, Inc., 1977).

3.   Ibid.
4.   Ibid.
5.   Ibid.

**Part III
Higher Education Analysis**

Part III
Introduction

In part III, a new econometric model of student choice among postsecondary alternatives is presented. In preparation for the introduction of this model, chapter 7 reviews the relevant empirical literature on the demand for postsecondary education. Chapter 8 then develops our model specification, describes the sample data, and presents our empirical results. Chapter 9 describes some preliminary policy forecasts made with the estimated model.

Chapter 3 also provides a detailed discussion of the full range of choices open to high school graduates. The higher education and vocational education choice models (presented in chapters 8, 9, and 11) have a limited focus on certain aspects of that broad choice set. This simplification is made for two reasons: (1) lack of availability of aggregate data characterizing certain options (although individuals making such decisions almost certainly have the data relevant to their own choice), and (2) the necessity to simplify the mathematical model for computational purposes. These simplifications are reasonable, but the results here should be read alongside and compared with the results of other chapters (especially chapters 3, 6, and 10).

7 Previous Studies of the Demand for Postsecondary Education

Over the past twenty years considerable research effort has been made into studying students' postsecondary educational decisions, particularly college enrollment decisions.

The earliest research on demand for higher education was largely sociological. Two large-scale longitudinal studies of high school students were begun in 1959 and 1960: a study of 10,000 high school seniors conducted by Medsker and Trent in 1959, and Project TALENT, which initially included 400,000 high school students in grades 9 through 12 in 1960. Both studies began to report results on college-going behavior in the early 1960s. They confirmed the importance of several factors that previously had been assumed to influence college-going behavior.

Project TALENT data illustrated the importance of family income and parental education (with a combined socioeconomic status scale) in determining the enrollment rates for high school graduates, even when measured abilities were equal. Medsker and Trent reported on the influence of high school peer relationships and the availability of a college within the graduates' community on enrollment changes.[1] A longitudinal study was later conducted by the Bureau of the Census.[2] This study further confirmed the importance of several variables used by Medsker and Trent and in Project TALENT. The census study also demonstrated the effect of high school tracking on college-going patterns.

The importance of these longitudinal studies cannot be overemphasized. They have provided much focus to the development of higher education policy and have refined the insights with which subsequent researchers have been able to address the question of demand for college. They do, however, have several weaknesses that limit their utility for policy-making. First, the studies locate important factors but fail to give quantitative magnitude to their independent effects. For example, Medsker and Trent found that a low-cost, nearby college was an important stimulator of enrollment. But their analysis does not answer several questions. How low cost? How nearby? How important? Second, the studies do not specify the relative magnitude

This chapter was derived from a paper presented to the Southern Economic Association in 1974 by Dr. David Mundel (then a member of the faculty at the Kennedy School of Government, Harvard University, and now at the Congressional Budget Office), who was associated with this project in its initial stages.

129

of the effects of the various factors that influence enrollment. Third, the studies are not tied explicitly to variables that can be altered by policy changes. For example, the studies do not enable evaluation of the impact of financial aid programs that would change the prices faced by lower- and moderate-income students.

Recently, a number of economists have studied the determinants of demand for college. The principal purposes of these studies were to overcome the weaknesses of such sociological studies and to investigate the effect of those attributes (income and prices) which are characteristics of both economic studies and policy alternatives. These studies have been both time-series and cross-sectional in nature.

Campbell and Siegel measured the effect of income and college prices on aggregate enrollment in the United States following World War I.[3] Galper and Dunn conducted a similar study, which concentrated on the effects of family income and Army recruitment on enrollment.[4] Both of these time-series studies fall short of providing the policy relevance and understanding that is needed. They leave out many important variables that influence enrollment (such as supply of various kinds of colleges, proximity, or selectivity) and they lack explicit connections to policy variables that government and institutional decision-makers can influence. Both studies also fail to differentiate between the enrollment effects caused by separate demand and supply behaviors.

One of the earliest cross-sectional studies of determinants of educational attainment was conducted by Morgan, David, Cohn, and Brazer.[5] This study was not focused on demand for college and lacked specific connection with policy variables. Later, several other cross-sectional studies were attempted. Stephen Hoenack studied the price responsiveness of demand for the University of California in an effort to develop an optimal pricing (or subsidization) policy for the university.[6] The Hoenack study had both strengths and weaknesses. A strong point in the study was the treatment of admissions. Because of the eligibility index used by the University of California, Hoenack was able to partially account for the impact of college selectivity. The two major weaknesses of the study resulted from observations of high schools rather than individuals and the use of distance as the sole determinant of price variations. This last problem severely limited the utility of Hoenack's model in evaluating the impact of policies that change the prices faced by specific groups of students.

In a more recent study, Feldman and Hoenack used Project TALENT data to estimate the effects of various price changes on enrollments in different types of institutions.[7] This study used state observations as data and thus was limited by a small sample size. The use of state observations ignored the fact that more price variation and proximity variation occurs within states than among states. Furthermore, statewide average tuitions for specific types of colleges were used as price data inputs. The Feldman and Hoenack study also ignored the problems caused by selective admissions policies and the variation in institutional attributes that exist within each single class of institutions. Thus, the price elasticities that the authors reported appear somewhat less accurate than those necessary to evaluate the impact of specific policies.

Corazzini, Dugan, and Grabowski[8] refined Feldman and Hoenack's analysis by using observations of college-going behavior stratified by socioeconomic status quartiles for each state rather than using simple statewide aggregates. The price variables were those used by Feldman and Hoenack, and thus, although the price elasticities behaved as expected (inverse to family status), the patterns and magnitudes must be viewed somewhat skeptically. The Corazzini study also ignored the implications of selective admissions policies and the distances students must travel to colleges.

Tuckman and Ford[9] attempted to use the price elasticities calculated by Hoenack and Corazzini, Dugan, and Grabowski to estimate the demand for community colleges in Dade County, Florida. Although this study is one of the few that has attempted both to develop estimates of the impact of demand determinants and to make enrollment projections, its generalizable utility is constrained by its specific geographic orientation and its use of travel costs as the sole source of price variation. A more recent study by Anderson, Boman, and Tinto has also investigated the effects of geographical accessibility on college attendance.[10] Its general finding was that proximity to a college has little effect on enrollment rates except among lower-income, lower-ability students. Although this finding has important policy relevance, several aspects of this study constrain its long-term utility. First, the student data is somewhat dated; the California, Illinois, Massachusetts, and North Carolina samples were drawn from 1966 high school seniors and the Wisconsin sample from 1957 seniors. Second, several factors that influence enrollment (such as price, financial aid, and admission policies) were omitted from the analysis and thus the estimated effect of distance may not be an accurate assessment. Third, commuting distance was assumed rather than estimated within the model.

The methodological precursors of our work are two studies by Radner and Miller[11] and by Kohn, Manski, and Mundel.[12] These studies pose an explicit model of the student's decision process in selecting among postsecondary alternatives and use observations of student behavior to estimate that model. The two studies are similar not only in the way they approach the study of enrollment decisions but also their data is from the 1966 SCOPE survey sample, which interviewed 34,000 high school seniors and reinterviewed a subset one year after graduation. The two studies differ primarily in the details of the behavioral models they assume and in the extensiveness of the data used.

A major problem with the Radner and Miller study was that the authors were constrained to use a very small subset of the available SCOPE data, thus inhibiting sample stratification. Another problem is the specification of the price variable. First, institutionally quoted prices (tuition, fees plus room and board) were used as price variables, rather than the actual prices facing particular students. This error would tend to overstate the prices faced by students with "financial need." Second, the price entered for colleges which the student did not attend were the average quoted prices for categories of institutions. This averaging limits the adaptability of the model to more detailed analyses at the stage or national level.

A more extensive study of the SCOPE data was conducted by Kohn, Manski, and Mundel. These authors used the 1966–67 Illinois and North Carolina samples to estimate the effect of tuition, distance, room and board costs, institutional characteristics (including average student ability, field offering, and dormitory capacity), and student characteristics (including ability, income, and parental education) on student demand. The chief limitations on its utility are the dated quality of the data and the limited geographic dispersion of the sample. The authors attempted to estimate the impact of financial aid but data inadequacies prevented them from doing so. Consequently, the reported price effects may be inaccurate. This study is also limited by the lack of an ability level stratification within the estimation procedure.

Recently, cross-sectional studies of student demand have been conducted by Barnes, Erickson, Hill, and Winokur;[13] Christensen, Melder, and Weisbrod;[14] and by Carroll and Relles.[15] Unlike the Radner and Miller and the Kohn, Manski, and Mundel studies, the statistical models in these efforts do not follow from any behavioral model of the college choice process. Consequently the behavioral meaning of the resulting coefficients is questionable.

Notes

1. L. L. Medsker and J. W. Trent, *Beyond High School: A Study of 10,000 High School Graduates* (Berkeley: Center for Research and Development in Higher Education, University of California, 1967).

2 Bureau of the Census, *Factors Related to High School Graduation and College Attendance: 1967*, series p-20, no. 185 (July 11, 1969).

3. R. Campbell and B. Siegel, "The Demand for Higher Education in the United States, 1919–1964," *American Economic Review* (June 1967), pp. 482–94.

4. H. Galper and R. M. Dunn, Jr., "A Short-Run Demand Function for Higher Education in the United States." *Journal of Political Economy* (September-October 1969), pp. 765–77.

5. J. Morgan, David W. Cohn, and H. Brazer, *Income and Welfare in the United States* (New York: McGraw-Hill, 1962).

6. S. Hoenack, "The Efficient Allocation of Subsidies to College Students," *American Economic Review* (June 1971), pp. 302–311.

7. P. Feldman, and S. Hoenack, "Private Demand for Higher Education in the United States," *The Economics and Financing of Higher Education in the United States*, (Washington D.C.: The Joint Economic Committee, 1969).

8. A. Corazzini, D. J. Dugan, and H. Grabowski, "Determinants and Distributional Aspects of Enrollment in U.S. Higher Education," *Journal of Human Resources* (Winter 1972), pp. 39–50.

9. H. P. Tuckman and W. S. Ford, *The Demand for Higher Education: A Florida Case Study* (Lexington, Mass.: Lexington Books, 1972).

10. C. A. Anderson, M. J. Boman, and V. Tinto, *Where Colleges Are and Who Attends* (New York: McGraw-Hill, 1972).

11. R. Radner and L. S. Miller, *Demand and Supply in U.S. Higher Education* (Berkeley: Carnegie Commission on Higher Education, 1975).

12. M. Kohn, C. Manski, and D. Mundel, "An Empirical Investigation of Factors Influencing College-Going Behavior," *Annals of Economic and Social Measurement* (Autumn 1976); also *Rand Corporation Report* R-1470-NSF (1974).

13. G. W. Barnes, E. W. Erickson, W. Hill, and H. S. Winokur, *Direct Aid to Students: A "Radical" Structural Reform* (Washington, D.C.: Inner City Fund, 1972).

14. S. Christensen, T. Melder and B. Weisbrod. "Factors Affecting College Attendance," *Journal of Human Resources*, Vol. X, No. 2, Spring 1975, p. 174–188.

15. S. Carroll and D. Relles. "A Bayesian Model of Choice among Higher Education Institutions," *Rand Corporation Report* R-2005-NIE/LE (June 1976).

8

A Model of Postsecondary Choice

This chapter will focus on the formulation and estimation of a model designed to analyze the postsecondary choices of high school students. Preliminary policy forecasts are presented and analyzed in chapter 9.

An Overview of the Research

Analytical Approach

Our basic behavioral premise is the assumption that graduating high school seniors face a set of possible educational and work alternatives and that, among those available, they select the one they most preferred at the time. We also assume that individual valuations of alternatives can be thought of as functions of measurable attributes of alternatives and of characteristics of individual decision-makers.

Each alternative is characterized by a vector, Z of attributes. Some of these "attributes" may in fact be functions of both characteristics of the individual (for example, SAT scores) making the choice, as well as "true" attributes of the alternative (such as cost). Others may be alternative specific "indicators"–for example, a variable that indicates that the alternative is a four-year college. Thus with individual i and alternative j will be associated a vector of attributes,

$$Z_{ij} = (Z_{1ij}, Z_{2ij}, \cdots, Z_{Kij})$$

where K is the number of attributes. We assume that the individual chooses one of the alternatives based on a valuation of each of them. The valuation by individual i of alternative j, $U(Z_{ij})$, is assumed to be a linear combination of the elements of Z_j:

$$U(Z_j) = \beta_1 Z_{1j} + \beta_2 Z_{2j} + \cdots + \beta_K Z_{Kj} + \epsilon_{ij} = Z_{ij}\beta + \epsilon_{ij}$$

where ϵ is a random term (explained below). The $\beta(\beta_k, k = 1, \cdots, K)$ are the parameters to be estimated. They reflect the relative importance of corresponding variables in the determination of the "desirability" of alternatives.

This chapter reflects primarily the work of David A. Wise, Charles F. Manski, and Winship C. Fuller.

Under appropriate assumptions about the distributions of the random ϵ's, it can be shown that the probability that the individual chooses the jth alternative is:

$$P_{ij} = \frac{e^{Z_{ij}\beta}}{e^{Z_{i1}\beta} + e^{Z_{i2}\beta} + \cdots + e^{Z_{iJ}\beta}}$$

where J is the number of alternatives in the individual's choice set. This "conditional logit model" is the one previously used by Kohn, Manski and Mundel (1974) and by Radner and Miller (1975).[1]

The basic objective of our work, and that of the Radner and Miller and the Kohn, Manski, and Mundel studies preceding it, has been to provide the policymaker with a means of forecasting the changes in student behavior that would result from anticipated changes in the structure of the educational system or from proposed modifications to educational policy. It is self-evident that the achievement of such a forecasting capability requires the development of a satisfactory model of student decision-making. This model should be realistic enough to mirror current student behavior accurately and rich enough to allow forecasts of behavior in anticipated or hypothesized future scenarios. These considerations have motivated our approach.

Model Specification and Data Sources

Having assumed that each student behaves in accord with our model, we must specify the set of alternatives faced by each student and the variables that determine individual valuations of them.

We assume that the alternatives available to a student include the following:

1. all colleges to which the student applies and is accepted
2. the public two-year college closest to the student's home
3. all public vocational programs to which the student applies and is accepted
4. all private vocational programs within 60 miles of the student's home
5. a full-time work alternative
6. a part-time work, part-time school alternative
7. for males, a military service alternative
8. for females, a homemaking alternative

Variables that are assumed to affect individual choices include (1) the "quality" of the alternatives; (2) student academic ability; (3) tuition and fees;

(4) room and board costs; (5) transportation costs; (6) financial aid; (7) income associated with alternatives; and (8) family income, sex, and race.

We also use dummy variables to capture unobserved aspects of several types of alternatives. The particular form of the objective function and the measures used to represent each decision-relevant factor will be set out in the second section of this chapter.

The data requirements for making inferences about the parameters of the objective function, U, are straightforward. For each member of a sample of students, the student's chosen postsecondary alternative and at least some alternatives available but not chosen should be known. Moreover, we should have measures on variables characterizing each available alternative along decision-relevant dimensions and measures characterizing the student along dimensions influencing his behavior.

The National Longitudinal Survey was our primary data source. The NLS base-year student survey plus the supporting surveys of student high school records and of high school characteristics provide extensive socioeconomic, demographic, and educational attainment data for each of a sample of over 20,000 1972 high school seniors. The NLS first year follow-up student survey provides the student's chosen postsecondary alternative as well as those of schools applied to but not attended. For each school applied to, the admissions decision is known and where admitted, the financial aid, if any, offered to the student by the school.

The crucial data not provided by the NLS are the characteristics of a student's available alternatives. For college alternatives, the required data were readily obtained from the American Council on Education's 1972 Institutional Characteristics File. This file contains detailed enrollment, cost, and educational data for 2,603 collegiate institutions. Obtaining suitable data on vocational schools and on the work alternative, however, was somewhat more difficult.

For vocational schools we used the U.S. Office of Education 1970-1971 Vocational Education Directory as a primary source. It provides limited program and enrollment data for 11,721 American vocational schools but lacks data on program lengths and costs. To cover this important gap, we turned to the Survey of Post-Secondary Career Schools conducted by the National Commission on the Financing of Post-Secondary Education. This 1973 survey of 227 schools offering over 1,400 vocational programs allowed us to estimate average lengths and costs by detailed program type. These estimates were then applied to the programs listed in the OE Directory.

In dealing with work alternatives, we did not attempt to differentiate among the various types of jobs a high school graduate might hold. Rather, we characterized a single "work" alternative by the yearly income a given student might expect to earn. The procedure for estimating expected income is described elsewhere.[2] Here we remark only that data on local labor market conditions were required for the estimation. Such data, not directly available from the NLS, were secured from U.S. Bureau of Labor Statistics reports.

The Place of Our Analysis in a Larger Context

Education and work choices made by individuals right after graduation from high school are important determinants of their educational attainment and subsequent careers. Decisions at this time in their lives, however, form only one layer of the series of decisions that collectively determine their levels of education and occupations. Thus, it should be remembered where in this series of decisions our analysis fits.

There surely are no precise time or age limits which bound all decisions that affect the quantity and type of individuals' education and their careers; however, a series of important decisions or choices, some occurring before and some after the ones on which we concentrate, can be outlined (see table 8-1). Some are made by institutions (colleges or other schools) and others by individuals.

The first decision in this series is an application choice made by the high school student. The individual can either apply to a college or school or make no applications; he or she also decides whether to apply for financial aid. This initial choice can be interpreted as revealing a demand schedule for postsecondary education. An admittance decision, as well as a financial aid decision, is made by the school to which the student applies, which can be interpreted as a supply schedule. Next, the student must select an alternative from both the schools to which he or she has been admitted as well as certain nonschool alternatives. We might think of the result of this choice as revealing effective demand; it is in fact the outcome that we observe ex post. Of course, it is derived from both "demand" and "supply" schedules. Finally, after a year or so, there may be a change in the status of those who entered college or university a year earlier, as well as in the status of those who did other things. Some of those who initially entered college may drop out or change schools, while others not in school during the first year may enter at this point. It would be inappropriate to view all college-going individuals as identical if some have a much greater probability of dropping out than others. It is easy to see that this series of decisions could be extended forward or backward with increasing complexity. This short outline provides some idea of where our current analysis fits into the considerably broader framework we hope to pursue in subsequent research.

Model Specification

The Alternatives

Each individual is assumed to have a variety of schooling alternatives available, as well as military service, homemaking, and full-time work. The alternative of combining work and going to school, both on a part-time basis, is also allowed. The individual's actual choice is defined (except where noted) by status in October 1972, in the fall immediately following graduation from high school. This information was obtained in the follow-up survey administered during the fall of 1973. The specific alternatives and availability criterion are as follows:

1. Four-year colleges
   a. Each four-year school that the individual applied to *and* to which he was accepted.
   b. Any four-year college that the individual is attending, if it is not one of the above.
   (Each four-year college alternative is actually broken into two alternatives, one for *living at home* and the other for living *on campus*. The only exception is for schools that have no on-campus living facilities.)
2. Two-year college
   a. Any two-year college that the student applied to *and* to which he or she was admitted.
   b. The *public* two-year college that is closest to his or her high school and in the same state, if it is not included in the two-year colleges above.
   c. Any two-year college that the individual attended if it is not in one of the above categories of two-year colleges.
3. Nursing schools
   a. Those to which the student applied and was admitted.
   b. Any nursing school that the individual is attending, if it is not included under (a).
   (This alternative is assumed *not* to be available to men.)
4. Public vocational schools
   a. Any that the student applied to *and* to which he or she was accepted.
   b. Any public vocational school that the individual attended if it is not in the above list.
   (Vocational school programs are classified by subject matter and by duration, as explained below.)
5. Private vocational schools (excluding nursing)
   a. The closest one to the student's high school is included *if* it is within 60 miles.
   b. Any other private vocational school if the student is attending it.

Table 8-1

Decisions Affecting Education and Career Choices

Decision (Decision-Maker)	Choice	Alternatives
Decision 1 (Student)	Application to school or college	Type of university Junior college Vocational school
	Application for financial aid	Yes No
Decision 2 (Institution)	Admission	Yes No
	Financial Aid	Yes, no Type How much
Decision 3 (Student)	Choice of education or work right after high school	Type of university Junior college Work
Decision 4	School status one year later	Continue in same school Change schools Drop out Enter late

6. Work:
   a. Available to each student.
7. Military:
   a. Available to each male student.
8. Homemaking:
   a. Available to each female student.
9. Part-time school and part-time work:
   a. Available to each student.

To clarify these alternatives and availability criteria, each individual in the survey listed the three schools that represented his or her "first three choices"; we do not know whether he or she applied to any others. (In practice, only a small proportion of students apply to more than three schools.) In addition, some students reported attendance at a school to which we had no record of application. Thus, this group of schools was included in the choice set.

The nursing school alternative is likely to exclude nursing programs that
are integrally related to four-year colleges or universities. A nursing student
in a four-year college would almost surely be classified as attending a four-
year college. Thus, the nursing alternative should be thought of as pertaining to three-year registered nursing programs and other nursing programs of
shorter duration.

Vocational schools are unlike other four- and two-year schools in that
the cost of attendance, as well as other attributes, appear to vary substantially
by the types and length of individual programs. Most colleges charge by the
semester and students enroll by the semester regardless of the particular courses
being taken. Vocational schools are much more heterogeneous. For this reason
we will classify vocational "schools" by type of program (such as clerical) and
duration of training. This means that, even though there is only one vocational
school in an area, an individual could still face several vocational school alternatives, depending on the number of types of programs that the school offers.
Alternatives could include a trade and industrial program of less than 12 months,
for example, as well as one lasting two years or more. Thus, the following vocational school alternatives are allowed:

Nursing:
    Public
    Private

Trade and Industrial:
    Public: less than 12 months
              12 to 24 months
              more than 24 months
    Private: less than 12 months
              12 to 24 months
              more than 24 months

Health Programs other than Nursing:
    Public: less than 12 months
              greater than 12 months
    Private: less than 12 months
              greater than 12 months

Home economics:
    Public
    Private

Marketing and Distribution:
    Public: less than 12 months
              greater than 12 months
    Private: less than 12 months
              greater than 12 months

Business and office:
    Public: less than 12 months
                 greater than 12 months
    Private: less than 12 months
                 greater than 12 months

Technical:
    Public
    Private

Public and private schools are distinguished not only because costs of attendance vary substantially among each, but also because private schools normally have an open enrollment policy whereas public vocational schools do not.

Not every alternative potentially available to a student is listed. For example, a student might choose among any number of junior colleges in a home state, while we have allowed only one or two. Our goal, however, is not to include every possible junior college, all of which may look quite similar relative to other alternatives, but rather to include one alternative that is "representative" of junior colleges.

The Variables

The variables that are assumed to determine an individual's valuation of an available alternative are described below. The variables assumed to influence choice are academic aptitude, cost, aid, family income, high school characteristics, distance, race, and local labor market conditions.

Academic aptitude of decision-makers, as measured by SAT scores, is assumed to influence the choice process in two ways, first through the aptitude of the individual who is choosing among alternatives and, second, through the average academic aptitude of all persons choosing each of the alternatives. In particular, the academic aptitude variable used in the analysis is individual aptitude minus the average aptitude of all persons selecting the alternative under consideration. For example, if the alternative is a four-year college, the value of the academic aptitude variable would be the individual's aptitude minus the average aptitude of persons who attend that college, with the college average being obtained from the institutional characteristic file.

It is anticipated that individuals will prefer alternatives chosen by persons of comparable aptitude to their own; that is, they will tend not to choose alternatives that will put them in situations with other persons of much higher or much lower aptitude than their own. This contention is borne out by the results. For noncollege alternatives the average was determined by the average of persons in the sample who selected each of them. For some individuals it was necessary to predict SAT scores from various other student attributes and characteristics. The actual academic aptitude variable used is specified in table 8-2.

All costs associated with an alternative as well as the various forms of aid are divided by a family income variable, estimated from the NLS data on parental occupation and education. The effect of tuition cost, in addition to depending on family income, is allowed to vary by the length of the program when the alternative is an educational one. Thus, there are three tuition categories (variables): one for educational programs lasting less than 12 months, another for those lasting from 12 to 24 months, and one for programs over 24 months. All costs are on an annual basis. The rationale for the separate categories is that the effect of costs that are expected to be incurred for only one year, for example, is likely to be different from the effect of a cost expected for four years.

A variable measuring the cost of room and board takes on a positive value only if the school alternative under consideration provides on-campus residence,[3] otherwise it is zero. It is divided by family income and is on an annual basis (two semesters).

The aid variables are also interacted with income through division by estimated family income. Four types of aid are distinguished: scholarship aid tied to attendance at a particular school; loan aid, also assumed to be tied to a particular school; work aid associated with particular school; and direct aid to the student, assumed to be available for attendance for any four-year college if the student reported receiving such aid. Scholarship aid is divided into two categories—programs less than or equal to 24 months, and those greater than 24 months. One work aid variable pertains to programs lasting from 12 to 24 months and the other to those lasting more than 24 months. Only one loan aid variable pertains to programs lasting more than 12 months. Finally, direct aid is not distinguished by program length. These length categories were determined by the availablity of observations in the sample.

An individual's high school is characterized by two variables: the percentage of students that go to colleges, and the percentage that go to other schools, primarily vocational schools. The first variable enters only if the alternative is a four- or two-year college and is zero otherwise. The second is nonzero only if the alternative is a vocational school.

The distance variable equals the logarithm of the distance to the alternative if choosing that alternative requires commuting and it is an educational alternative; it is zero otherwise. The effect of this distance presumably reflects both travel time and cost.

A dichotomous race variable takes on the value one only if the alternative is a four-year college and the individual is black, and zero otherwise.

Local labor market conditions are reflected in the student's expected annual income from working. This wage variable was estimated from several student and labor market characteristics. The variable takes the value zero for all but the work alternative.

Table 8-2
Variables Used in Choice Model

Academic aptitude 1 $\quad \equiv \begin{cases} A + 100 \text{ if } A \leqslant -100, \\ 0 \text{ otherwise} \end{cases}$

Academic aptitude 2 $\quad \equiv \begin{cases} -100 \text{ if } A \leqslant -100, \\ A \text{ if } -100 < A \leqslant 0, \\ 0 \text{ otherwise} \end{cases}$

Academic aptitude 3 $\quad \equiv \begin{cases} A \text{ if } 0 < A \leqslant 100, \\ 100 \text{ if } A > 100, \\ 0 \text{ otherwise} \end{cases}$

Academic aptitude 4 $\quad \equiv \begin{cases} A - 100 \text{ if } A > 100, \\ 0 \text{ otherwise} \end{cases}$

Tuition cost 1 $\quad \equiv \begin{cases} \text{tuition plus fees} \div \text{family income, if program is less than} \\ \text{1 year,} \\ 0 \text{ otherwise} \end{cases}$

Tuition cost 2 $\quad \equiv \begin{cases} \text{tuition plus fees} \div \text{family income, if program is greater} \\ \text{than 1 year but less than or equal to 2 years,} \\ 0 \text{ otherwise} \end{cases}$

Tuition cost 3 $\quad \equiv \begin{cases} \text{tuition plus fees} \div \text{family income, if program is greater} \\ \text{than 2 years,} \\ 0 \text{ otherwise} \end{cases}$

Living cost $\quad \equiv \begin{cases} \text{room plus board if the alternative is live on-campus,} \\ 0 \text{ otherwise} \end{cases}$

Scholarship aid 1, 2 $\quad \equiv \begin{cases} \text{scholarship aid} \div \text{family income if the program is less} \\ \text{than or equal to 2 years,} \\ 0 \text{ otherwise} \end{cases}$

Scholarship aid, 3 $\quad \equiv \begin{cases} \text{scholarship aid} \div \text{family income if the program is greater} \\ \text{than 2 years,} \\ 0 \text{ otherwise} \end{cases}$

Work aid 2 $\quad \equiv \begin{cases} \text{work aid} \div \text{family income if the program is between 1} \\ \text{and 2 years,} \\ 0 \text{ otherwise} \end{cases}$

Table 8–2 (Continued)

Work aid 3	$\equiv$	work aid ÷ family income if the program is greater than 2 years, 0 otherwise
Loan aid 2, 3	$\equiv$	loan aid ÷ family income if the program is greater than 1 year, 0 otherwise
Direct aid 1, 2, 3	$\equiv$	aid ÷ family income for all program lengths, 0 for noneducation alternatives
High school students in college	$\equiv$	percentage of students from person's high school who go to college if the alternative is a four-year college, 0 otherwise
High school students in other schools	$\equiv$	percentage of students from person's high school in schools other than four-year colleges if the alternative is a non-four-year school, 0 otherwise
Distance	$\equiv$	logarithm of distance to a *school alternative* if the student is to commute to the school, 0 otherwise
Wage	$\equiv$	expected annual income if the alternative is full-time work, 0 otherwise
Race	$\equiv$	1 if the alternative is a four-year college and the person is black, 0 otherwise
Four-year on-campus	$\equiv$	1 if the alternative is a four-year live on-campus alternative, 0 otherwise
. . .		
Part-time work and school	$\equiv$	1 if the alternative is work part time and go to school part time, 0 otherwise

Finally, there are nine alternative specific variables. For example, one such variable indicates a four-year-college–on-campus alternative. It takes the value one for this alternative and zero otherwise. The remaining eight alternative specific variables identify two-year colleges, nursing or other health school alternatives, trade and industrial schools, business and office or marketing school alternatives, full-time work, military, homemaking, and part-time work–part-time school. The live at home four-year college alternative serves as the norm. It may be assumed that the alternative specific term relative to it is zero and the others represent deviations from it. The rationale for these variables is that alternatives are likely to have common characteristics associated with them which are not captured by the other variables we have included explicitly. In fact, the part-time work–part-time school alternative is characterized only by the alternative specific variable; all the other variables have zero values for this alternative.

The variables and their definitions are summarized in table 8-2, where A represents an individual's SAT minus the average SAT score for the alternative under consideration. (In this specification academic aptitude is assigned the value zero for the part-time work part-time school alternative. This will be changed to correspond to the formulations for other alternatives in future work.)

Parameter Estimates and Forecasts

Estimates of the parameters in this model were obtained using a random sample of 4,507 observations from the larger NLS sample. We will first discuss individual coefficient estimates, followed by discussion of a predictive test. Finally, chapter 9 uses the model to examine the effect of labor market conditions and student aid policies on the demand for postsecondary education.

All our results are tentative and subject to revision after more extensive analysis. In particular, the estimated effects of educational policies, although likely to reflect general orders of magnitude reasonably well, should be taken only as illustrative at this time.

Coefficient Estimates

Parameter estimates based on the whole sample are presented in column 1 of table 8-3. We have also divided the sample into two subgroups, depending on estimated family income, one for persons with family income below and the other above $10,664. The initial specification described in the previous section and used as a basis for the estimates in column 1 constrains income to interact with cost and aid variables in a particular way. The estimates in columns 2 and 3 allow all parameters to vary between the two income levels. In this latter specification, the cost and aid variables are *not divided by family*

Table 8–3
Parameter Estimates

Variable	Total Sample	High-Income Group[a]	Low-Income Group[a]
Academic aptitude 1	0.00313	0.00373	0.00290
	(0.00049)	(0.00072)	(0.00069)
Academic aptitude 2	−0.00397	−0.00476	−0.00295
	(0.00101)	(0.00142)	(0.00149)
Academic aptitude 3	0.00093	0.00171	0.00088
	(0.00106)	(0.00142)	(0.00162)
Academic aptitude 4	−0.00412	−0.00334	−0.00436
	(0.00048)	(0.00061)	(0.00082)
Tuition cost 1	−29.92600	−0.00237	−0.00347
	(5.65100)	(0.00081)	(0.00076)
Tuition cost 2	−0.32850	0.00086	−0.00044
	(1.59710)	(0.00025)	(0.00027)
Tuition cost 3	−2.20660	0.00004	−0.00039
	(0.83533)	(0.00010)	(0.00015)
Living cost	−10,47900	−0.00085	−0.00081
	(1.34800)	(0.00016)	(0.00023)
Scholarship aid 1, 2	31.80900	0.00325	0.00388
	(5.11030)	(0.00104)	(0.00070)
Scholarship aid 3	4.74430	0.00065	0.00056
	(1.42090)	(0.00025)	(0.00021)
Work aid 2	74.34600	0.00809	0.00764
	(13.71800)	(0.00259)	(0.00178)
Work aid 3	5.98570	0.00045	0.00096
	(3.57950)	(0.00060)	(0.00056)
Loan aid 2, 3	7.63610	0.00037	0.00114
	(1.88420)	(0.00026)	(0.00030)
Direct aid 1, 2, 3	11.04200	0.00102	0.00134
	(2.85540)	(0.00045)	(0.00042)
High school students in colleges	0.13295	0.10300	0.11771
	(0.02455)	(0.03418)	(0.03711)
High school students in other schools	0.13319	0.21302	0.07913
	(0.11015)	(0.17671)	(0.14253)
Distance	−0.06727	−0.06151	−0.08019
	(0.02306)	(0.02963)	(0.03716)
Wage	0.00008	0.00008	0.00010
	(0.00004)	(0.00005)	(0.00005)
Race	−0.39131	−0.34056	−0.37628
	(0.16566)	(0.28223)	(0.21218)
Four-year campus	0.81777	1.01620	0.13301
	(0.14745)	(0.19794)	(0.25068)
Two-year college	−2.05140	−2.14140	−2.07560
	(0.13045)	(0.18590)	(0.20495)
Nursing or other health	−1.07520	−1.84420	−0.70442
	(0.49087)	(0.80980)	(0.63813)

Table 8-3 (Continued)

Variable	Total Sample	High-Income Groups[a]	Low-Income Group[a]
Trade and industrial	−4.23610	−5.94850	−3.56860
	(0.42523)	(0.72312)	(0.56340)
Business and office	−3.18400	−4.59550	−2.65250
or marketing	(0.42407)	(0.66081)	(0.59634)
Work	0.02952	−0.13635	−0.13231
	(0.26446)	(0.36344)	(0.39680)
Military	−2.44070	−2.53460	−2.62500
	(0.25133)	(0.35055)	(0.37141)
Homemaking	−1.92720	−2.19360	−1.98550
	(0.22803)	(0.32495)	(0.33480)
Part-time work	−2.29380	−2.03300	−2.73870
Part-time school	(0.22330)	(0.30364)	(0.33783)
Number of observations	4,507	2,159	2,348

[a]The cost and aid variables are not divided by family income in this specification.

income. The reason for trying both formulations is to provide some check on the validity of the more constrained specification. We will discuss first the estimates in column 1.

The importance of academic aptitude in an individual's perception of alternatives is shown in figure 8-1. This diagram shows the effect on the function U in equation 3 of changes in academic aptitude. Recalling that the aptitude variable in the diagram is an individual's SAT score minus an average score for the alternative, referred to as SAT, in general the estimated desirability of an alternative to an individual tends to increase as aptitude approaches the average pertaining to the alternative. Our estimates show a high point below the point where the two are equal (where our variable equals zero) and a slight increase as the individual score exceeds the average with a drop again after the individual exceeds the average by 100 points. This "double-peaked" result may be due either to the break points that we selected or to some underlying characteristic of decision-makers. For example, if there were two groups of individuals, some tending to prefer alternatives with averages higher than their own and others preferring lower averages, then this pattern could be rationalized; in fact, almost any pattern could be produced. All but the coefficient on the third aptitude variable are significantly different from zero at standard levels of significance.

The coefficients on tuition cost are all negative, but vary dramatically by program length, as the following demonstrates.

Tuition cost 1 = − 29.93
Tuition cost 2 = − 00.33
Tuition cost 3 = − 02.21

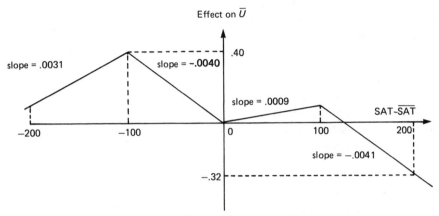

Figure 8-1. Effect of Aptitude Differences

The highest value is for programs of short duration. Theoretically it is difficult to predict any particular pattern because the coefficients should depend not only on current costs but also on expectations about the value of each alternative (versus all others) for such variables as future income, occupation, and life-style.

The aid variable coefficients are also reproduced as follows:

Scholarship aid 1, 2,	=	31.81
Scholarship aid 3	=	4.74
Work aid 2	=	74.34
Work aid 3	=	5.99
Loan aid 2, 3	=	7.64
Direct aid 1, 2, 3	=	11.04

Note first that the signs of the coefficients are opposite to those of the cost variables and the two groups of coefficients are roughly of the same order of magnitude. In particular, the scholarship aid variables just about mirror the tuition cost variables. Unfortunately, we were unable to distinguish aid for programs lasting less than a year from those lasting from one to two years. Two surprises emerge from these estimated results. First, there seems to be no identifiable distinction between the value attached to different types of aid. One might expect, for example, that the coefficients on work aid and loan aid would be consistently lower than those on scholarship aid and direct aid, but they are not. Second, the coefficient on work aid for two-year programs appears to be questionably large, which may be caused by a relationship between work aid and quality of training, for example, in some vocational programs.

Also, the value of aid in programs of two years or less is undoubtedly over-stated because some persons indicated that they applied to junior colleges and vocational schools, were accepted, and were offered aid. For these schools, the value of any aid that the student reported was included in the appropriate aid variable. But other junior colleges and training programs, especially the nearest ones, were part of the individual's choice set. For these schools we did not have any information on the aid that the student would receive, and we thus assigned a value of zero to the appropriate aid variables. But surely this aid would have been positive for some students. Therefore, because students are likely to attend those junior colleges and vocational schools where they applied and were accepted, the coefficient on aid for these programs is likely to be overstated.

Living cost is also estimated to affect choice in a manner which is commen-surate with the effect of tuition cost and aid. The value of the relevant coeffi-cient is –10.5. Thus, although individual coefficients on cost and aid variables suggest some questionable differences among programs, the general consistency in magnitudes among the various cost and aid coefficients is reassuring.

In future work we plan to respecify the cost and aid variables. Specifically, we will allow the coefficient on cost to vary by school type (for example, by four-year college, two-year college, and so on), rather than by length of program. We may, however, continue to allow differences by length for some vocational programs. A similar procedure will be followed for the various types of aid. In addition, we have had to settle for rather gross estimates of tuition costs for vocational schools because of inadequate data. This means that, in particular, the exact parameter estimates corresponding to programs of two years or less must be viewed with considerable skepticism, even though the order of magni-tude of the coefficients in general seems to be reasonable. In future work, then, we will also attempt to get more precise cost estimates for these schools. This should be possible using a more recent survey of vocational schools than was initially available.[4] Finally, in future work we should consider a different and less detailed definition of vocational school alternatives. This possibility is discussed more fully with reference to the results presented below.

Peer group or community characteristics appear to influence individual decisions in that the coefficients on both our high school characteristics vari-ables are positive. In particular, the coefficient on the percentage of students in an individual's high school who go to college is estimated to increase the likelihood that he or she will go to college. The coefficient on the proportion of an individual's high school classmates who go to other schools is of com-parable magnitude but not very precisely measured. Also, the coefficient on distance is negative, as we would expect.

Local labor market conditions also appear to influence choice. The esti-mated coefficient on the expected wage is positive and significantly different from zero at standard significance levels. This coefficient is quite small, how-ever, when compared with the cost and aid coefficients. Race appears to have a small negative influence on the likelihood of college attendance.

Finally, most of the alternative specific terms are significantly different from zero. Apparently there are characteristics of alternatives that have a measurable influence on choice but that we have not captured in the other variables. We point out that all the alternative specific terms, except those for work and four-year off-campus college attendance, are negative and of roughly, the same order of magnitude. They should be thought of as representing the value of unmeasured characteristics of these alternatives relative to those for the four-year–off-campus alternative. The on-campus term is relatively large and positive, while the work alternative term has a small positive value.

The estimates in columns 2 and 3 of table 8–3 will not be discussed in detail. We shall point out some general characteristics of the two sets of coefficients, however, while recalling that the cost of aid variables are not divided by family income in this specification.

As one might expect, the coefficients on cost and aid variables tend to be larger for the low-income group than the high. In fact, two of the tuition cost coefficients for the high income group are positive, but not significantly different from zero.[5] An informal check on our previous specification is provided by comparing the coefficients in columns 2 and 3 with those in column 1, with the appropriate column 1 coefficients divided by the mean income in the sample (about $10,000). This gives coefficients that lie midway between the estimates for the high- and low-income groups, which is what we would expect if the effects of income are reasonably well captured by our initial formulation.

The coefficient on the expected wage is considerably larger for the low-income than for the high-income group. This suggests that our wage variable should also be allowed to interact with wealth, possibly through division by family income. Our current specification does not allow such interaction, but future work will take this into account.

Finally, the coefficients on academic aptitude suggest a relationship between aptitude and the desirability of alternatives like that depicted in figure 8–1. The coefficients (slopes) for the low-income groups are generally smaller than for the high group, and with the coefficients for the total sample between them. We offer no convincing explanation for this pattern, although some plausible rationalization could be hypothesized.

A Predictive Test

To test the predictive ability of the model, we compared actual and predicted choices for a different sample of students than was used for estimation purposes. To this end, we selected a second sample of 4,583 persons from the NLS tape. For each person in this sample, we predicted the probability of selecting each of the alternatives and summed them. The resulting percentage distribution across alternatives is compared with the actual distribution in table 8–4. The two distributions are reasonably close; however, we are not able to predict choices among alternative vocational school categories with any degree of precision. But the total predicted and actual number of persons in all vocational school categories, and the corresponding percentages, are quite close (37 versus 43 and .7 versus .8, respectively).

It is not surprising that predicting choices among vocational schools seems to be the weakest part of our analysis. Not only are the categories rather arbitrarily defined, but the estimated cost figures of particular alternatives are likely to include substantial errors. In addition, we were never sure that any particular length category actually existed for a given individual, because our information about the vocational schools in the area of each high school did not indicate the length of the program options available. On the average, though, the defined vocational school alternatives are likely to be reasonably representative of actual alternatives. Thus we can predict reasonably well in the aggregate, but cannot distinguish very well among our defined alternatives.

In future work these alternatives will be redefined to correspond more closely to those which we know to exist. This will necessarily involve giving up some detail about program length. We will also in future work be able to get more accurate measures of cost from a more extensive survey of vocational schools now available.[6]

Finally, it is not surprising that we can forecast reasonably well using a sample of persons similar to the sample used for estimation. Both were randomly selected from the same larger sample. If our model fits the data used in estimation, we would also expect it to fit a different but quite similar sample reasonably well. A better test of the "structural" specification of the model would be to estimate the model on a set of data defined by values of the independent variables and then use that model to predict for values of independent

Table 8–4
Actual Versus Predicted Distributions, A Forecast Example

Alternative	Frequencies		Percentage Distribution	
	Actual	Predicted	Actual	Predicted
Four-year college, on-campus	519	519.0	11.3	11.3
Four-year college, live at home	572	552.1	12.5	12.0
Two-year college	518	473.1	11.3	10.3
Vocational and trade schools	37	43.0	0.7	1.0
Work full-time	2533	2587.8	55.3	56.5
Military	85	96.6	1.9	2.1
Homemaker	123	120.9	2.7	2.6
Part-time school, part-time work	196	189.0	4.3	4.1
Total number		4,583		

variables outside the range so defined. For example, we could obtain estimates using only alternatives with tuition costs below some level, then use the resulting estimates to predict probabilities of choices for alternatives with tuitions above this level. (This would be comparable to predicting the effect of aid values well beyond the range of aid data used for estimation, as done in one hypothetical policy simulated in chapter 9.) If our parameter estimates are reasonably accurate, we should be able to predict quite well outside the range of the independent variables used for estimation. We will perform this test in future work.

Notes

1. See those papers as well as the original McFadden article (1973) for discussions of theoretical and computational properties.

2. See appendix A in UCI's *Experiences of Recent High School Graduates: The Transition to Work or Postsecondary Education*, as submitted to NCES, DHEW.

3. In practice, schools that indicate a positive room and board cost per student. It would include any living arrangement other than living at home.

4. 1975 Postsecondary Career Schools Enrollment and Programs Survey, NCES, DHEW.

5. One rationalization for a positive coefficient is that the cost measures some quality differences that are not otherwise captured by the model.

6. 1975 Postsecondary Career Schools Enrollment and Programs Survey, NCES, DHEW.

9

Simulations for Policy Analysis

This chapter analyzes several illustrative policies using the choice model developed and discussed in chapter 8. The way in which a changing labor market could affect student choices is analyzed in the first section of this chapter, followed by a segment which examines the results of increased tuition and financial aid in public schools. Effects of changes in the amounts of direct aid offered to students are then simulated in the third section.

A Shift in Labor Market Opportunity

Our primary reason for developing a model of postsecondary educational choice is to be able to predict the effects on student choices of such government policies as tuition subsidization and other aid programs. But considerable interest, in economics at least, also centers around the effect of labor market conditions on educational choice. That question and the potential effects of some hypothetical government aid programs will be discussed in this section.

We pose the following question: what would be the effect on work and educational choices of a 10 percent increase in the expected annual wage from working full time, with other influences on the choice set remaining constant? We would like to ask the question with respect to some representative individual; but instead of considering the effect on a single person, we will assume that a representative person might look something like the "average" person in our sample. Therefore, in asking what the expected effects would be, averaged over all persons in our sample, we have increased the expected wage of each individual in the sample by 10 percent, calculated the probaiblity, for each person, of choosing each alternative, and summed them. The resulting frequency distribution may be compared with the predicted distribution based on the initial expected wage rates by considering the numbers in table 9-1. The first two columns pertain to the total sample, the next two to the high SAT and high family income subsample, and the last two to the low SAT and family income group. The numbers in the "before" columns pertain to *predicted* frequencies before the increase in the expected wage.

In general, after the increase in the wage, the predicted number of persons selecting college alternatives falls, while the number choosing the work alternative

This chapter reflects the work of David A. Wise, Charles F. Manski, George J. Nolfi, Winship C. Fuller, and Valerie I Nelson.

Table 9-1

The Effect of An Exogenous Shift in the Expected Wage

Alternative	Total Sample Before	Total Sample After	High SAT and Income Before	High SAT and Income After	Low SAT and Income Before	Low SAT and Income After
Four-year college, on campus	492.0	489.0	304.8	303.3	40.2	39.8
Four-year college, live at home	519.7	516.2	275.7	274.2	66.1	65.4
Two-year college	465.9	453.8	129.8	126.8	135.9	132.1
Vocational and trade schools	49.1	47.8	11.4	11.1	18.5	17.9
Work full-time	2569.6	2598.3	442.7	450.6	1084.8	1093.9
Military	96.9	96.4	17.9	17.9	39.2	39.0
Homemaker	118.9	116.1	15.8	15.5	57.3	55.9
Part-time school, part-time work	189.7	184.2	47.8	46.6	66.5	64.5
Total number of persons	4,503		1,246		1,509	

increases. We can also get some idea of the orders of magnitude by considering the elasticity of the number of persons selecting the work alternative with respect to the wage increase. A 10 percent increase in the wage leads to approximately a 1 percent increase in the number of persons in the total sample who elect to work full time; the actual elasticity is .112. The elasticities for the high SAT and income and the low SAT and income subgroups are .178 and .084, respectively. These numbers are comparable in magnitude to some common estimates of the elasticity of hours worked with respect to the wage in labor supply studies. Our estimates, of course, should not be given the same interpretation as wage elasticities in labor supply studies.

The elasticity is higher for the high SAT-income groups than for the low group. This is likely to result from differences in the initial alternatives available to the two groups. The alternatives, and in fact the initial choices, of the high SAT-income group are more heavily weighted toward four-year colleges to begin with, whereas the low SAT-income group is less likely to have available and to choose these alternatives. Therefore, the possibilities for shifting are greater for the first than for the second group.

These estimates are based on some very restrictive assumptions; namely, that everything else remains unchanged, including such factors as the monetary value to individuals of different types of education. While this may be true for a particular individual or small groups of individuals in a given geographic area, it is not likely to be true for the general population of high school graduates. (Also, there is some evidence that the return to education may be falling, on the average, in the economy as a whole.) We have also not considered possible supply side reactions on the part of colleges and universities to a general increase in the wage rate. Nonetheless, the numbers may be thought of indicative of the effect of labor market opportunities and work choices.

Increased Tuition and Aid in Public Schools

Most public colleges and universities are highly subsidized in the sense that student tuition and fees cover only a portion of the actual cost per student.

One rationale for this policy is that higher education provides social benefits beyond those accruing to individual students and should therefore be subsidized. It has been argued, however, that the extent of this subsidy for any particular individual should depend on his or her ability to pay. We have, therefore, simulated the predicted effects on our sample of two hypothetical policies that reflect these concerns. These policies would increase tuition costs in public two- and four-year schools to something like the average cost per student. At the same time, they base actual public tuition paid on family income, while tuitions in private schools are left unchanged. The details are as follows:

Program 1

Tuition in four-year public schools was raised to $2,100 and in two-year schools to $1,400.

$$
\text{Tuition paid} = \begin{cases} 0, \text{ if family income} \leqslant 9{,}000, \\[2mm] \left(\dfrac{\text{family income}}{10{,}000} - \dfrac{9{,}000}{10{,}000}\right) \times \text{tuition, if} \\[2mm] \qquad 9{,}000 < \text{family income} \leqslant 19{,}000 \\[2mm] \text{tuition, if family income} > 19{,}000 \end{cases}
$$

All initial aid levels were left unchanged.

Program 2

Same as program 1 but:

$$
\text{Tuition paid} = \begin{cases} 0, \text{ if family income} \leqslant 10{,}665, \\[2mm] \left(\dfrac{\text{family income}}{5{,}665} - \dfrac{10{,}665}{5{,}665}\right) \times \text{tuition, if} \\[2mm] \qquad 10{,}665 < \text{family income} \leqslant 15{,}665 \\[2mm] \text{tuition, if family income} > 15{,}665. \end{cases}
$$

The effects of these programs are determined by the size of the tuition coefficients relative to the other coefficients. Aid given here is in the form of tuition reductions; in the next section we will investigate the predicted effects of aid given directly to students.

The simulated effects of these two programs on all persons in the sample and on the high and low income groups separately are shown in part a of table 9-2, with summary statistics shown in part b. Because our hypothetical policies

Table 9–2
Increased Tuition and Aid in Public Schools

(a) Programs 1 and 2 (Frequencies)

Alternative	Base			Program 1			Program 2		
	Total Sample	High Income	Low Income	Total Sample	High Income	Low Income	Total Sample	High Income	Low Income
Four-year college, campus; public	305.79	203.01	92.80	305.85	210.53	95.3	304.94	209.09	95.88
Four-year college, campus; private	186.30	146.79	39.51	186.55	147.33	39.2	186.80	147.66	39.14
Four-year college, home; public	328.86	198.02	130.87	330.17	195.45	134.7	329.79	194.43	135.39
Four-year college, home; private	180.87	132.67	58.20	190.82	133.12	57.7	190.98	133.37	57.61
Two-year college; public	451.27	213.57	237.94	452.65	213.56	239.3	453.01	213.79	239.47
Two-year college; private	14.66	8.68	5.97	14.66	9.69	5.9	14.66	8.70	5.97
Vocational and trade schools	49.21	22.24	26.96	49.17	22.33	26.84	49.24	22.39	26.89
Work full-time	2569.60	1080.80	1488.90	1567.00	1084.20	1482.90	2567.40	1085.50	1482.00
Military	96.90	42.04	54.86	95.83	42.16	54.67	96.84	42.21	54.63
Homemaker	118.92	46.49	72.44	118.78	46.65	72.13	118.79	46.70	72.09
Part-time school part-time work	189.69	85.41	104.29	189.54	85.76	103.79	189.64	85.95	103.69
Total number of persons	4,503	2,190	2,313	4,503	2,190	2,313	4,503	2,190	2,313

(b) Summary Statistics (Predicted; in Thousands of Dollars)

	Total Sample	High Income	Low Income	Total Sample	High Income	Low Income	Total Sample	High Income	Low Income
Direct aid	195.0	103.4	92.6	195.1	101.0	94.1	195.1	100.9	94.2
Percentage of total aid	30.1	31.1	29.0	30.2	31.5	22.9	30.2	31.5	28.9
Scholarship aid	216.7	115.9	100.9	212.5	106.8	105.7	212.6	106.9	105.7
Percentage of total aid	33.3	34.8	31.6	32.9	33.3	32.4	32.9	33.4	32.4
Work aid	77.1	30.8	46.3	76.8	29.9	46.9	76.9	30.0	46.9
Percentage of total aid	11.8	9.3	14.5	11.9	9.3	14.4	11.9	9.4	14.4
Loan aid	161.4	82.1	79.3	161.9	82.7	79.2	161.9	82.6	79.3
Percent of total aid	24.8	24.7	24.9	25.1	25.8	24.3	25.1	25.8	24.3
Total aid	651.1	332.3	319.1	646.3	320.4	325.9	646.4	320.3	326.0
Total tuition paid	1304.0	940.8	363.2	1298.8	1069.7	229.2	1357.9	1161.6	196.4
Tuition minus aid	652.7	608.5	44.2	662.5	749.2	− 96.7	711.5	841.2	− 129.7

distinguish public from private schools, we separate public and private schools in the reported results for each of the two- and four-year college alternatives.

Neither policy produces large shifts in individual choices, but we do observe some increase in the number of low-income persons electing to attend public colleges and somewhat smaller decreases for high-income persons. The increase in the low-income group is about 1.7 percent under program 1 and 2 percent under program 2. The negative effects for the high income groups are 0.8 percent and 0.2 percent, respectively. Although a casual comparison of the coefficients on the wage rate and on tuition points toward these numbers being small, the tuition variable used here is tuition divided by family income, with average family income being somewhat over $10,000. Thus, even though tuition is changed substantially for some persons (an average decrease of about $400 for low-income persons under program 2), the change in tuition divided by income is much smaller.

Aggregate changes in the predicted difference between tuition paid and aid can be seen by looking at the last line of table 9-2, part b. The increases for the high-income groups are approximately offset by decreases for the low-income group, yielding small net changes. For the high-income group, the increases in this aggregate are about 23 and 38 percent, respectively, for the two programs, while the low-income group in fact receives more in aid than is paid in tuition.

The Effect of Direct Aid Programs

We have simulated the effect of four different direct aid programs on our sample of 4,503 persons. As with the tuition subsidization programs, we have distinguished the private and public four- and two-year colleges. By direct aid we mean money given directly to the student to be used for any educational program he or she chooses. In some cases we have restricted aid to be no more than the tuition cost of the program chosen, while in others we have allowed aid to be greater than tuition. The amount of aid is again conditional on family income, but the formula differs somewhat from the tuition subsidization used in the previous section. Finally, in some instances we have raised the tuition costs in public colleges, while in others we have left them at their original levels. The precise specifications of each program are as follows:

Program 1

> Tuition in public two-year colleges is assumed equal to $1,400 if it was initially below this level.
>
> Tuition in public four-year colleges is assumed equal to $2,100 if it was initially below this level.
>
> Direct aid is available for use at any school but *cannot exceed the cost of tuition.*

$$\text{Direct aid} = \begin{cases} 2{,}100\text{, if family income} \leqslant 5{,}000, \\[6pt] \left(\dfrac{20{,}000}{15{,}000} - \dfrac{\text{family income}}{15{,}000}\right) \times 2{,}100 \quad \begin{array}{l} \text{if } 5{,}000 < \text{family} \\ \text{income} < 20{,}000, \end{array} \\[12pt] 0\text{, if family income} > 20{,}000 \end{cases}$$

Program 2

Same as program 1, but aid *can* exceed tuition cost.

Program 3

Same as program 1, but tuitions in public schools are *not raised*, they are left at initial levels.

Program 4

Same as program 1, but tuitions are *not* raised, and aid *can* exceed tuition cost.

Predicted frequency and percentage distributions across alternatives are shown for these four direct aid programs in part (a) of table 9-3, with summary statistics indicating the amount of aid and tuition paid in total shown in part (b).

The first two columns of the part (a) and the first column of part (b) are derived from the *predicted* values based on the initial sample, before any changes were made in the tuition and aid variables.

In general we find that, as expected, the number of persons choosing to work full time decreases substantially while the number choosing educational alternatives increases. In particular, the proportion of persons choosing to go to public two-year colleges increases from about 10 percent to between 25 and 30 percent. The only exception is under program 3, in which tuition is not raised and aid cannot exceed tuition. Under this plan, persons who are potential entrants to two-year schools find that they cannot gain much in the form of aid by going. These results partially result from the disparity between our coefficients on tuition and those on direct aid; one does not just offset the other. This suggests that in future work we should consider some constraints on our tuition and aid coefficients, or, when simulating a program like 3, it might be more appropriate to use only tuition coefficients because the program is essentially a tuition subsidization one. This is not the case, however, when aid is allowed to exceed tuition cost.

The magnitude of the total increases in aid required to support these programs are depicted in part (b) of table 9-3. Except under program 3, the resulting aggregate aid is five to six times initial aid. The amount paid in tuition, of course, varies greatly depending on whether or not public school tuition is increased. Programs 1 and 2 tend to transfer money to colleges through aid to students, whereas program 4 transfers considerable

Table 9-3
Direct Aid Programs

(a) Predicted Distributions, Programs 1, 2, 3, and 4

Alternative	Base Frequency	%	Program 1 Frequency	%	Program 2 Frequency	%	Program 3 Frequency	%	Program 4 Frequency	%
Four-year college, campus; public	305.79	6.79	336.98	7.49	328.51	7.30	314.54	6.99	346.06	7.69
Four-year college, campus; private	186.30	4.14	242.89	5.39	209.88	4.66	259.42	5.76	205.60	4.57
Four-year college, home; public	328.66	7.30	374.89	8.33	362.66	8.05	338.28	7.51	385.99	8.57
Four-year college, home; private	190.87	4.24	144.93	3.22	218.89	4.86	154.43	3.43	213.87	4.75
Two-year college; public	451.27	10.02	1,160.20	25.76	1,302.70	28.93	551.72	12.25	1,313.30	29.17
Two-year college; private	14.66	0.33	12.27	0.27	22.48	0.50	14.82	0.33	22.23	0.49
Vocational and trade schools	49.21	1.07	112.82	2.50	140.62	3.13	148.48	3.27	137.69	3.06
Work full-time	2,569.60	57.06	1,829.30	40.62	1,656.20	36.78	2,350.40	52.20	1,622.70	36.03
Military	96.90	2.15	69.92	1.55	63.73	1.42	89.21	1.98	62.49	1.39
Homeworker	118.92	2.64	83.65	1.86	74.76	1.66	108.20	2.40	73.21	1.63
Part-time school, part-time work	189.69	4.21	134.02	2.98	121.50	2.70	172.55	3.83	118.73	2.64
Total number of persons	4,503		4,503		4,503		4,503		4,503	

(b) Summary Statistics (Predicted; in Thousands of Dollars)

	Base	Program 1	Program 2	Program 3	Program 4
Direct aid	196.0	2,771.3	3,457.5	1,059.1	3,509.3
Percentage of total aid	30.1	94.1	87.8	91.7	87.9
Scholarship aid	216.7	84.8	225.6	53.3	226.3
Percentage of total aid	33.3	2.9	5.7	4.6	5.7
Work aid	77.1	21.4	80.8	8.2	81.5
Percentage of total aid	11.8	0.7	2.1	0.7	2.1
Loan aid	161.4	66.9	174.7	34.2	175.6
Percentage of total aid	24.8	2.3	4.4	3.0	4.4
Total aid	651.3	2,944.4	3,938.6	1,155.0	3,992.7
Total tuition paid	1,304.0	3,991.2	4,230.3	1,561.2	1,792.0
Tuition minus aid	652.7	1,046.7	291.7	406.2	-2,200.7

money to the student that is not subsequently paid out as tuition. Program 3 increases both aid and tuition only slightly relative to the other programs. It also has the least effect on the choices of individuals.

A more complete analysis would take account of the cost in aid of obtaining a particular distribution of school and work choices. It would also be more explicit about the number of wealthy versus poorer students who choose each alternative.

**Part IV
Vocational Education
Analysis**

10 Institutional Aid and the Creation of Two-Price Markets

Government financial support of postsecondary education, whether in the form of grants or loans to students or operating subsidies to institutions, stems from a common set of public beliefs: that a college education develops the cultural and social maturity of youth and thereby contributes to a better society; that research and development leads to scientific and technical advances and stimulates economic growth; that professional and technical training is necessary for the functioning of a modern economy; and that postsecondary education provides the opportunity for upward social mobility and expanding economic opportunities for minorities and ethnic groups in our society.

Cultural norms, parental pressures, and the opportunity for job advancement all encourage youth to pursue education beyong high school, but government financial aid provides an additional important incentive. Subsidies that lower the direct price of college or vocational school, through either low tuition at subsidized institutions or direct grants and loans to be applied against tuition or living expenses, are designed in general to encourage average students to continue their education beyond high school and, more specifically, to make education available to low-income groups who would otherwise have insufficient resources to pay for college.

Behind this standard rationale for government subsidy, however, lies an overlapping patchwork of state, local, and federal funding to students and to institutions. Partly by historical accident and partly to preserve state and local autonomy over their own institutions, federal and state governments have pursued quite different means of supporting postsecondary education. In 1862, the federal government began to assist land-grant universities through the Morrill Act and, by the mid-1960s, had invested heavily in construction at colleges and universities. However, the 1965 Higher Education Act and its 1972 Amendments focused the federal role on financial aid to students through grants and loans and, in particular, targeted on disadvantaged and low-income groups.

An exception to the federal policy of direct aid to students, rather than institutions, is in vocational education. The Vocational Education Act of 1963 expanded federal grants to states for vocational education programs in public high schools, vocational-technical institutes, and community colleges. This policy of institutional aid to vocational education has been maintained through the 1960s and the 1970s, despite the large-scale shift toward student aid embodied in the 1972 Higher Education Amendments.

This chapter is primarily the work of Valerie I. Nelson.

165

Financial support to postsecondary education by state and local governments has, in contrast, been primarily through institutional aid. The bulk of subsidy is through general-purpose grants to statewide systems of colleges, universities, and vocational schools. Following the stimulus to land-grant universities of the Morrill Act of 1862, states in the late 1800s began to develop public colleges and universities; tuition was set at low levels to encourage attendance. The greatest expansion in public systems, however, came in the 1960s and the early 1970s with the tremendous growth in community colleges and vocational-technical schools. Recently, state scholarship programs aiding the student directly have been established, but they still constitute a small fraction of total subsidies by states to higher education. Although an assortment of city colleges across the country are subsidized by local governments, these government units primarily provide direct aid to the network of vocational-technical institutes constructed after the 1963 Vocational Education Act.

In this criss-crossing of federal, state, and local aid to students and institutions, one sector of postsecondary education has been remarkably absent— private nonprofit and proprietary schools and colleges. Grants and loans to students can generally be used at both public and private institutions, but the broad base of state and local subsidies to institutions has been targeted exclusively on public systems. Private colleges and universities such as Harvard, Stanford, or Amherst and proprietary vocational schools such as Katherine Gibbs ordinarily preceded the public school system in most areas of the country. However, when states began to develop their own networks of institutions, they excluded such private institutions from subsidy. In many cases, public support of private religious colleges was prohibited by state constitutions, but constitutional amendments or direct contracting for services (which would have been allowed) were never seriously considered by state education officials.

The inevitable result of this subsidy patchwork has been the creation of "two-price" systems of postsecondary education: on the one hand, heavily subsidized public systems of colleges, universities and vocational-technical institutes with no or low direct tuition to the student; on the other hand, an array of private institutions with tuition charges supplemented only by whatever private endowment or government research and development funds could be found from outside sources. The resulting differences in tuition between public and private institutions are substantial: in 1974–75, public colleges and universities charged an average of only $503 per year in tuition and fees, while private schools averaged $2,290. Among vocational programs there was a similar tuition differential: $299 for an average public program in 1973–74 and $1,387 for a proprietary or nonprofit private school.

Several general comments can be made about this "two-price" system of higher education and vocational education. First, there is no clear and consistent rationale for subsidizing public but not private schools. The social and economic benefits of higher education that have been used to justify public support are associated just as much with students attending private schools and colleges. In the early years of government support, it may have been argued that the low tuition at public schools was targeted at low- and moderate-income students, while private institutions continued to serve the affluent. In recent years, however, experience has shown minimal differentiation in student clienteles; several studies suggest that the distribution of students by SES scales in public and proprietary vocational schools is roughly comparable and only slightly higher in private than in public colleges.

Second, there have been a variety of proposals at the federal and state levels to extend institutional aid in some form to nonprofit and proprietary institutions. The 1968 Amendments to the Vocational Education Act, in fact, encourage states to contract with proprietary vocational schools for the provision of vocational training "where such private institutions can make a significant contribution to attaining the objectives of the State plan, and can provide substantially equivalent training at a lesser cost, or can provide equipment or services not available in public institutions." Such contracts are rarely made, however. In 1972, the American Council on Education and other higher education organizations proposed federal institutional aid to colleges and universities, including both public and private institutions. States such as Massachusetts and New York have considered direct per-pupil subsidies for in-state students in private colleges. Finally, recent proposals to raise the level of tuition and fees at public colleges in such states as New Jersey and Maryland would reduce these substantial price differentials between public and private institutions.

Third, however, there has been no general framework of analysis among researchers or policymakers about the meaning and implications of a "two-price" system in higher education or about the predicted outcomes of policies designed to narrow or perpetuate this price differential. Several broad generalizations, based on cursory examinations of trends and casual observances of differences in programs among schools, have often been made by educators. Clearly, low relative tuition gave public institutions a competitive advantage over private institutions in recent expansion in enrollments. As a result, an increasing share of students have entered the public sector; in 1958, 60 percent of students were in public colleges, whereas this figure had increased to 79 percent by 1974. Competition from low-priced public vocational programs appears to have actually cut student enrollment in proprietary schools in half between 1963 and 1972–73. It is clear that many private institutions continue to attract large numbers of students despite their higher tuition, possibly because the quality of their programs may be higher than those offered in public schools. In 1970, for example, less than half of graduate degrees were from private institutions, but 71 percent of the faculty in the five strongest departments ranked by quality in each field are in the private institutions.[1] Private colleges have also often been the most innovative in introducing new courses and open learning programs.[2]

However, no systematic analysis of the dynamics of a two-price system or its implications for the behavior of students and institutions has yet been made. The National Center for Postsecondary Education (NCFPE) and other research groups have simulated the effect of various tuition and financial aid schemes on the distribution of student enrollments among institutions, but none of these empirical models of the higher education system have incorporated institutional behavior as an important factor.[3] Elasticities of demand at varying tuition levels are carefully estimated for students, but the response of institutions to the structure of prices in the system is not rigorously tested within these models.

This gap in systematic analysis of postsecondary education institutions can be explained, in part, by a more general lack of theoretical models in the political science and economics literature. Some economists have characterized institutions by their public, nonprofit, or profitmaking status and suggested general models of institutional behavior. Nonprofit and public institutions, it is argued, will invest more heavily in facilities and equipment than will profitmaking institutions, for example.[4] But such generalizations have not been tested against data on colleges, nor have they been related to the more general questions of the implications of a tuition differential or the interrelated responses of student enrollment to tuition changes.

The purpose of this section of the report is to describe, in brief, the simple dynamics of two-price markets and to test one specific element in the paradigm against the empirical data on vocational education choices. This discussion is preliminary and should be seen in the context of the inadequacy of past research on the tuition differential. The empirical tests of the paradigm in vocational education are imperfect because of the nature of the NLS sample, but it is anticipated that these sample problems will be overcome in future analysis. In addition, a similar analysis of the two-price system for colleges and universities is expected.

The Dynamics of Two-Price Markets

Two-price systems of public and private institutions are perhaps most obvious and certainly most publicly debated in the case of higher education, where the substantial tuition differential is of concern to many private educators. But the mix of low-price public and high-price private institutions is typical of a wide range of other education and social service areas as well, including vocational education, day care, mental health and health care, employment counseling, and legal aid. Indeed the thrust of one piece of Great Society legislation after another in the mid-1960s was to channel federal funds to public and nonprofit agencies across the country. An implicit part of the federal bargain with such agencies was a low price or fee for services to the consumer, a price both substantially below the actual cost of providing the service and below the price charged by the existing private institutions.

The rationale for federal support was simple and straightforward—subsidies would provide incentives for public consumption and encourage institutions to improve their service offerings. But, as in the case of public support of higher education beginning over 100 years ago, certain existing profitmaking and non-profit agencies were systematically excluded from receiving the federal subsidy. The inevitable result was the creation of a series of two-price systems in the social service areas of the economy.

The objectives of federal support were simple enough but the implementation of most Great Society legislation has been difficult and troublesome. In recent years, many explanations have been offered for the "failure" of these initiatives—including the now obvious fact that their stated goal of quickly alleviating poverty were overly optimistic. But out of the critiques of specific service areas emerge another common set of themes: the drain on the federal budget far exceeds what was expected; programs often service white middle-class groups and do not reach many of the poor; and public agencies at times may be characterized by waste, low quality, or offerings unresponsive to consumer preference. These critiques mirror similar questions about colleges and universities: the lack of explicit targeting on low-income students and the higher quality of private than public institutions.

Conditions obviously vary from one social service sector to another, but it can be argued that such problems arise in part from the dynamics of the two-price system. Several conceptually simple but profound consequences may follow from the introduction of a publicly subsidized option into a social service area that has in the past been dominated by private institutions. Much depends on the specific policies and actions taken by consumers, federal bureaucrats, and the individual local agencies receiving the subsidy. In the abstract, each of these actors may respond in the manner envisioned when the authorizing legislation was passed; however, the price differential in a two-price system does, in several important aspects, allow public agencies to subvert the intent of Congress and act against the public interest.

The potential difficulties are readily apparent if two-price systems are thought of as marketplaces for consumer purchases. Assume, for simplicity, that there is an existing private market of consumers and producers purchasing and selling one standard service at one common price. Next, introduce a subset of new institutions offering the identical service at a substantially lower market price. If consumers have correct information, it is quite predictable that demand for the new offering will skyrocket. Not only will new consumers be attracted for the first time but in addition, all those who previously paid the higher price will perceive a windfall advantage. Indeed, no cost-conscious consumer would buy from the private, unsubsidized producer unless he were forced to. The first conclusion is that there will be a substantial shift in demand from the unsubsidized to the subsidized option.

Second, assume a limit on the level of federal subsidy and the resulting level of services that can be provided by the new public agency. By necessity, the agency must ration its service among all those who demand it at the new low price. Ideally, the public agency, which is responsive to the intent of Great Society legislation, will target its services first and foremost on disadvantaged consumers who probably were not previously in the market at all, because the price was too high. But the agency, facing skyrocketing demands for its services, has the added option of rationing to the middle class, which is also attracted to the low price. The second conclusion is that rationing will be needed, and that the new agency may choose to ration to middle-class, rather than disadvantaged, consumers.

To the extent that the public agency does admit middle-class consumers and exclude disadvantaged consumers, it will draw business away from existing private institutions. Each consumer served by the new agency, who previously was willing to purchase at a higher price, is now no longer in the private marketplace. Private institutions will therefore see their clientele being whittled away, and ultimately they may be forced to go out of business completely. The third conclusion is that expansion of the public offering at a low price may simply displace private purchases, with minimal addition to total consumption.

These three conclusions are fairly obvious: with identical products, the consumer will always choose the one with a lower price. Thus, the introduction of a publicly subsidized option and the creation of two-price markets will lead to excess demand for the subsidized offering, the necessity for rationing and the potential for it to be misapplied, and finally the possible displacement of the private market by adverse competition from the new agency.

A fourth possible consequence of two-price market dynamics is conceptually more complex than the first three. Up to this point, the assumption has been made that the service was identical, except for its price, for the consumers in the subsidized and unsubsidized agencies. However, public agencies may discover that they can alter the quality, type, location, and other characteristics of their service and still have sufficient demand to justify operating at full capacity. More and more consumers may decide voluntarily to return to the private market as the public option is altered, but as long as there is still excess demand the public agency will not be affected.

Ultimately, however, excess demand for the public option can be reduced to zero by sufficient differentiation of offerings between the public and private agencies. This equilibrium point will be characterized by a *price-value tradeoff* in the marginal consumer's perception of the public and private options. On the one hand, the public agency offers a low price but also a low value option, while the private agency charges a higher price but also offers a higher value option. Some consumers will strongly prefer one option over the other, but a market equilibrium is established through that middle range of consumers who are just indifferent between the two and who perceive a tradeoff between price and value.

A price-value tradeoff may arise in three distinct respects. First, the quality of the service measured along one or several clear-cut dimensions may be lower in the public agency; this occurs if public bureaucrats become lax and inefficient in their production of the services. Second, public agencies may offer services with certain characteristics which are in the public interest, but for which the students are not willing to pay—for example, the provision of emergency rooms in community hospitals or liberal arts courses in vocational schools. Third, a price-value tradeoff may arise when professionals orient programs around their own needs for professional recognition or according to somewhat biased views about what the consumer needs.

Several points should be stressed about the nature of this price-value trade-off. If the two-price market is in equilibrium and there is no excess demand for the public service, then the marginal consumer does perceive higher value in the private than in the public agency. From this fact, it follows that such consumers, if given the federal subsidy directly, would switch to private agencies for the higher value service. Finally, unless there are compensating social benefits from the public but not the private service, the federal government is subsidizing agencies unnecessarily. From the point of view of the marginal consumer, the new public agency offers a package no more attractive than that of the existing public market.

The Case of Vocational Education

Vocational education is one social service area where a two-price market has clearly been created and is being perpetuated by institutional subsidies from the federal government. Federal legislation in the 1960s provided a strong identifiable stimulus for constructing a state-local network of vocational-technical institutes and programs in community colleges. But, as in other service areas, the expansion of programs took place without recognition of, cooperation with, or subsidy of the extensive array of proprietary vocational schools in the private sector. Not surprisingly, a two-price market has emerged, with predictable problems of excess demand, inequities of access, and nonresponsiveness of programs not far behind.

This two-price system in vocational education has been analyzed in detail by Nelson[5]; the outlines of this work are presented in the remainder of this chapter, including some discussion of the intent of federal legislation, the high school graduate's decision to enroll, the choice of institution, and the predictable impact of federal subsidies (for example, rationing and the resulting inequities in access, displacement versus expansion, a price-value tradeoff and the tradeoff between tuition and length of program). Further analysis of this price-value tradeoff using the NLS data is described in chapter 11.

Federal Legislation in Vocational Education: The Intent

Federal involvement in vocational education can be traced back to 1917 with passage of the Smith-Hughes Act authorizing federal subsidies to the states for vocational programs in public high schools. However, the most significant federal initiative has been the Vocational Education Act of 1963 and its 1968 Amendments, which increased subsidies from $52 million in 1962 to $468 million in 1974. State and local governments contribute an additional $2,965 million to support vocational programs in local public high schools, area vocational-technical institutes, and community colleges.

Vocational education was never a major component in the Great Society or War on Poverty; neither was it a major federal education program. In 1967 only $256 million was appropriated by the federal government for vocational education, compared to $4.5 billion for higher education, $3.2 billion for elementary and secondary general education, and $1.8 billion for remedial work and training programs sponsored under the Manpower Development and Training Act and other labor legislation. Nevertheless, it shared with other Great Society initiatives the hopes of alleviating unemployment and poverty through the expansion of a social service network. Both the 1963 and 1968 legislation were motivated by widespread public support and expert advice on vocational education as a means to deal with automation and structural shifts in the economy and with high unemployment rates of youths in the ghettos. The clear mandate of Congress was to expand vocational education opportunities beyond what were available at the time, in particular to extend access to disadvantaged groups and previously neglected minorities.

The stated purpose of the Vocational Education Act of 1963 begins: "to strengthen and improve the quality of vocational education and to expand the vocational education opportunities in the Nation." Federal grants to states were authorized:

to assist them to maintain, extend, and improve existing programs to vocational education, to develop new programs of vocational education. . . so that persons of all ages in all communities of the State . . . will have ready access to vocational training or retraining which is of high quality, which is realistic in the light of actual or anticipated opportunities for gainful employment, and which is suited to their needs, interests, and ability to benefit from such training.

This short introductory passage outlines the basic elements of the Great Society social services strategy as applied to vocational education. The objectives are to improve and to broaden the base of services, particularly to groups in the population not adequately served by existing programs. Indeed, the act promises universal access to "persons of all ages in all communities of the State." The strategy to achieve these objectives is financial assistance to state departments of education. Typically, the federal government will not provide programs directly, but will encourage direct public provision through the public schools. The grants will provide the resources for and require schools to "strengthen" their programs—that is, to serve their communities in ways that in the past had been either contrary to the schools' inclinations or perceptions of need, or beyond local resources and capabilities.

There was particular reason for concern over the need to stimulate and improve vocational education programs. In 1962, a Panel of Consultants on Vocational Education appointed by President John F. Kennedy had reviewed programs in the public schools and concluded that they were failing to provide up-to-date subjects, excluding the disadvantaged, and offering low-quality programs. In particular, 53 percent of enrollments were in home economics courses that did not lead to employment, classes were often held in the basements of schools with obsolete equipment, and programs were seriously underfunded by local school districts.

The VEA of 1963 and the 1968 Amendments, therefore, stressed that programs should be expanded to include the disadvantaged, established a criterion for funding which encouraged programs leading to "gainful" employment, placed additional requirements on states and local education agencies (LEA's) to conform to federal objectives, and provided for research and development grants to develop innovative programs of vocational education.

Two particular aspects of the legislation relate directly to postsecondary education opportunities and the experiences of high school graduates in the NLS. In 1962, only 14,000 students were enrolled in public vocational programs at the postsecondary level. At that time there were few community colleges; most of these catered to liberal arts students who would eventually transfer into four-year colleges.

The VEA of 1963, however, specifically set aside funds for both construction of area vocational-technical institutes and for development of postsecondary level programs. Vocational-technical institutes, which would enroll students from an entire city or from several neighboring school districts, had begun to develop within states without explicit federal encouragement and, in many cases, were offering high quality vocational education with up-to-date equipment. In particular, they aggregated the resources of several small rural schools without sufficient means to purchase their own equipment and hire trained teachers. Some support for area vocational technical schools had already been instituted in the National Defense Education Act of 1958, but, in the Vocational Education Act of 1963, the federal stimulus of area school was increased through the subsidization of construction expenses.

The 1963 act also required states to spend a minimum of 33 percent of federal funds on vocational-technical programs that would enroll both secondary and postsecondary students and/or on programs for postsecondary and adult students. In 1968, a new provision required that 25 percent of federal funds be spent on "persons who have completed or left high school and who are available for study in preparation for entering the labor market." These funds could be distributed to public community colleges as well as to area vocational-technical institutes.

The impact on programs and enrollments of these new legislative provisions was substantial. Between 1965, when funds were authorized, and 1968, 898 construction and remodeling projects had been undertaken. While in 1963 there were only 405 regional vocational/technical institutes, by 1969 there were 1,303. This construction was a direct result of the commitment of 42.6 percent of the 1965 federal funds to construction, 35.8 percent in 1966 and 28.6 percent in 1967. In addition, the number of students enrolled in postsecondary vocational education rose dramatically, from 144,000 in 1963 to 1,573,000 in 1974 (see table 10-1).

It is also clear that public school programs have improved in quality since 1963. Vocational education in general is no longer relegated to the basement or reserved for the low achievers in the class. In particular, many of the new vocational-technical institutes and community colleges offer up-to-date training on expensive, new equipment, and their graduates do well in the labor market.

However, accompanying this expansion in programs and the elevation in their status, several old as well as new and unforeseen problems for vocational education have developed. First, despite repeated exhortation and substantial increases in funding by the federal government, most states have failed to provide quality vocational education to minority and center-city areas; resources are instead focused primarily on the middle-class suburbs. Second, public sector enrollments have increased since 1963, but to a large extent at the expense of the private sector; proprietary school enrollments have been cut

Table 10-1
Enrollments and Expenditures, 1963-74

	Total Enrollments	Postsecondary Enrollments	Expenditures[a]	
			Total	Federal
1963	4,217,000	144,000	308	55
1964	4,566,000	171,000	332	55
1965	5,431,000	207,000	604	157
1966	6,070,000	442,000	799	233
1967	7,047,000	500,000	1,004	260
1968	7,534,000	593,000	1,192	262
1969	7,979,000	706,000	1,368	254
1970	8,794,000	1,013,000	1,841	300
1971	10,495,000	1,141,000	2,347	396
1972	11,602,000	1,304,000	2,660	466
1973	12,072,000	1,350,000	3,033	482
1974	13,535,639	1,572,779	3,433	468

[a]In millions of dollars.

approximately in half since 1963. Third, while most vocational education classes are no longer held either literally or figuratively in the basement, public schools do appear to be offering programs that are excessively rigid and academic in orientation. Finally, and quite unexpectedly, the budget allocation of resources to vocational education has become an issue of some controversy. The offering of improved courses that are attractive to large numbers of middle-class students has generated resentments among those excluded by the systems and has amplified pressures for additional funding of new programs.

The ideal school district, from the perspective of the federal government, would implement the legislative intent of expanding opportunities to new groups of students in the community. It would actively seek out and select from its potential waiting lists of students those who would not otherwise enter training. Its low price would be used to attract not only those unwilling to pay the private market price, but those disadvantaged low-income groups who could not otherwise afford it. It would also attempt to fulfill the legislative intent with high-quality innovative programs that would be, in the words of the legislation, "realistic in the light of actual or anticipated opportunities for gainful employment, and . . . suited to their [students'] needs, interests, and ability to benefit from such training."

However, there are potential pitfalls in this simple story. The new or expanded public institution has both the discretion and the local political and educational incentives to ration access in such a manner that it accepts primarily those in the middle class who probably would otherwise have gone into the private sector and it excludes potential new entrants and the disadvantaged. In the process, it can wipe out substantial sections of the private market with no net increase in training among youth. Finally, it can survive as an institution if its seats are filled to capacity; but, within that constraint, it can pursue its own needs, not the student's, and create a price-value trade-off in the market for students that results in a low price accompanied by a low market value for public programs. Each of these steps, of course, subverts the intent of the VEA of 1963.

Notes

1. Richard M. Cyert, "The Market Approach to Higher Education," paper presented at American Council on Education 57th Annual Meeting. San Diego, California, Oct. 10, 1974.

2. George J. Nolfi and Valerie I. Nelson, *Strengthening the Alternative Postsecondary Education System: Continuing and Part-Time Study in Massachusetts*, statewide master plan for adult, continuing and nontraditional postsecondary education (vol. I, Summary Report and Recommendations; vol. II, Technical Report, 1973). See also George J. Nolfi, Valerie I. Nelson, Betty Karro,

and Patrick Dolan, *A Study of the Potential and Capacity for Innovation in American Higher Education and of Federal Policy Possibilities* (Cambridge, Mass: UCI, 1971), background studies prepared for "Newman II" Task Force of the Dept. of Health, Education and Welfare, for the "Second Newman Report."

3. National Commission on the Financing of Postsecondary Education, *Financing Postsecondary Education in the United States* (Washington, D.C., December 1973).

4. See for example, J. Newhouse, "Toward a Theory of Non-Profit Institutions: An Economic Model of a Hospital," *American Economic Review* (March 1970); and Martin Feldstein, "Hospital Cost Inflation: A Study of Non-Profit Price Dynamics," *Harvard Institute of Economic Research*, Discussion Paper no. 139 (October 1970).

5. Valerie I. Nelson, "Public Provision and Private Markets: Vocational Education and the Great Society," Ph.D. Dissertation, Economics Department, Yale University, 1977.

11

Vocational Education Choice Model

This chapter presents and analyzes some estimates of the determinants of vocational education choices; conditional logit estimation was the empirical tool. These results are important as a test of the price-value tradeoff, one aspect of the two-price market described in chapter 10. Numerous other questions could and eventually will be asked about vocational students and schools, such as: Who goes? What role does high school track or family background play in the decision to enroll? Who expects to go, but then does not? And finally, what function do training institutions such as the military or unions have in vocational education? These questions, while important, are not addressed in this section of the report. Instead, this work has focused on developing and testing a market model of public and private education, and all empirical estimation has been directed to that end.

In Chapter 10, a number of hypotheses were made about the dynamics of two-price markets and sketchy empirical data was presented for the case of vocational education. The NLS does not provide the data necessary for testing the first three hypotheses about the two-price market: (1) that when a low-price public option is introduced to an existing private market, there will be excess demand for the new service; (2) that when agencies ration access to their programs, they may not target on the disadvantaged; and (3) that some fraction of any expansion in the public provision of services may constitute a displacement of private agencies.

However, the NLS does provide the data for a partial test of the hypothesis that a price-value tradeoff can develop in a two-price market such as vocational education. The term "price-value tradeoff" implies an equilibrium has been reached in which the marginal consumer perceives high price, high value in the private option and low price, low value in the public option, and is just indifferent between the two. The tradeoff develops when public institutions differentiate the characteristics of their offering from that of private institutions in such a manner as to reduce the direct value of the service to the consumer. In doing so, the professionals and bureaucrats designing the programs may be serving the public interest, their own interests, or their own beliefs about the appropriate design of program. As described in Nelson,[1] researchers and

---

This chapter is primarily the work of Valerie I. Nelson and Winship C. Fuller (also involving the adaptation and respecification of the choice model developed in Chapter 8).

policymakers disagree about the social implications of the conflict between students and educators.

Questions of social benefits aside, the survey research reviewed in Nelson does suggest that students balance such considerations as cost, length of program, location, and style of instruction in making school choices. It appears that the price-value tradeoff in vocational education is manifested in the following form: low tuition cost in the public sector is offset by longer programs and more academic, less flexible instruction. Many students are willing to pay the higher tution charged at proprietary schools because they finish sooner and learn through more practical methods of instruction.

The NLS data makes possible a more rigorous test of this price-value tradeoff in vocational education because it reveals the actual behavior of students, not just their attitudes as expressed in responses to questionnaires. All high school graduates in 1972 faced a slightly different array of vocational education choices in their local areas; schools varied by tuition, length of program, subject, and location within the public and proprietary sectors. When the NLS sample of students is supplemented by NCES data detailing the actual range of school choices for each student, it is possible to estimate the enrollment response to each of these institutional characteristics. When compared across public and private schools, these coefficients provide a measure of the price-value tradeoff in the overall two-price system.

The High School Graduate's Decision to Enroll in
Vocational Education

The high school graduate who pursues postsecondary vocational education is primarily interested in attaining job skills, rather than in such avocational pursuits as auto mechanics or cooking. As such, the decision to enroll is a very serious step involving substantial commitments of time and money in the short run. However, the student also expects that the investment will pay off in higher wage, salary, and other job benefits over a lifetime. As with any typical investment, there are, of course, significant uncertainties and, therefore, risks involved. For example, jobs may not materialize in particular fields, or the student may be ill-suited to a particular training program or type of work. These short-term costs, long-term benefits, and uncertainties make vocational education a very important step in the student's career plans.

First, the direct and indirect costs of vocational programs beyond high school are substantial. Tuition and fees for a typical program in 1974 averaged $1,387 in proprietary schools and $299 in public vocational-technical institutes. Equally or more important is the loss of foregone income while the student is in school and out of the labor market. He or she may not be able to work full time for a few months or up to two or more years; part-time study may be even longer. A 1973 sample of students showed that average foregone income losses ranged from $1,193 to $6,422, depending on the program. Union apprentices and employer trainees do not pay direct tuition but sustain the indirect costs of lower earning levels during the training period.

Second, the decision to pursue a particular program of vocational education is closely tied to, and tends to lock the student into, specific long-term career goals. The Department of Labor defines several hundred distinct craft, technical, and office occupations, each requiring a specific set of skills at less than the collegel B.A. level. Vocational education programs usually focus on one or a narrow range of these jobs beyond graduation, and these skills are not easily transferable across the labor market. For example, it a student goes to a specialized barber school or into a nursing program, there is a minimal comparability of skills between the two occupations. If jobs are not available in such specialized fields, then the graduate usually is forced to drop back down the occupational ladder (for example, from executive secretary to clerk-typist), rather than being able to cross over into other jobs requiring comparably high but quite different skills.

However, if graduates do succeed in finding jobs in their field of training, they reap significant wage and other benefits. The advantages of skilled over unskilled jobs are many: higher annual earnings, greater employment stability and opportunities for promotion, better working conditions, and greater job satisfaction. Over the long term, these higher earnings and other benefits will offset the short-term costs of training. The average rate of return for a year of vocational education in proprietary schools has been estimated to be about 10 percent.[2]

The choice of a particular program of vocational education will depend, in part, on the student's assessment of the difference in short-term training costs and expected long-term wage benefits across a wide range of occupations. Some students do have strong preferences from the start about one career or another, regardless of monetary payoffs or rate of return. A girl may have dreamed of becoming a nurse for years, for example, and virtually ignores all other options. But other students are less committed to particular jobs and look closely at varying prospects for wages and job security associated with a whole set of vocational education options and jobs. These students will make their plans in response to clear signals from the labor market about the most favorable opportunities, zeroing in on those occupations where wages appear to be rising and abandoning those where they are falling. By and large, it is those students who do not have a strong commitment to the liberal arts experience who are dropping out of college in response to the financially more attractive options in vocational education and the resulting skilled jobs in the economy.

The Choice of Institution

Though the student's eye is primarily on labor options, he or she also must decide among a tremendous range of institutions within the vocational education sector. For each specific career objective, there are usually a variety of alternative sources of training: public or proprietary schools, community colleges, union apprenticeships, the military, correspondence schools, government manpower training programs, community organizations, and employer training programs. Even within the same training field, programs vary substantially across these major institutional types by cost, teaching method, schedule of courses, types of faculty, location, and other characteristics. By comparison, the college student faces quite limited variation in the programs offered by two- and four-year public and private colleges.

Students, therefore, are confronted by a matrix of institutional and occupational choices when they consider vocational education. Each occupation has several sources of training, and each type of training institution has a myriad of occupational choices. For example, the student may go to a private school or a union program to become an electrician, a plumber, or a truck driver. Even in unionized job areas, such as the construction and building trades, proprietary schools and the military provide substantial training. Similarly, most airplane mechanics are trained in the military, but proprietary schools and employer training programs also play a role.

Students learn about these options through parents and friends, guidance counselors, information guides, employers, television and newspaper ads, and many years of personal observations about jobs and their relative income and status. Manuals, such as *The Occupational Outlook Handbook* published by the Department of Labor, catalogue jobs and the type of work involved, skills required, institutional sources of training, and the outlook for employment in future years. Such guides as *Lovejoy's Career and Vocational School Guide*, available in bookstores, and numerous local directories also provide information on jobs and training.

From an investment standpoint, students will assess these options for the short-term costs and long-term benefits. The primary economic factors that vary among institutions offering similar subject fields are tuition charges, length of program (which determines foregone income), and wage rates following graduation. But students also express individual tastes and preferences for teaching methods, student clientele, scheduling, credentials, geographic location, and other program characteristics.

The decision to enroll in vocational education turns out to be complicated, involving such factors as the costs and benefits of training, wages and nonmonetary aspects of jobs, tuition charges and teaching styles of institutions, and the individual's unique tastes and preferences. The important point from the perspective of the following analysis is that students are responsive to changes among these basic conditions over time. Any change in relative wage rates among occupations or in tuition charges or other factors among institutions will disrupt the established flow of students. Enrollments will increase for higher-paid occupations and for lower-cost training alternatives and vice versa. The responsiveness of students to these wage and tuition changes determines the size of these shifts in enrollments from year to year.

Ideally, a wide range of institutional characteristics should be used to describe the choices confronted by each student when considering vocational education. The literature suggests that students will examine such characteristics as tuition, financial aid, length of program, range of subjects and credentials offered, distance, school reputation for labor market success of graduates, scheduling of classes, size of school, type of student enrolled, extent of placement and other services offered, style of instruction, and balance of liberal arts versus skill training.

However, the data actually available on the thousands of proprietary and public vocational schools across the country are limited. Though extensive information has been collected on colleges and universities by the American Council on Education and other agencies, the small proprietary vocational schools have been largely ignored by researchers and policymakers. In 1974, however, the National Center for Education Statistics conducted a survey of proprietary and public vocational schools, which provides information on tuition and fees, length of program, and subject field of each program offered by the school. Distance to the nearest vocational school has in addition been calculated using information from the 1973 Directory of Postsecondary Occupation.

Therefore, using statewide averages of schools as calculated from the NCES data, the student's vocational education choices can be characterized by cost, length of program, subject, and distances. The following sections of this chapter describe the specification of the model, data sources, parameter estimates, and their implications. Problems encountered in the estimation of this choice model and the results of some simulated policy changes are also described.

The structure of the choice model used is similar in most important respects to the basic demand model presented in chapter 8. Slight modifications in the sample drawn from the NLS tape, in the variables derived, and in the specification of choices were made where appropriate to focus in detail on the vocational education sector. In addition, the NCES data tape on proprietary and public vocational schools was discovered late in the project and several improvements in the demand model proposed by staff could be implemented only in this later segment of the overall project effort.

Specification of Choices in Vocational Education

As described earlier, the high school graduate faces a multiplicity of vocational education choices, both in terms of subject fields and prospective jobs and in terms of intitutional sources of training. The primary considerations in selecting vocational education appear to be the student's aspirations and interests for a specific type of job following graduation; a secondary consideration is the institutional source of training. Most occupations allow several options for training, including military, employer, union, and government manpower training, as well as formal education in vocational schools.

Eventually, we hope to specify the full range of choices actually confronted by each student in an expanded choice model. This model would entail assembling and incorporating additional data on military, union, employer, and manpower training programs. However, the model estimated here only specifies those vocational education choices which are within formal educational institutions.

Each student is generally assumed to have, for each major subject field, three alternatives for formal vocational schooling: the vocational track in the public community college; the local public voc-tech institute; and a number of proprietary vocational schools specializing in distinct occupational areas. These three types of schools vary systematically in such critical attributes as length of program, tuition, credential offered, distance, scheduling, school reputation, style of instruction, and the other characteristics. When students choose one of these three alternatives, they are essentially expressing their preference for one particular combination of attributes over another; for example, a 10-month program without a formal credential may be preferred over a two-year program with an Associate's degree. These community college programs, voc-tech, institutes and proprietary schools have several typical attributes.

Community colleges initially focused on liberal arts transfer students, but the recent federal subsidies and growing career orientation of students has led to greatly expanded offerings in vocational programs at community colleges. Although students may now major in a vocational curriculum, they are generally required to attend the full two-year program and to supplement their vocational courses with substantial liberal arts requirements. Community colleges are similar to four-year colleges in that they are generally part of statewide networks with extensive campuses, an academic classroom approach to teaching, and the style and flavor of an academic institution.

To some students who have not liked high school in the past, this academic orientation may be a deterrent to enrollment in a community college. In addition, the vocational program normally requires the full two-year workload of courses and therefore a substantial financial loss in terms of foregone income. There are, however, some distinct advantages associated only with the community college: the associate's degree, the option while in school to transfer into liberal arts, and the option of going on to college after graduation.

Vocational-technical institutes, which were developed primarily in the 1960s in response to federal construction and operating subsidies, are clearly organized around the vocational preparation of students. Nevertheless, they share certain features with community colleges: an academic classroom orientation in teaching style, liberal arts requirements to supplement vocational courses, and fairly rigid scheduling of classes in the 9-hour, 5-day, and 9-month format of high schools.

Voc-techs differ from community colleges, however, in two important respects: length of program and credential. Programs are generally shorter than the two years required for the community college, and thus, foregone income loss is reduced. However, voc-techs are not generally accredited to grant degrees and course credit is not usually transferable into four-year college programs. Students, therefore, have less flexibility to alter their plans and pursue liberal arts or to continue their education in college. They also forego the prestige of the associate's degree.

Proprietary and independent nonprofit schools offer a quite distinct alternative to either the public community college or the voc-tech institute. They typically are small (50 to 500 students), profit-oriented organizations specializing in training for one particular skill. Courses are generally organized in short, intensive modules, and the format is more practical than academic in orientation. Classes are run at various hours to be convenient to the working person, and, at graduation, vocational proprietary schools usually award certificates or diplomas. Few grant degrees, although many offer A.A.-equivalent programs without the general education component, and the competencies gained by students are comparable.

The advantages to students from attending a proprietary school are the short time required for attendance, the flexiblity in scheduling, the practical teaching style, and the strong job orientation of the program. On the other hand, proprietary schools are accredited to grant only certificates or diplomas, and once students enter a program they are restricted to the particular occupational fields in which the school specializes.

The Choice Model and the Price-Value Tradeoff

Although the community college, the voc-tech institute, and the proprietary school generally share a typical set of attributes, schools do vary from one city or state to another. For example, tuition is universally higher in proprietary schools than in voc-techs or community colleges, but the precise differential between public and private institutions varies from state to state. Similarly, the academic orientation of teaching will tend to be stronger in community colleges than in proprietary schools, but there may be some instances when the reverse holds. It is this variation in attributes among the three alternatives, from one local area to another, which makes possible empirical estimation of factors affecting a student's decision.

The demand model described in chapters 8 and 9 assumes that the probability of choosing any alternative varies with both the attributes of each alternative and with the characteristics of the student. The parameters in the choice model approximate the direction and size of response of student enrollments to changes in these attributes of the schools.

The hypothesis that a price-value tradeoff can develop in vocational education is tested through estimating the choice model in the following way.

Tuition, one important attribute of vocational schools, is, by virtue of federal, state, and local subsidies, substantially lower in community colleges and voc-techs than in proprietary schools. There must, therefore, be some compensating characteristics of proprietary schools that attract students despite their higher price. If a local vocational education marketplace is in equilibrium (without rationing), then the marginal student must perceive a higher value of nonprice characteristics in the proprietary school than in either public school alternative.

The next step in testing the price-value tradeoff comes by comparison of parameter estimates with the actual observed characteristics of public or private schools. These parameter estimates provide some measure of the importance students assign to various attributes in their selection of a school. If public and private schools are found to vary systematically in offsetting directions, then a price-value tradeoff does exist. For example, public schools charge substantially lower tuition than private schools, but they may also score lower on such other attributes as length of program that are revealed to be important to students. Comparing tuition and program length among the three types of schools across the country will indicate whether such a tradeoff actually exists.

The limitations on data prevent a full investigation of the price-value trade-off in vocational education; critical attributes such as teaching style or flexibility of scheduling are simply not available for each individual school. The estimation therefore focuses on those characteristics for which data are available, albeit in imperfect form—that is, tuition, length of program, and distance. Estimation of a choice model with alternatives that vary according to these characteristics will, at a minimum, illuminate the importance of these factors in students' choices and suggest the presence of a price-value tradeoff or the lack of it among public and private options.

Model Specification and Alternatives

Alternatives

The structure of the choice model used here is similar to that developed for the basic demand model, except in the range of vocational education choices specified. Each individual is assumed to have the same four-year college, two-year community college academic program, work, military, homemaking, and part-time school and part-time work, and work alternatives available. In addition, each student has twenty-four vocational education options broken down among the three institutional categories of community college vocational program, voc-tech institute, and proprietary school and among the eight occupational-subject categories of agribusiness, marketing and distribution, health, nursing, home economics, business and office, technical, and trade and industrial.

The alternatives and the distribution of students among them within this sample are shown in table 11-1.

Variables

The variables assumed to influence choices are similar, and in many cases identical, to those specified for the basic demand model in chapter 8. They include academic aptitude, distance, length of program, and tuition per month for vocational programs. In addition, alternative-specific dummy variables are used for the choice of both part-time work and part-time school and for the combined vocational subject categories of (1) health and nursing, (2) business, office, marketing, and distribution, (3) technical and agribusiness, and (4) trade and industrial.

Table 11-1
Distribution of Students Among Choice Categories

Choice Category	Number of students
Vocational education (24 possible categories)	343
3 Institutional types:	
Proprietary schools	97
Public vocational schools	157
Community colleges—vocational	89
8 Subject categories	
Agribusiness	2
Marketing, distribution	28
Health	38
Nursing	24
Home economics	39
Business, office	81
Technical	29
Trade, industrial	110
Academic community college	232
Two-year private college	36
Work full time	1,335
Four-year college	565
Military	73
Homemaker	54
Both work and school part time	33

Note: The sample included 2671 high school graduates of 1972 (male and female, with 74,906 choices being available among them.

Data on Schools

Data on tuition and distance, college options, and on community college vocational programs across the country were identical to that used for the basic demand model; the basic source was the ACE. As in the earlier model, all students have the option of the *nearest* community college, and we assume that all eight vocational subject categories are offered. Length of program is postulated as 20 months and tuition per month is calculated from tuition and fees data on the ACE tape.

Characteristics of public voc-tech institutes and proprietary schools are estimated from the 1975 NCES survey of postsecondary occupational programs. This NCES survey is only a sample (1,686) of all the vocational schools across the country; therefore, these data have been used to calculate a hypothetical "composite:' of voc-tech and proprietary school alternatives for each state.

The variables developed from this source are tuition per month and length of program for each of the eight subject categories. Though voc-tech institutes may be state or locally operated, both tuition and length of program required for each occupational subject area are likely to be set by the state department of education. Proprietary school tuition and fees and length of program will vary from state to state possibly with differences in the cost of living and in the particular nature of jobs within each of the eight subject areas. The precise calculations of tuition per month for each subject category in each state are presented elsewhere. Because data were missing in a number of cells, estimates for a given subject and a given state were calculated on the basis of both statewide averages of tuition across all schools and national averages for the subject category as a whole.[3]

Parameter Estimates and Forecasts

Estimates of the parameters in the model were obtained using a sample of 2,671 high school graduates from the NLS. This sample differs from that used in chapters 8 and 9 in that it is more representative of the students pursuing vocational education. It remains, with the usual exceptions based on the exclusion of students for missing data, a "random" sample from the NLS.

Coefficient Estimates

The coefficients and standard deviations of the estimates are presented in table 11-2. Estimates of the effect of academic aptitude are roughly comparable to those for the higher education choice model. The two major variables impacting on vocational education choices are tuition per month and length of program; both are negative in sign and highly significant. The coefficient of the variable representing distance factors is positive and significant, a counterintuitive result. However, as explained below, this variable is the only one (other than aptitude) that is applicable to academic college as well as vocational education choices. A positive coefficient here arises from two facts: first, voc-tech and proprietary school distances are measured from a data source that overestimates the actual distance, while community college and college distances are measured relatively accurately; and, second, the distance variable is picking up other factors not adequately measured for those students choosing college.

The particular specification presented in table 11-2 is limited in the range of variables included. A brief comparison with estimates presented in chapter 8 will show, for example, that such critical variables as college tuition, financial aid, and wage in the local labor market are not included, nor are such alternative-specific variables as work, military and homemaker. However, attempts to estimate the vocational education choice model incorporating any or all of these variables were unsuccessful. The matrix to be inverted in the estimation process appeared to approach singularity due to multi-collinearity among the variables and, because of rounding procedures in the computer program, the matrix became ultimately non-invertible. This problem of estimation can be traced to a significant difference between the specification of choices utilized here and those in chapter 8. Because this segment of the research focused on vocational education, 24 vocational alternatives (8 subject categories and 3 institutional types) were postulated for each student. As a result, about 65,000 of the 75,000 choices available to the 2,671 students were in vocational education. Ultimately, however, only 343 of the 2,671 students chose a vocational school option; thus, the result is a sample dominated by vocational education

Table 11-2
Variables and Estimated Coefficients

Variable	Coefficient	Standard Deviation
Tuition per month (vocational schools and community colleges)	−97.51	6.41
Length of program	− .175	.007
Distance	.099	.015
Aptitude variables		
A(1)	.0040	.0005
A(2)	− .0015	.0010
A(3)	− .0007	.0010
A(4)	− .0035	.0044
Subject dummies		
Health and nursing	− .904	.152
Business, office, marketing and distribution	− .682	.126
Technical and agribusiness	− 1.456	.203
Trade and industrial	− .038	.129
Both part-time dummy	− 3.22	.189

choices which are infrequently taken (less than 15 percent). In practical terms, any attempts to use dummy or other variables which spanned the entire vocational education sector (that is, if all vocational education choices were assigned a value of 0 or of 1) created a problem of near singularity. Similarly, dummy variables could be used for several subsets of subject categories, but not all, because no linear combination of variables (such as occurs with dummies) could be allowed to span the entire set of vocational education choices that dominate the sample.

Despite the estimation problems, these results are presented with some confidence in their validity. The coefficients of tuition per month and program length were estimated consistently in sign and approximate size through several alternative specifications. In particular, as subject dummies were added, these coefficients were minimally affected. In the future, however, the choice model will be estimated with fewer vocational categories and more nonvocational categories to minimize this multicollinearity problem.

Predictions and Three Forecasts

When these parameter estimates are used to predict the choices of individuals within the sample, the results can then be compared with the actual choices made.[4] The fit here is not as close as was obtained for the higher education choice model because alternative-specific dummy variables could not be included. As a result, academic aptitude is the only variable that is used to predict a person's choice between the military and work, for example. Clearly these estimates must be imprecise.

The fit within the vocational education choices is much better, however, because coefficients could be estimated for more relevant variables and subject dummies. Part (a) of table 11–3 shows the actual and predicted numbers of students choosing each of the three institutional types; community college vocational program, voc-tech institute, and proprietary school. In general, the model overpredicts vocational school attendance (450 predicted versus 343 actual); however, the distribution of choices among the three institutional types is apparently captured by the two predictive variables of tuition per month and length of program.

An interesting pattern emerges from comparing actual and predicted choices under alternative specifications of the model. When tuition per month is included, but length of program is not, the model overpredicts substantially the percentage of choices among the two low-price public options and underpredicts proprietary school attendance. In other words, if students considered price alone, proprietary schools would have far fewer students than they do now.

When the length of program variable is added to the specification, however, the distribution of enrollments between proprietary schools and public

Table 11-3
Distribution of Choices

(a) *Vocational Education Choices*

	Actual		Predicted	
	Number	*%*	*Number*	*%*
Community college vocational	89	26	62	14
Voc-tech institute	157	46	241	54
Proprietary school	97	28	147	33
Total	343	100	450	100

(b) *Proprietary versus Voc-tech Choices*

	Actual		Predicted	
	Number	*%*	*Number*	*%*
Voc-tech institute	157	62	241	62
Proprietary school	97	38	147	38
Total	254	100	388	100

voc-techs is accurately predicted. Considering these two options alone, the data presented in part (b) of table 11-3 point toward direct tuition cost and length of program, which explains a large part of the student's choice between these two institution types.

With only these two variables in the specification, however, enrollments in community colleges are underpredicted (62 predicted versus 89 actual). Low tuition and long programs alone do not thus capture all the dominant concerns of students interested in vocational education; other attributes must be involved that have not been measured here. This conclusion is not surprising. Community colleges have several important advantages over both the voc-tech institute and the proprietary school; among these are the associate's degree, the option while in school to transfer into liberal arts, and the option of going on into college after graduation. The fact that this model underpredicts community college enrollments relative to voc-tech institute and proprietary school enrollments on the basis of only tuition and length may actually therefore be seen as confirming the underlying model we have postulated to explain students' choices.

Table 11-4 presents the predicted results of several illustrative policy changes on the part of the public system: tuition at public colleges raised by $100 per month; length of public programs lowered by 15 percent; and a combination of the two. These results are not unexpected when compared to the original predicted distribution of students. When public tuition is raised, enrollments at voc-tech institutes drop dramatically. When public programs are shortened, enrollments rise. The results also demonstrate the effect on total enrollments of such changes in policy. A rise in public tuition

Table 11–4
Policy Simulations

	Base		Public Tuition by $100/mo.		Public Length by 15%		Both Public Tuition and Public Length	
	Number	%	Number	%	Number	%	Number	%
Proprietary	147.0	52.7	153.9	46.4	144.2	29.8	152.5	43.7
Public Voc.	240.6	53.5	112.8	34.0	279.1	57.6	131.8	37.8
Public C.C.	62.1	13.8	65.3	19.6	60.9	12.6	64.8	18.5
Total	449.7	–	332.0	(−26.1)	484.2	(+ 7.7)	349.1	(−22.3)

does push significant numbers out of vocational education entirely; a ahortening of time required in public school draws students into vocational education.

Conclusions

Estimation of this choice model does confirm the hypothesis that tuition per month and program length are significant attributes affecting student choices and that some additional, unmeasured attribute of community colleges effects choices as well. One more step is required in testing the price-value tradeoff: a comparison of these attributes among public and private schools. Table 11-5 shows the mean figures for tuition per month and length of program for each of these institutional categories. It is clear that, on the average, public schools cost less and attract students with this low price. However, long programs deter students and, in this regard, proprietary schools are valued more highly by students than public schools.

Two caveats are in order. First, these figures and the parameter estimates of the model indicate that, indeed, a balance of "price" and "value" attributes exists across the wide spectrum of public and private schools and is important in the students' decision-making process. The figures say nothing about the processes by which a price-value tradeoff develops, nor whether it is in the student's or the public's best interests. The additional months required for students to attend public schools may pay off in ways that the student does not understand at the time of the decision, or they may benefit society as a whole.

Second, no general equilibrium analysis has been applied to the actions and interactions of the public and private sector. Public and private schools are competitive and interdependent in ways that have not been fully dealt with here. Clearly, the low subsidized tuition of public voc-techs allows them to offer longer programs than proprietary schools and continue to attract

Table 11-5
Institutional Characteristics

| Variable | Means | | |
	Private	Public	Community College Vocational
Tuition per month (relative to family income)	$290	$40	$36
Length of program (months)	10.7	15.7	20
Distance (miles)	19.2	20.2	6.2

students. However, the equilibrium price-value tradeoff may well vary from one state to the next as tuition becomes higher or lower by state policy. For example, one state with a higher than average tuition may actually be forced to have shorter programs than another state with a lower tuition and the same share of vocational enrollments. Ultimately, statewide comparisons, simulations, and alternative market equilibria can be tested through closer examination of the data. This task will be undertaken in future work.

These qualifications aside, however, there is clear evidence of a price-value tradeoff in students' assessments and ultimate choices of public and private sector schools. Proprietary schools can continue to compete against the expanding public sector because they offer something to offset the high tuition cost. The shorter program means that the benefits of higher earning levels following graduation begin much sooner and the total of direct and indirect costs of tuition, foregone income, and earnings following early graduation may actually be less than for public schools.

Notes

1. Valerie I. Nelson, "Public Provision and Private Markets: Vocational Education and the Great Society," Ph.D. Dissertation, Economics Department, Yale University, 1977.

2. Richard Freeman, "Occupational Training in Proprietary Schools and Technical Institutes," *Review of Economics and Statistics* (August 1974).

3. The precise values used in each of these categories are available in the full report *Expreiences of Recent High School Graduates: The Transition to Work or Postsecondary Education*, Nolfi and others (Cambridge, Mass.: University Consultants, Inc., 1977).

4. Precise values are given in ibid.

Bibliography

Advisory Commission on Intergovernmental Relations, Report of the Commission. *Block Grants: A Roundtable Discussion.* Washington, D.C.: U.S. Government Printing Office, October 1976.

Alexander, Karl L., and Bruce K. Eckland. *High School Context, College Quality, and Educational Attainment: Institutional Constraints in Educational Stratification.* Baltimore, Md.: Center for Social Organization of Schools, John Hopkins University, July 1976.

Alexander, Karl L., and Edward L. McDill. *Selection and Allocation Within Schools: Some Causes and Consequences of Curriculum Placement.* Baltimore, Md.: Center for Social Organization of Schools, John Hopkins University, Maryland, May 1976.

Alexander, Karl L., and Edward L. McDill. *Social Background and Schooling Influences on the Subjective Orientations of High School Seniors.* Baltimore, Md.: Center for Social Organization of Schools, John Hopkins University, November 1974.

Allen, Robert E., and Thomas E. Gutteridge. *The Career Profiles of Business Majors From Two-Year Public and Proprietary Colleges.* Buffalo: State University of New York, 1973.

American Association of State Colleges and Universities. *Basic Facts About Tuition and Educational Opportunity.* Washington, D.C., May 1976.

American Association of State Colleges and Universities. *Education to Meet Present and Future Career Needs.* Report from Second National Conference on Career Education, Washington, D.C., November 1974.

American Council on Education. *The Labor Market for College Graduates.* Policy Analysis Service Reports, vol. 1, no. 4 (June 1975).

Anderson, C. A., M. J. Boman, and V. Tinto. *Where Colleges Are and Who Attends.* New York: McGraw-Hill, 1972.

Anderson, Stephen M. *The Adult Basic Education Program.* Washington, D.C.: National Center for Education Statistics.

Anderson, Stephen M. *The Dropout Prevention Program.* Washington, D.C.: National Center for Education Statistics.

Astin, Alexander W. *Financial Aid and Student Persistence.* Los Angeles: Higher Education Research Institute, 1976.

Astin, Alexander W., Margo R. King, John M. Light, and Gerald T. Richardson. *The American Freshman: National Norms for Fall 1974.* Los Angeles: Cooperative Institutional Research Program, University of California, 1975.

Atelsek, Frank J., and Irene L. Gomberg. *Student Assistance: Participants and Programs—1974-75.* Washington, D.C.: Higher Education Panel Reports, no. 27, American Council on Education, December 1975.

Atwater, Dixie L. *Higher Tuition for Nonresident Students: Its Legal and Administrative Status.* Washington, D.C.: ICF Incorporated, March 1975.

Bailey, J. P., Jr., and F. E. Collins. *Entry into Postsecondary Education.* Paper presented at the Annual Meeting of the American Educational Research Association, Research Triangle Park, North Carolina, April 1977.

Barnes, Gary, and others. *Enrollment Patterns Under Modifications to the Basic Grant Program.* Washington, D.C.: ICF Incorporated, June 1975.

Barnes, Gary, Edward W. Erickson, W. Hill, and G. Watts, Jr. *Extension of the College-Going/College Choice Model to the NLS Class of 1971 Data,* report submitted to the Office of the Assistant Secretary of Planning and Evaluation of DHEW. Washington, D.C.: ICF Incorporated, June 1975.

Barnes, Gary, Edward W. Erickson, W. Hill, and H. S. Winokur. *Direct Aid to Students: A "Radical" Structural Reform.* Washington, D.C.: Inner City Fund, 1972.

Belitsky, A. H. *Private Vocational Schools and Their Students' Limited Objectives, Unlimited Opportunities.* Cambridge, Mass.: Schenkman, 1969.

Ben-Porath, Yoram. "The Production of Human Capital and the Life-Cycle of Earnings," *Journal of Political Economy*, 75, pp. 352-65.

Berg, Ivar. *Education and Jobs: The Great Training Robbery.* New York: Praeger, 1972.

Berk, Sarah F., Richard A. Berk, and Catherine Berheide. *The Non-Division of Household Labor*, Chicago: Northwestern University.

Black, Michael S. *Student Attitudes Toward Vocational Education.* Columbus: The Center for Vocational Education, Ohio State University, March 1976.

Bond, Sheryl. "Postsecondary Education in Accredited Private Vocational Schools." Ph.D. dissertation, School of Education, Indiana University, August 1974.

Boroson, Warren. "The New Campus Careerism," *Boston Herald-American,* May 12, 1976.

Box, G. E. P., and D. R. Cox. "An Analysis of Transformations," *Journal of the Royal Statistical Society*, ser. B, vol. 26, pp. 211-43.

Brickell, Henry M., Carol B. Aslanian, and Laurel J. Spak. *Data for Decisions— An Analysis of Evaluation Data Needed by Decision-Makers in Educational Programs.* New York: Policy Studies in Education, March 1974.

Brimmer, Andrew F. "Income Distribution and Economic Equity in the United States—Perspectives in Black and White." Lecture presented at the 1976 Annual Meeting of the American Association for the Advancement of Science, Boston, Mass., February 1976.

Browning, Edgar K. "How Much More Equality Can We Afford?" *The Public Interest* 43 (Spring 1976) pp. 90-110.

Burdetsky, Ben. "Troubled Transition: From School to Work," *Worklife* (November 1976).

U.S. Bureau of the Census. *Factors Related to High School Graduation and College Attendance: 1967*, ser. P-20, no. 185 (July 11,1969).

California State Legislature, Select Committee on the Implementation of Career Education. *Competency in Marketable Skills*, hearings, Los Angeles, November 14, 1974.

California State Legislature, Select Committee on the Implementation of Career Education. *Labor Perceptions of Marketable Skills Through Public Education*, hearings, San Francisco, January 17, 1975.

Campbell, R., and B. Siegel. "The Demand for Higher Education in the United States, 1919-1964," *American Economic Review* (June 1967), 482-94.

Carnegie Commission on Higher Education. *College Graduates and Jobs: Adjusting to a New Labor Market Situation*. New York: McGraw-Hill, April 1973.

Carnegie Foundation for the Advancement of Teaching. *More Than Survival: Prospects for Higher Education in a Period of Uncertainty*. San Francisco: Jossey Bass, 1975.

Carroll S. and Relles P.: "A Bayesian Model of Choice Among Higher Education Institutions," *Rand Corporation Report,* R-2005-NIE/LE (June 1976).

Carter, W. Thomas. *The Career Opportunities Program—A Summing Up*, vol. 3. New York: New Careers Training Laboratory, Queens College, 1975-76.

Center for Educational Research and Evaluation. *National Longitudinal Study of the High School Class of 1972; A Capsule Description of First Follow-Up Survey Data.* Report prepared for National Center for Education Statistics, Washington, D.C., August 1975.

Center for Educational Research and Evaluation: *National Longitudinal Study Third Follow-Up Field Test Instrument—Revised Draft.* Washington, D.C. (September 1975).

Center for Human Resource Research. *The National Longitudinal Survey Handbook.* Columbus: Ohio State University, October 1975.

Center for Vocational Education. *Plan for a Study of Transferable Skills.* Columbus: Ohio State University, February 1976.

Center for Vocational Education. *Proceedings of the Tenth Anniversary Program: Career Development of Women.* Columbus: Ohio State University, 1975.

Chamberlain, Gary. "Identification in Variance Components Models," unpublished manuscript, Harvard University, Cambridge, Mass., 1976.

Chamberlain, Gary. *Education, Income and Ability Revisited*, rev. ed. Cambridge, Mass.: Harvard University Economics Department, July 1975a.

Chamberlain, Gary. "Unobservables in Earnings Functions: Applications in the Malmo Data," unpublished manuscript, Harvard University, Cambridge, Mass., 1975b.

Chamberlain, Gary, and Zvi Griliches. "Unobservables with a Variance-Components

Structure: Ability, Schooling, and the Economic Success of Brothers," *International Economic Review* 16 (1975), pp. 422-49.

Charner, Ivan. *Paid Education Leave: A Sociological Perspective*, Education and Work Group/NIE (February 1976).

A. Christensen, T. Melder, and B. Weisbrod. "Factors Affecting College Attendance," *Journal of Human Resources*, vol. 10, no. 2, pp. 174-88.

Christian, C. E. *The Proprietary Student: A Pilot Study*. Washington, D.C.: Higher Education Research Institute, Inc. July 1975.

Christoffel, Pamela, and Lois D. Rice. *Federal Policy Issues and Data Needs in Postsecondary Education*. Washington, D.C.: College Entrance Examination Board, 1976.

Coleman, James S. "How Do the Young Become Adults?" Paper presented at the American Educational Research Association Annual Meeting, April 1972.

Coleman, James S. *Equality of Educational Opportunity*. Washington, D.C.: Office of Education, U.S. Department of Health, Education, and Welfare, 1966.

College Entrance Examination Board, Panel on Financing Low-Income and Minority Students in Higher Education: *Toward Equal Opportunity for Higher Education*. Princeton, N.J.; 1973.

Consortium on Financing Higher Education. *Federal Student Assistance: A Review of Title IV of the Higher Education Act* (April 1975).

Copa, George H., Donald E. Irvin, and Clyde Maurice. *Status of Former High School Students: Procedure for Local Assessment*. Summary Report of a Statewide Sample Class of 1974. Minneapolis: Minnesota Research Coordinating Unit for Vocational Education, University of Minnesota, February 1976.

Copa, George H., and Donald E. Irvin, Jr. *Occupational Supply and Demand Information: A Format with Implications for Planning Education for Work*. Minneapolis: Minnesota Research Coordinating Unit for Vocational Education, University of Minnesota, September 1974.

Corazzini, A., D. J. Dugan, and H. Grabowski. "Determinants and Distributional Aspects of Enrollment in U.S. Higher Education," *Journal of Human Resources* (Winter 1972), pp. 39-50.

Corrallo, Salvatore B., and Junius A. Davis. "Impact of Financial Aid on Postsecondary Entrance and Persistence." Paper Presented at the Annual Meeting of the American Educational Research Association, New York, April 1977.

Cyert, Richard M. "The Market Approach to Higher Education." Mimeographed paper presented at American Council on Education, 57th Annual Meeting, San Diego, California, October 10, 1974.

Dagenais, M. G. "The Use of Incomplete Observations in Multiple Regression Analysis," *Journal of Econometrics* 1 (1973), pp. 317-28.

Dempster, A. P. *Elements of Continuous Multivariate Analysis*. Reading, Mass.: Addison-Wesley, 1969.

DiCesare, Constance Bogh. *Changes in the Occupational Structure of U.S. Jobs.*
    Reprinted from March 1975 *Monthly Labor Review.* Washington, D.C.:
    U.S. Department of Labor, Bureau of Labor Statistics.
Dillon, Don. *Toward Matching Personal and Job Characteristics.* Reprinted from
    Occupational Outlook Quarterly, Spring 1975. Washington, D.C.: U.S.
    Department of Labor.
Draves, Bill. *Teaching Free: An Introduction to Adult Learning for Volunteer
    and Part-Time Teachers.* Manhattan, Kansas: The Free University Network,
    1976.
Dunteman, George H., and Samuel S. Peng. *National Longitudinal Study of the
    High School Class of 1972: Planning and Activity States Analyses.* Research
    Triangle Park, N.C. Research Triangle Institute, September 1975.
Eisner, Elliot W., Joseph Schwab, and Decker Walker. *Career Education: The
    State of the Idea: Its Prospects for the Future.* Report Prepared for the
    National Institute of Education. Stanford: Stanford University, October
    1974.
El-Khawas, Elaine H. *Better Information for Student Choice: Report of a
    National Task Force.* Washington, D.C.: American Council on Education,
    March 1977.
El-Khawas, Elaine H. *New Expectations for Fair Practice: Suggestions for In-
    stitutional Review.* Washington, D.C.: American Council on Education,
    September 1976.
El-Khawas, Elaine H. *Public and Private Higher Education: Differences in Role,
    Character and Clientele.* Policy Analysis Service Reports, vol. 2, no. 3.
    Washington, D.C.: American Council on Education, December 1976b.
Erickson, Edward, Watts Hill, Jr., Herbert S. Winokur, Jr., Dixie Atwater, and
    Ursula Guerrieri. "Proprietary Business Schools and Community Colleges:
    Resources Allocation, Student Needs, and Federal Policies," Cambridge,
    Mass.: ICF Incorporated, June 1972.
Federal Interagency Committee on Education. *Some Observations on Open
    Learning and Non-Traditional Education.* Based on the Second National
    Conference on Open Learning and Non-Traditional Education, Washington,
    D.C., July 1975.
Feingold, Norman S. "Career Guidance and the Changing World of Work."
    Keynote address at the National Association of Industry-Education Coopera-
    tion Conference, Buffalo, New York, May 1974.
Feldmand, P., and S. Hoenack. "Private Demand for Higher Education in the
    United States." *The Economics and Financing of Higher Education in the
    United States.* Washington, D.C.: The Joint Economic Committee, 1969.
Feldstein, Martin. "Hospital Cost Inflation: A Study of Non-Profit Price
    Dynamics," Harvard Institute of Economic Research, *Discussion Paper*
    139 (October 1970).

Fennema, Elizabeth. *Influences of Selected Cognitive, Affective and Educational Variables on Sex-Related Differences in Mathematical Learning and Studying.* Madison: University of Wisconsin, October 1976.

Ferguson, R. L., and E. J. Maxey. *Trends in the Academic Performance of High School and College Students.* ACT Research Report no. 70. Iowa City, Iowa: ACT Publications, January 1976.

Fetters, William B. *Changes in Attitudes One and One Half Years After Graduation,* National Longitudinal Study of the High School Class of 1972. Washington, D.C.: U.S. Department of HEW/National Center for Educational Statistics, 1975.

Fife, Jonathan D. *Applying the Goals of Student Financial Aid.* Washington, D.C.: American Association for Higher Education, 1975.

First National Bank of Boston. *Occupational Forecast for the Boston Standard Metropolitan Statistical Area: 1970-1980, 1980-1985.* Report for the School Committee of the City of Boston, November 1975.

Fox, Lynn H. "The Effects of Sex Role Socialization on Mathematics Participation and Achievement." Paper prepared for the Education and Work Group, National Institute of Education, Washington, D.C.: December 1976.

Frankel, Steven M. *Executive Summary—An Assessment of School-Supervised Work Education Programs.* Washington, D.C.: HEW, Office of Education, September 1973.

Freeman, Richard B. *The Declining Economic Value of Higher Education and the American Social System.* New York: Aspen Institute for Humanistic Studies, 1976.

Freeman, Richard B. *The Over-Educated American.* New York: Academic Press, 1976b.

Freeman, Richard. "Occupational Training in Proprietary Schools and Technical Institutes," *Review of Economics and Statistics* (August 1974).

Freeman, Richard B. *The Decline of the Economic Value of College Education.* Cambridge, Mass.: Harvard University, September 1975.

From School to Work: Improving the Transition. Policy Papers Prepared for the National Commission for Manpower Policy.

Froomkin, Joseph. *Changing Credential Objectives of Students in Postsecondary Education.* Washington, D.C.: Joseph Froomkin, Inc., December 1974.

Fulton, Richard. "Preparation for Work—The Role of Proprietary. Postsecondary Institutions." Remarks Prepared for SREB Legislative Work Conference, Memphis, Tennessee, August 23, 1973, p. 3.

Gallaway, Lowell E. "Labor Mobility, Resource Allocation, and Structural Unemployment, *American Economic Review* 53 (September 1963).

Galper, H., and R. M. Dunn, Jr. "A Short-Run Demand Function for Higher Education in the United States," *Journal of Political Economy* (September-October 1969), pp. 765-77.

Ganschow, Laurie H. *Case Studies in Practical Career Guidance—Number 1.*

Baltimore Placement and Follow-up Program/Baltimore City Public Schools. Palo Alto, Calif.: American Institute for Research, June 1973.

General Accounting Office. *What Is the Role of Federal Assistance for Vocational Education?* Washington, D.C.: Comptroller General of the U.S., December 1974.

Gilroy, Curtis L. *Investment in Human Capital and Black-White Unemployment.* Reprinted from July 1975 *Monthly Labor Review.* Washington, D.C.: U.S. Department of Labor.

Gladieux, Lawrence E. *Distribution of Federal Student Assistance: The Enigma of the Two-Year Colleges.* Washington, D.C.: College Entrance Examination Board, June 1975.

Glickman, Albert S., Barry E. Goodstadt, Abraham K. Korman, and Alan P. Romanczuk, *Navy Career Motivation Programs In An All-Volunteer Condition:* 1. *A Cognitive Map of Career Motivation.* Silver Spring, Md.: American Institutes for Research, March 1975.

Griffin, Larry J. *On Estimating the Economic Value of Schooling and Experience: Some Issues in Conceptualization and Measurement.* Baltimore, Md.: Center for Social Organizations of Schools, The John Hopkins University, January 1977.

Griffin, Larry J. *Specification Biases in Estimates of Socioeconomic-Returns to Schooling.* Baltimore, Md.: Center for Social Organization of Schools, The John Hopkins University, January 1976.

Griliches, Zvi. "Estimating the Returns to Schooling: Some Econometric Problems," Harvard Institute of Economic Research Discussion Paper no. 433, *Econometrica* (1975a).

Griliches, Zvi. "Wages and Earnings of Very Young Men," *Journal of Political Economy* (1975b).

Griliches, Zvi, and G. Chamberlain. "Notes on 'Indexed' Dependent Variables," unpublished manuscript, Harvard University, 1976.

Griliches, Zvi, and William M. Mason. *Education, Income, and Ability.* Cambridge, Mass.: Harvard University, Department of Economics, June 1972.

Griliches, Zvi, and V. Ringstad. *Economics of Scale and the Form of the Production Function.* Amsterdam and London: North-Holland Publishing Company.

Grossman, Allyson Sherman. *Women in the Labor Force: The Early Years.* Reprinted from November 1975 *Monthly Labor Review.* Washington, D.C.: U.S. Department of Labor, Bureau of Labor Statistics.

Gurin, Patricia, and Betty Mae Morrison. *Education, Labor Market Experiences, and Current Expectancies of Black and White Men and Women.* Ann Arbor: Survey Research Center, University of Michigan, September 1976.

Guzzardi, Walter Jr. "Education for the World of Work," *Fortune* (October 1975).

Hauser, Robert M., William H. Sewell, and Duane F. Alwin. "High School

Effects on Achievement," in William H. Sewell, Robert M. Hauser, and David L. Featherman (eds.), *Schooling and Achievement in American Society.* New York: Academic Press, 1976.

Hausman, Jerry, A., and David A. Wise. *A Conditional Probit Model for Qualitative Choice: Discrete Decisions Recognizing Interdependence and Heterogenoces Preference.* Cambridge: Massachusetts Institute of Technology. April 1976.

Hearings Before the Subcommittee on Elementary, Secondary, and Vocational Education; H.R. 19 and Related Bills, Feb. 18, 19, 25, 26 and March 3, 6, 10, 18, 19, 1975.

Heckman, J., and S. Polachek. "Empirical Evidence on the Functional Form of the Earnings-Schooling Relationship," *Journal of the American Statistical Association* 69 (1969), 350-51.

Hill, Russell C. *Dropping Out of High School: The Effects of Family, Ability, School Quality and Local Employment Conditions.* Washington, D.C.: Department of Health, Education and Welfare, 1975.

Hoenack, S. "The Efficient Allocation of Subsidies to College Students," *American Economic Review* (June 1971), pp. 302-311.

Hoffman, Ben. *Alternative Continuing Education Future: An Analysis of 5,711 Manitoba Grade 10, 11 and 12 Student Responses to Ten Scenarios.* Province of Manitoba: Postsecondary Research Reference Committee, October 1976.

Hoffman, Bernard B. "Students' Decisions on Postsecondary Study: The Manitoba Experience," *Educational Planning* 1976.

Hoffman, Jonathan. *The Guide to Vocational Education in America: Trends to 1978.* Westport, Conn.: Market Data Retrieval, 1975.

Holmstrom, Engin I. "Higher Education and Social Mobility: A Promise Still Kept." Paper presented at the Annual Meeting of the American Association for Higher Education, Chicago, March 1976.

Holmstrom, Engin I. *"Older" Freshmen: Do They Differ from "Typical" Undergraduates?* Washington, D.C.: American Council on Education, Research Report, vol. 8, no. 7, 1973.

"How Can Colleges Deal with the Increasing Incidence of Student Weakness in Basic Learning Skills," *Change* (March 1977).

Howe, Harold II. *The Value of College: A Non-Economist's View.* New York: Ford Foundation, November 1975.

Jackson, Tom, and Davidyne Mayleas. *The Hidden Job Market.* New York: The New York Times Co., 1976.

Jacobson, Robert L. "Private Colleges Seek 'Balanced' Student Aid Stabilized Enrollment," *The Chronicle for Higher Education* (February 22, 1977a).

Jacobson, Robert L. "Two-Year Colleges Prepare to Fight for 'New Clientele'" *The Chronicle for Higher Education* (March 1977).

Jencks, Christopher S., and Marsha D. Brown. "Effects of High Schools on

Their Students," *Harvard Educational Review* 45: 273-324.

Jessee, Ronald N. *The Follow-Through Program*. Washington, D.C.: National Center for Ed. Statistics.

Johnston, J. *Econometric Methods*, 2 ed. New York: McGraw-Hill, 1972.

Joreskog, Karl G., and M. Van Thillo. "LISREL—A General Computer Program for Estimating a Linear Structural Equation System Involving Multiple Indicators of Unmeasured Variables," *Research Report 73-5* (1973), Uppsala University, Statistics Department. (Also available from Educational Testing Service, Princeton, N.J.)

Joseph Froomkin, Inc. *A Study to Identify the Trends in the Sources of Student Support for Post-Secondary Education*. Washington, D.C.: Joseph Froomkin, Inc., December 1974.

Kincaid, H., and E. Podeska. *An Exploratory Survey of Proprietary Vocational Schools*. Palo Alto: Stanford Research Institute, 1966.

Kohn, M., C. Manski, and D. Mundel, "An Empirical Investigation of Factors Influencing College Going Behavior," *Annals of Economic and Social Measurement* (Autumm 1976); also *Rand Corporation Report* R-1470-DSF, 1974.

Lawley, D. N., and A. E. Maxwell. *Factor Analysis as a Statistical Method*, London: Butterworth, 1971.

Lee, Arthur M. *Learning a Living Across the Nation, vol. 4. Project Baseline—4th National Report. Part 1: Narrative Report*. Flagstaff: Northern Arizona University, December 1975a.

Lee, Arthur M., and Dorris Fitzgerald. *Learning a Living Across the Nation, vol. 4. Project Baseline, 4th National Report—Part 2: Statistical Almanac*. Flagstaff: Northern Arizona University, October 1975b.

Lee, John B., Daryl E. Carlson, Jerry S. Davis, and Ann M. Hershberger. *Student Aid: Descriptions and Options*. Menlo Park: Stanford Research Institute, October 1975.

Leibowitz, Arleen. "Home Investments in Children," *Journal of Political Economy* 82 (1974), S111-S132.

Levinsohm, J., J. A. Riccobono, and R. P. Moore, *National Longitudinal Survey of the High School Class of 1972: Base-Year and First Follow-Data Users Manual*. Research Triangle Park, N.C.: Center for Educational Research and Evaluation, 1975.

Major, Thomas S. *PDEM-1, A Quantitative Model for Forecasting Post-Secondary Demand and Enrollment, vol. 4*. University of Manitoba, December 1974.

Manski, C. F. "The Conditional/Polytomous Logit Program: Instructions for Use," unpublished manuscript, Carnegie-Mellon University, 1974.

Marconi, Katherine. *Sociological Research on Employment Patterns of Youth*. Washington, D.C.: George Washington University, Graduate School of Arts and Sciences, January 1974.

Marsden, Lorna, Edward Hawey, and Ivan Charner. *Female Graduates: Their*

Occupational Mobility and Occupational Attainments. Washington, D.C.: 1977.

Mason, Thomas R., ed. *Assessing Computer-Based Systems Models.* San Francisco: Jossey-Bass, 1976.

Mawby, Russell G. "The Greatest Opportunity." Remarks at the Opening Session of the Annual Assembly of the Council for the Advancement and Support of Education, Washington, D.C.: July 1976.

McGuire, Joseph W. "The Distribution of Subsidy to Students in California Public Higher Education," *The Journal of Human Resources* p. 1-3.

Medsker, L. L., and J. W. Trent. *Beyond High School: A Study of 10,000 High School Graduates.* Berkeley: Center for Research and Development in Higher Education, University of California, 1967.

Medved, Michael, and David Wallechinsky. *What Really Happened to the Class of '65?* New York: Random House, 1976.

Meleen, Paulette, Suzzanne Gordon, Kermit Baller, Kristina Engstrom, Bruce Nickerson, and Jo Schuchat. *Identifying and Planning for New Emerging Occupations: A Suggested Guide.* Belmont, Mass.: Contract Research Corporation, 1976.

Miller, Leonard S. *College Admissions and Financial Aid Policies as Revealed by Institutional Practices: A Progress Report Prepared for TIMS xx11 International Meetings.* Berkeley, Cal.: School of Social Welfare, Fall 1975.

Miller, Leonard S., and Roy Radner. *Demand & Supply in United States Higher Education.* Berkeley, Ca.: Technical Report sponsored by the Carnegie Commission on Higher Education, 1975.

Morgan, J., W. Cohn David, and H. Brazer. *Income and Welfare in the United States.* New York: McGraw-Hill, 1962.

National Advisory Council on Vocational Education. *Report on Urban Vocational Education,* Washington, D.C., Dec. 6, 1974.

National Assessment of Educational Progress/Education Commission of the States. *Proceedings of Year OB Offerors' Conference.* Denver, 1975.

National Center for Education Statistics. "Effectiveness of High School Job Training: Assessment of Class of 1972 One and One-half Years after Graduation," *Bulletin* 22 (August 29, 1975).

National Center for Education Statistics. *National Longitudinal Study of the High School Class of 1972. A Capsule Description of Second Follow-Up Survey Data.* Washington, D.C.: NCES, October 1974.

National Commission on the Financing of Postsecondary Education. *Financing Postsecondary Education in the United States.* Washington, D.C., December 1973.

National Commission on the Financing of Postsecondary Education. *Survey of Postsecondary Career Schools.* Washington, D.C., June 1973.

National Commission for Manpower Policy. *From School to Work. Improving the Transition.* Washington, D.C.: U.S. Gov. Printing Office, 1976.

National Education Association. "Educators Sees no Major Erosion of Basics, Lists Counterbalancing Gains," *News Communications* (November 1975).

National Longitudinal Study of the High School Class of 1972. Summary of Proceedings of Informal Session at the AERA Annual Meeting, San Francisco, 1976.

Nelson, Valerie I. *Public Provision and Private Markets: Vocational Education.* New Haven: Yale University Economics Department, PhD Thesis, 1977.

Nolfi, George J., and Valerie I. Nelson. *Strengthening the Alternative Postsecondary Education System: Continuing and Part-Time Study in Massachusetts.* Statewide master plan for adult, continuing, and nontraditional postsecondary education. Vol. I, Summary Report and Recommendations. Vol. II, Technical Report, 1973. Study performed for the State of Massachusetts.

Nolfi, George J., Valerie I. Nelson, Betty Karro, and Patrick Dolan. *A Study of the Potential and Capacity for Innovation in American Higher and of Federal Policy Possibilities.* Cambridge, Mass.: University Consultants, Inc., 1971. Background studies prepared for "Newman II" Task Force of the Dept. of Health, Education and Welfare, for the "Second Newman Report."

Olson, Lawrence. *The Allocation of Time to Vocational School Training* Rochester, N.Y.: University of Rochester, August 1976.

Palmer, James D. "Utility Measures for Education: An Enduring Value." Paper presented at the American Association for the Advancement of Science Annual Meeting, Boston, February 1976.

Parnes, Herbert A., and others. *Career Thresholds*, vols. 1-4. Columbus: Center for Human Resources Research, Ohio State University, 1970-73.

Parreca, Anthony G., and John J. Stallard. "Common Affected Domain Competencies of Students among Vocational Areas. Presented at the American Educational Association Convention, San Francisco, April 1976.

Perg, Samuel S., and William B. Fetters. "College Student Withdrawal: A Motivational Problem." Paper presented at the Annual Meeting of the American Educational Research Association, New York, April 1977. Research Triangle Park, N.C.

Plsurde, Paul J. *Experience with Analytical Models in Higher Education Management.* Amherst: Center for Educational Management Studies, University of Massachusetts, June, 1976.

Profile of Characteristics of the Graduating Classes of 1977, 1978 and 1979. From Postsecondary Outcomes Research, sponsored by the Postsecondary Research Reference Committee of the Province of Manitoba 1977.

Project Talent. *The Project Talent Data Bank: A Handbook.* Palo Alto: American Institute for Research, 1972.

Radner, R., and L. S. Miller. *Demand and Supply in U.S. Higher Education.*
    Berkeley: Carnegie Commission on Higher Education, 1975.
Radner, Roy, Leonard S., Miller, Douglas Adkins, and Frederick E. Balderston.
    Demand and Supply in U.S. Higher Education. A report prepared for
    the Carnegie Commission on Higher Education. New York: McGraw-Hill,
    1975.
Rand Corporation. *Effects of Secondary Education on Post-Secondary School
    Careers.* Santa Monica: Rand Corporation, March 1975.
Recent Research on Private Higher Education. A compilation of Policy Analysis
    Service Reports, vol. 2, no. 2. Washington, D.C.: American Council on
    Education, August 1976.
"Report of the College Scholarship Service Student Advisory Committee on
    What 250 Students Say about Financial Aid Problems." *The College Board
    Review* 100 (Summer 1976).
*Report of Congressional Budget Office Conference on the Teenage Unemploy-
    ment Problem: What are the Options?* Washington, D.C.: Government
    Printing Office, October 1976.
Report of the Federal Interagency Committee on Education: *Toward a Federal
    Strategy for Protection of the Consumer of Education.* Virginia Y. Trotter,
    Chairman. U.S. Dept. of HEW, July 1975.
Report of the National Advisory Council for Career Education on *The Efficacy
    of Career Education*, 1976.
Report of the Subcommittee on Population Education, Federal Interagency
    Committee on Education on *Population Education and the Federal Role.*
    Louis M. Hellman, Chairman. U.S. Dept. of HEW, November 1976.
Report of the Subcommittee on Research, Development, Dissemination and
    Evaluation. *Federal Educational, Research, Development, Dissemination
    and Evaluation Efforts.* Harold L. Hodgkinson, Chairman. U.S. Dept. of
    HEW. Washington, D.C. December 1976.
Research Triangle Institute. *NLS Third Follow-Up Field Test Instrument—
    Revised Draft—Form A.* Research Triangle Park, N.C.: Research Triangle
    Institute, September 1975.
Research Triangle Institute. *Conceptual Model of the National Longitudinal
    Study.* Research Triangle Park, N.C.: Research Triangle Institute, July
    1973a.
Research Triangle Institute. *Operation Follow-Up. First Follow-Up Question-
    naire Form A.* National Longitudinal Study of the High School Class of
    1972. Research Triangle Park, N.C.: Research Triangle Institute, Fall
    1973b.
Riccobono, John A. and George H. Dunteman, *National Longitudinal Study
    of the High School Class of 1972: Preliminary Analyses of Student
    Financial Aid.* Research Triangle Park, N.C.: Research Triangle Institute,
    September 1975.

Richard, Ray. "Student Boom Defies Gravity of Recession." *Boston Globe* (September 1975).

Rivlin, Alice M., Director. Background paper of the Congress of the United States. *Policy Options for the Teenage Unemployment Problem.* Washington, D.C.: Government Printing Office, September 1976.

Rosen, Sherwin. "Human Capital: A Survey of Empirical Research," University of Rochester *Discussion Paper* 76-2 (1976).

Rosen, Sherwin. "Income Generating Functions and Capital Accumulation." Harvard Institute of Economic Research *Discussion Paper* 306. Cambridge: Harvard University, A73.

Russell, Neil, and M. P. Yakimishyn. *PDEM-1/A Summary Handbook for the Post-Secondary Demand and Enrollment Model-1.* University of Manitoba. February 1975.

Sandell, Steven H. "The Demand for College: The Effect of Local Colleges on Attendance." Paper presented to the American Educational Research Association, San Francisco, April 1976.

Schiller, Bradley L. "Equality, Opportunity, and the 'Good Job.'" *The Public Interest* 43 (Spring 1976).

Scully, Malcolm G. "Career-Oriented Studies: the Debate Intensifies," *The Chronicle for Higher Education* 1976.

Scully, Malcolm G. "Providing Better Information for Potential Students." *The Chronicle for Higher Education* (April 1977).

Selby, David. *Comments on Possible Policy Research Uses of Four Major Longitudinal Data Bases.* Washington, D.C.: Joseph Froomkin, Inc., October 1976.

Shapiro, Harvey D. "An Analysis of a Grim Job Market, review of *The Over-Educated American,* by Richard B. Freeman," *Chronicle of Higher Education* (December 6, 1976), p. 15.

Sherman, Julia. *Effects of Biological Factors on Sex-Related Differences in Mathematics Achievement.* Madison: Women's Research Institute of Wisconsin, 1976.

Spence, A. Michael. *Market Signalling: Informational Transfer in Hiring and Related Screening Processes,* Cambridge: Harvard University Press, 1974.

Stakelon, Anne E., and Joel H. Magisos. *Sex Stereotyping and Occupational Aspiration: An Annotated Bibliography.* Bibliography Series No. 29. Columbus: The Center for Vocational Education, Ohio State University, October 1975.

The States and Private Higher Education—A New Era Has Begun: What Problems and What Policies? A Report of the Carnegie Council on Policy Studies in Higher Education (February 1977).

Stern, Barry E. *Articulation of Education and Work.* Washington, D.C.: Department of Health, Education and Welfare, December, 1976.

Stowell John. "18% Fewer Jobs Available for '75 College Grads." *Boston Globe* 1975.

Strong, Merle E., Richard D. Boss, Susan J. Kosmo, Eugene S. Nelson, and Wayne A. Hammerstrom. *Review and Synthesis of Job Placement Literature.* Vol. I of a Research Project to Develop a Coordinated Comprehensive Placement System. Madison: Center for Studies in Vocational and Technical Education, University of Wisconsin, March 1975.

Strong, Merle E., Richard D. Boss, Susan J. Kosmo, Eugene S. Nelson, and Wayne A. Hammerstrom. *Survey and Analysis of Career Placement Activities.* Vol. II of a Research Project to Develop a Coordinated Comprehensive Placement System. Madison: Center for Studies in Vocational and Technical Education, University of Wisconsin, May 1975.

Strong, Merle E., Wayne A. Hammerstrom, Susan J. Kosmo, Richard D. Boss, John D. Hartz, and Eugene S. Nelson. *Data Base Establishment and Model Development for a Coordinated Comprehensive Placement System.* Final Report. Madison: Center for Studies in Vocational and Technical Education, University of Wisconsin, November 1975.

Strong, Merle E., Susan J. Kosmo, Wayne A. Hammerstrom, Richard D. Boss, and John D. Hartz. *A Coordinated and Comprehensive School-Based Career Placement Model.* Vol. III, *Coordinated Comprehensive Placement System.* Madison: Center for Studies in Vocational and Technical Education, University of Wisconsin, November 1975.

Systems Research Inc. "Examples of the Use of National and State Post-Secondary Education Financing Models." Technical paper prepared for the National Conference on Postsecondary Financing, Washington D.C., January 1975.

Temme, Lloyd V. *Occupation: Meanings and Measures.* Washington, D.C.: Bureau of Social Science Research, Inc., June 1975.

Tenison, Lawrence J. *Description and Specifications for the Linked NLS-Institutional Data Base.* National Longitudinal Study of the High School Class of 1972. A Technical Report. Washington, D.C.: College Entrance Examination Board, March 1976.

Theil, Henri. *Principles of Econometrics.* New York: Wiley, 1971.

Third Annual Report to the Congress of the Student Loan Marketing Association. Edward A. McCabe, Chairman of the Board. Washington, D.C.: National Student Loan Marketing Association 1976.

Trivett, David A. "Jobs and College Graduates." *ERIC Higher Education Research Currents* (November 1975).

Trivett, David A. *Open Admissions and the CUNY Experience. ERIC Higher Education Research Currents.* Washington, D.C.: American Association for Higher Education.

Tuckman, H. P., and W. S. Ford. *The Demand for Higher Education: A Florida Case Study.* Lexington, Mass.: Lexington Books, 1972.

U.S. Congressional Budget Office. *Employment & Training Programs.* Staff Working Papers. Washington, D.C.: U.S. Government Printing Office, May 4, 1976a.

U.S. Congressional Budget Office. *Policy Options for the Teenage Unemployment Problem.* Background Paper No. 13. Washington, D.C.: U.S. Government Printing Office, September 21, 1976b.

U.S. Congressional Budget Office Conference Report. *The Teenage Unemployment Problem: What Are the Options?* Washington, D.C.: U.S. Government
Printing Office, October 1976c.

U.S. Department of Commerce, Bureau of the Census. *Current Population
Reports. Population Characteristics. Educational Attainment in the United
States: March, 1975.* Washington, D.C.: U.S. Government Printing Office,
1975.

U.S. Department of Health, Education and Welfare, National Center for Education Statistics. *Survey of Program and Enrollment in Noncollegiate Postsecondary Schools with Occupational Programs, 1973,* Washington, D.C.:
U.S. Government Printing Office, 1975.

U.S. Department of Health, Education and Welfare, Office of Education.
Office of Planning, Budgeting & Evaluation. *Annual Evaluation Report on
Educational Programs—Fiscal Year 1972.* Washington, D.C.: U.S. Govern-
ment Printing Office, March 1973.

U.S. Department of Labor, Bureau of Labor Statistics. *Jobs for Which
Apprenticeships Are Available.* Washington, D.C. 1976.

U.S. Department of Labor, Bureau of Labor Statistics. *Jobs for Which Junior
College, Technical Institute, or Other Specialized Training Is Usually
Required.* Washington, D.C. 1976.

U.S. Department of Labor, Bureau of Labor Statistics. *The Changing Structure
of New England Employment—1947-1973.* Regional Report No. 74-9.
Boston: New England Regional Office, 1973.

U.S. Department of Labor, Bureau of Labor Statistics. *Children of Working
Mothers, March 1974.* Special Labor Force Report 174. Washington, D.C.:
U.S. Department of Labor, 1975.

U.S. Department of Labor, Bureau of Labor Statistics. *Educational Attainment
of Workers—March 1974.* Special Labor Force Report 175. Washington,
D.C.: U.S. Government Printing Office, 1975.

U.S. Department of Labor, Bureau of Labor Statistics. *Educational Attainment
of Workers, March 1975.* Special Labor Force Report. Washington, D.C.:
U.S. Department of Labor, July 1975.

U.S. Department of Labor, Bureau of Labor Statistics. *Employment and Unemployment in 1974.* Special Labor Force Report 178. Washington, D.C.:
U.S. Department of Labor, 1975.

U.S. Department of Labor, Bureau of Labor Statistics. *Jobseeking Methods
Used by American Workers.* Bulletin 1886. Washington, D.C.: U.S.
Government Printing Office, 1975.

U.S. Department of Labor, Bureau of Labor Statistics. *Marital and Family
Characteristics of the Labor Force, March 1974.* Special Labor Force Report
1973. Washington, D.C.: U.S. Department of Labor, 1975.

U.S. Department of Labor, Bureau of Labor Statistics. *Marital and Family Characteristics of the Labor Force, March 1975.* Special Labor Force Report. Washington, D.C.: U.S. Department of Labor, July 1975.

U.S. Department of Labor, Bureau of Labor Statistics. *Multiple Jobholders in May 1974.* Special Labor Force Report 177. Washington, D.C.: U.S. Department of Labor, 1975.

U.S. Department of Labor, Bureau of Labor Statistics. *Multiple Jobholders in 1975.* Special Labor Force Report, July 1975.

U.S. Department of Labor, Bureau of Labor Statistics. *Employment Outlook for 1976 College Graduates in New England.* Boston: New England Regional Office, 1976.

U.S. Department of Labor, Bureau of Labor Statistics. *New England Occupational Projections to 1980.* Regional Report No. 75-6. Boston: U.S. Department of Labor, New England Regional Office.

U.S. Department of Labor, Bureau of Labor Statistics News. *Employment and Unemployment by State and Area: 1974.* Washington, D.C.: U.S. Government Printing Office, April 1975.

U.S. Department of Labor, Bureau of Labor Statistics News. *Productivity and Costs in the Private Economy, First Quarter 1975 (and Data for Non-Financial Corporations Fourth Quarter 1974),* April 1975.

U.S. Department of Labor, Bureau of Labor Statistics. *Occupational Earnings in Selected Areas, 1973-74.* Washington, D.C.: U.S. Department of Labor, May 1974.

U.S. Department of Labor, Bureau of Labor Statistics. *Occupational Earnings and Wage Trends in Metropolitan Areas, 1974-75.* July 1975.

U.S. Department of Labor, Bureau of Labor Statistics. *Occupational Earnings in Selected Areas, 1974-75.* Washington, D.C.: U.S. Department of Labor, May 1975.

U.S. Department of Labor, Bureau of Labor Statistics. *Occupation Manpower and Training Needs—Revised 1974.* Bulletin 1824. Washington, D.C.: U.S. Government Printing Office, 1974.

U.S. Department of Labor, Bureau of Labor Statistics. *Occupational Outlook for the Mid-1980's.* Reprinted from the *Occupational Quarterly* 18 (Winter 1974).

U.S. Department of Labor, Bureau of Labor Statistics. *U.S. Workers and Their Jobs: The Changing Picture.* Bulletin 1919, 1976.

U.S. Department of Labor, Bureau of Labor Statistics. *Work Experience of the Population in 1974.* Special Labor Force Report. Washington, D.C.: U.S. Department of Labor, June 1975.

U.S. Department of Labor, Manpower Administration. *Apprentice Training: Sure Way to a Skilled Craft.* Washington, D.C.: Government Printing Office, revised 1974.

U.S. House of Representatives, Committee on Education and Labor. "Basic Educational Opportunity Grant Program." Hearings before a subcommittee on Postsecondary Education, House of Representatives, on H. Res. 745, 94th Cong., 1st Session, 1975.

U.S. House of Representatives, Committee on Education and Labor. "Higher Education Act Amendments of 1976." Hearings before a subcommittee on postsecondary education, House of Representative on H.R. 3470, 94th Congress, 1st and 2nd Session, 1976.

U.S. House of Representatives, Committee on Education and Labor. "Higher Education Loan Programs." Hearings before Special Subcommittee on Education, House of Reps., on H.R. 68, H.R. 314, and H.R. 12523, 93rd Cong., 1st and 2nd Sessions, 1974.

U.S. House of Representatives, Committee on Education and Labor. "The Student Financial Aid Act of 1975." Hearings before Subcommittee on Postsecondary Education, House of Reps., on H.R. 3471, 94th Congress, 1st Session, 1975.

U.S. House of Representatives, Committee on Education and Labor. "Student Financial Assistance Graduate Programs, State Programs and Grants." Hearings before the Special Subcommittee on Education, House of Reps., 93rd Congress, 2nd Session, 1974.

U.S. House of Representatives, Committee on Education and Labor. "Student Financial Aid (Institutional Aid)." Hearings before Special Subcommittee on Education. House of Reps. 93rd Cong., 2nd Session, 1974.

U.S. House of Representatives, Committee on Education and Labor. "Student Financial Assistance (Miscellaneous)." Hearings before Special Subcommittee on Education, House of Reps., 93rd Cong., 2nd Session, 1974.

U.S. House of Representatives. Committee on Education and Labor. "Student Financial Assistance (Seminars)." Hearings before the Special Subcommittee on Education, House of Reps., 93rd Congress, 2nd Session, 1974.

U.S. House of Representatives. Committee on Education and Labor. "Student Financial Assistance (Student Loan Programs)." Hearings before the Special Subcommittee on Education, House of Reps., 93rd Congress, 2nd Session, 1974.

U.S. House of Representatives, Committee on Education and Labor. "Student Financial Assistance (Theory and Practice of Need Analysis)." Hearings before Special Subcommittee on Education, 93rd Congress, 1st Session, 1973.

U.S. House of Representatives, Committee on Education and Labor. "Student Financial Assistance (Work Programs)." Hearings before the Special Subcommittee on Education, 93rd Congress, 2nd Session, 1974.

U.S. Office of Education, *Annual Report on Programs Administered by the U.S. Office of Education*. F4 1973.

U.S. Office of Education. *An Introduction to Career Education*. Washington,
    D.C.: U.S. Government Printing Office, 1975.
U.S. Office of Education, Office of Planning, Budgeting and Evaluation.
    Career Education in the Public Schools, 1974-75: A National Survey.
    July 1976.
U.S. President. Report transmitted to the Congress. *Employment and
    Training Report of the President*. Washington, D.C.: U.S. Government
    Printing Office, 1976.
U.S. Senate. *Federal and State Student Aid Programs*. 1972. S. Doc. 92-90.
    92nd Congress, 2nd Session, October 1972.
"Urban Students Gain Occupational Skills in New Facilities." *Commonwealth*.
    Boston, Mass.: Department of Education, vol. 5, no. 10 (November 1976).
Useem, Michael, and Miller, S. M. "The Upper Class in Higher Education,"
    Social Policy (January-February 1977).
Van Alstyne, Carol. "Tuition: Review of Proposed Rationales for Establishing
    Tuition Levels at Public Colleges and Universities in the South." Prepared
    for Discussion at the Legislative Advisory Council Meeting of Southern
    Regional Education Board, December 3, 1976.
Van Alystyne, Carol, and Sharon L. Coldren. *Financing Higher Education: Basic
    Facts Underlying Current Issues*. Washington, D.C.: American Federation
    of Teachers, January 1977.
Van Alystyne, Carol, and Sharon L. Coldren. *The Costs of Implementing Fed-
    erally Mandated Social Programs at Colleges and Universities*. Washington,
    D.C.: American Council on Education, June 1976.
Van Dusen, William D., Edmund Jacobson, and Alan Wagner. *Analysis of Stu-
    dent Costs of Attendance*. Washington, D.C.: College Entrance Examina-
    tion Board, December 1974.
Wachtel, Paul. "The Effect of School Quality on Achievement, Attainment
    Levels, and Lifetime Earnings," *Explorations in Economic Research*
    2 (1975), 502-36.
Wallace, T. D., and L. A. Ihnen. "Full-Time Schooling in Life-Cycle Models
    of Human Capital Accumulation," *Journal of Political Economy*, 83,
    pp. 137-55.
Weathersby, George B. "Institutional vs. Student Assistance: A Difficult
    Public Financing Choice." Paper presented at the American Association
    for Higher Education Annual Meeting, March 1976.
Weathersby, George. *A Design for Data Base Estimation of the Effects of
    HEA Title III Intervention*. Work Statement. Washington, D.C.: U.S. Office
    of Education, Office of Planning, Budgeting & Evaluation, April 23, 1975.
Weathersby, George B., Gregory A. Jackson, Frederic Jacobs, Edward P. St.
    John, and Tyler Tngley. *The Development of Institutions of Higher
    Education: Theory and Assessment of Impact of Four Possible Areas of
    Federal Intervention*. Final Report prepared for the U.S. Office of

Education. Washington, D.C.: Office of Planning, Budgeting and Evaluation, January 1977.

"Who Needs College?" *Newsweek* (April 26, 1976).

Who Pays? Who Benefits? National Invitational Conference on the Independent Student, Dallas, Texas. New York: College Entrance Examination Board, 1974.

Wilms, Wellford W. *The Effectiveness of Public and Proprietary Occupational Training.* Berkeley: Center for Research and Development in Higher Education, University of California at Berkeley, October 1974.

Wilms, Wellford W. *Profitmaking and Education.* Berkeley: Center for Research and Development in Higher Education, University of California, July 1973.

Wirtz, Willard, and the National Manpower Institute. *The Boundless Resource— A Prospectus for an Education-Work Policy.* Washington, D.C.: New Republic Book Company, 1975.

Wise, David A. *Academic Achievement and Job Performance.* Cambridge: Harvard University, Kennedy School of Government.

Wise, David A. *Personal Attributes, Job Performance and Probability of Promotion.* Cambridge: Discussion Paper No. 28D. Harvard University, John F. Kennedy School of Government, January 1975.

Wise, Robert, Ivan Charner, and Mary Lou Randour. *A Conceptual Framework for Career Awareness in Career Decision-Making.* Washington, D.C.: National Institute of Education, July 1976.

Witmer, David R. "Is the Productivity of Colleges Declining?" Paper presented at Third General Conference on Institutional Management in Higher Education of the OECD, Paris, France, September 1976.

Wolman, Jean, et al. *A Comparative Study of Proprietary and Non-Proprietary Vocational Training Programs,* vol. I. Palo Alto: American Institutes for Research in the Behavioral Sciences, 1972.

Yankelovich, Daniel, and Ruth Clark. "College and Noncollege Youth Values," *Change* (September 1974).

Zisman, Paul M. *Education and the Occupational Integration of Spanish American Immigrants.* San Francisco: R&E Research Associates, 1975.

About the Authors

George J. Nolfi was educated at the University of California at Berkeley (B.S., 1962), the Massachusetts Institute of Technology (Ph.D., 1965), and the John F. Kennedy School of Government at Harvard University (M.P.A., 1967). He has worked as a budget analyst with the Office of Management and Budget, and with a research and consulting firm before founding University Consultants, Inc., a Cambridge, Massachusetts-based policy analysis, contract research, and consulting firm, in 1969.

Dr. Nolfi has consulted with a variety of clients including federal and state agencies, private foundation, presidential or gubernatorial commissions or task forces (e.g., the Scranton Commission and the Newman Task Force) and individual institutions. The results of these studies have been published under the auspices of agencies including the Office of the Assistant Secretary of Education, HEW, the U.S. House of Representatives Subcommittee on Postsecondary Education, the National Institute of Education, several state agencies, and several institutions, by the client and University Consultants, Inc.

He has authored pending legislation dealing with financing educational opportunities for adults (Senate Bill 178 in the 1978 Session of the Massachusetts Legislature).

Dr. Nolfi has published widely on topics including post-secondary and recurrent education finance, education and work, lifelong learning, vocational education. His current interests include youth and education policy, retraining and unemployment, education finance, cost reduction in public services, innovation in postsecondary education, adapting education institutions to new clientele markets, and recurrent education.

Winship C. Fuller received the B.S. from Suffolk University in 1967, and the M.S. (1969) and Ph.D. (1977) from the Department of Economics at Tufts University. His dissertation, *The Transformation of Chinese Agriculture, 1949-1974,* used several alternative econometric methods to estimate an aggregate production function for the agricultural sector of the Chinese economy. This estimation process required extensive use of the computer facilities at several universities, as well as complete familiarity with numerous computer languages and software packages. Dr. Fuller has also taught several economics courses at Tufts University, Providence College, Rhode Island College, Lowell Technological Institute, and Wheaton College. He is currently an assistant professor of management at the University of Lowell and a senior member of the staff at University Consultants, Inc. His academic interests include further analysis of the extensive NLS data bank, additional research on the Chinese agricultural sector, and econometric investigations into both Greater Boston rental housing and faculty committee assignments at the University of Lowell.

Arthur J. Corazzini received the B.A. from Boston College and both the M.A. and Ph.D. in economics from Princeton University. His current academic research interests are in regional economic policy. He has served as the deputy chancellor of higher education for the State of Massachusetts and as a senior economist in the U.S. General Accounting Office in Washington, D.C. At present, he is associate professor of economics at Tufts University. He has been a senior associate of University Consultants, Inc. for this and other studies. Among his publications are articles on the demand for higher education in the *Journal of Human Resources* and an evaluation of counter cyclical revenue sharing completed for the General Accounting Office.

William H. Epstein received the B.A. from Swarthmore College in 1973 and the Ph.D. in economics from Harvard University in 1977, where his dissertation topic was schooling and occupation decisions. He is currently employed as a fiscal economist at the Office of Management and Budget in Washington, D.C. He was an associate of University Consultants, Inc. for this and other studies. His special interests include international trade and econometrics.

Richard B. Freeman received a B.A. from Dartmouth College in 1964 and a Ph.D. in economics from Harvard University in 1969. He has served as consultant for various governmental agencies, research economist for several academic concerns, and as member of the National Task Force on Education. His special field is labor economics and previous titles on this subject include *The Market for College-Trained Manpower* (1971), *The Overeducated American* (1976), and *Labor Economics* (1972). Dr. Freeman is currently a professor of economics at Harvard University. He has been a senior associate of University Consultants, Inc. for this and other studies.

Charles F. Manski received the B.S. (1970) and Ph.D. (1973) in economics from Massachusetts Institute of Technology and has been employed by the School of Urban and Public Affairs at Carnegie-Mellon University where he is currently an associate professor of economics. He was a senior associate of University Consultants, Inc. for this study. His dissertation, entitled *The Analysis of Qualitative Choice,* presented an analysis of the stochastic utility model of choice which involved the development and estimation of an econometric model of choice of colleges by high school students. He has also served as a member of the research staff at the Joint Center for Urban Studies of Massachusetts Institute of Technology and Harvard University and as a visiting professor in the Department of Economics of the University of California, Berkeley. His numerous publications include contributions to the *Journal of Econometrics,* the *Annals of Economic and Social Measurement, Econometrica,* and the *Transportation Research Record.* Currently, his academic interests include research into the design and testing of an algorithm for maximum likelihood estimation of the Multinomial

Probit Choice Model, as well as a study of robust estimation of Quantal Response Models.

Valerie I. Nelson has been a lecturer in the John F. Kennedy School of Government at Harvard University since 1974. Specifically, she is involved in teaching and case development and in administration of three-week student internships in the spring term. The course is a first-year requirement of the Masters Program in Public Policy and is based on cases and exercises in the identification of policy issues, in the selection and application of analytic skills and methodologies to the solution of public policy issues, and in written and oral presentations. Her education and research interests have been primarily in economics of education, beginning with the B.A. in economics from Radcliffe College and work with Samuel Bowles on schooling and income inequality. Further degrees include the M.Sc. in economics from the London School of Economics and the Ph.D. in economics from Yale University. Her dissertation title was *Public Provision and Private Markets: A Case Study of Vocational Education.* She has been a senior associate of University Consultants, Inc. for this and numerous other studies. Current research includes two-price markets in higher education and urban and regional economic development problems and policies.

David A. Wise received the B.A. from the University of Washington in 1961, after which he spent six years at the Department of Labor in Washington, D.C. He then earned the Ph.D. in economics (1972) from the University of California, Berkeley, where his prize-winning dissertation was entitled *Academic Achievement and Job Performance: Earnings and Promotion.* He is currently an associate professor in the Public Policy Program at the John F. Kennedy School of Government, Harvard University. He was an associate of University Consultants, Inc. for this study. His numerous articles are included in the *American Economic Review, Econometrica,* and the *Annals of Economic and Social Measurement.* His current interests include models of qualitative choice, postsecondary school and work choices, and the causes and possible cures of youth unemployment.